The International Library of Sociology

THE PSYCHO-ANALYTICAL APPROACH TO JUVENILE DELINQUENCY

Founded by KARL MANNHEIM

The International Library of Sociology

THE SOCIOLOGY OF YOUTH AND ADOLESCENCE
In 12 Volumes

I	Adolescence	*Fleming*
II	Adolescents and Morality	*Eppel*
III	Caring for Children in Trouble	*Carlebach*
IV	Casework in Child Care	*Kastell*
V	Children in Care	*Heywood*
VI	Delinquency and Opportunity	*Cloward et al*
VII	Family Environment and Delinquency	*Glueck*
VIII	German Youth: Bond or Free	*Becker*
IX	The Psychoanalytical Approach to Juvenile Delinquency	*Friedlander*
X	Studies in the Social Psychology of Adolescence	*Richardson et al*
XI	Working with Unattached Youth	*Goetschius*
XII	Youth and the Social Order	*Musgrove*

THE PSYCHO-ANALYTICAL APPROACH TO JUVENILE DELINQUENCY

Theory: Case-Studies: Treatment

by

KATE FRIEDLANDER

First published in 1947 by
Routledge and Kegan Paul Ltd

Reprinted in 1998 by
Routledge
11 New Fetter Lane, London EC4P 4EE

Printed and bound in Great Britain

British Library Cataloguing in Publication Data
A CIP catalogue record for this book
is available from the British Library

The Psychoanalytical Approach to Juvenile Delinquency
ISBN 0-415-17668-9
The Sociology of Youth and Adolescence: 12 Volumes
ISBN 0-415-17828-2
The International Library of Sociology: 274 Volumes
ISBN 0-415-17838-X

CONTENTS

PART III

TREATMENT

TABLE OF CASES

PREFACE

The actions of delinquents are harmful to community life. Law-abiding citizens, being conscious of their better social attitude, feel justified in condemning the behaviour of the offender and pressing for his punishment. They rationalize their attitude on the ground that they themselves undergo frustrations for the sake of the community, whereas the delinquent gratifies his desires to the discomfort of his fellow-citizens. They overlook the fact that for them life is much more satisfactory if they obey the laws of the community and that in the long run the delinquent himself suffers by his antisocial behaviour much more than society. Furthermore, they probably do not know that delinquency is a disease of society, just as cancer, for instance, is a disease of the individual.

During recent decades the problem of delinquency has been approached scientifically from various angles. It has been considered as a social problem, as a penological and criminological problem and—from the point of view of the individual offender—as a psychological problem.

More progress might have been made in modifying public opinion if the various sciences engaged in studying delinquency had co-ordinated their lines of investigation. The psychological approach, for instance, is in disfavour with some workers, who argue that the psychology of the individual does not explain the social implications of delinquency. That may be so, but without an understanding and a detailed knowledge of the individual's problems sociological research cannot proceed satisfactorily.

This book is an attempt to show which problems in the vast field of research in delinquency can be solved by psycho-analysis; and in what way sociological and criminological research workers can make use of psycho-analytical findings in order to further their own investigations. I do not wish to convey the impression that psycho-analysis can do more than explain certain manifestations of delinquency. This field of research is one which by its very nature needs the co-operation of sociology, criminology, penology and psychology (including psychiatry) if it is to achieve valuable results.

April 1945.

THE PSYCHO-ANALYTICAL APPROACH TO JUVENILE DELINQUENCY

INTRODUCTION

CHAPTER I

CRIMINAL LAW AND PUBLIC OPINION

The Criminal Justice Bill (5) which was before Parliament at the outbreak of the Second World War was an indication that the end aimed at by modern methods of dealing with delinquents and criminals is now definitely recognized to be the re-education and rehabilitation of the offender. This is shown by the extension of probation as a form of treatment for delinquency and by the emphasis laid on the provision of hostels and remand homes of various kinds, as well as of centres of observation. Since the beginning of this century, research in the field of criminology, penology, sociology, psychology and psychiatry has furnished the scientific facts which have led to the modification of the criminal law.

The question arises whether this modification of the law, though it provides many more facilities for treatment, especially of the juvenile offender, will be sufficient in itself to guarantee the best use of the available methods. In other words, has public opinion advanced enough to allow full use to be made of modern methods of treatment? A few facts will show that it was not the law alone which stood in the way of a more scientific approach to the handling of delinquents during recent decades, nor is it so to-day.

Mannheim (17) analyses those tendencies which seem to him to work in a direction entirely opposed to the re-education and individual treatment of offenders. In the economic field it is the principle of " less eligibility " which blocks the way to reform. At every stage of the development of better penological methods, for instance—whether these methods consisted in better diet in prisons, a wage system, vocational training, or after-care for Borstal boys—it could be observed that large sections of the public were opposed to their introduction, generally on the ground that better conditions for prisoners would put them above the poorest classes of the population and would therefore constitute a definite incitement to crime. In the social field, the stigma attached to various kinds of punishment shows that at bottom the idea of retribution and vengeance is still active in the mind of the public and of the authorities. Mannheim (17, p. 59) states that " Even now, during the debates on the Criminal Justice Bill, it is becoming increasingly obvious that this old idea (principle of less eligibility) still represents the most formidable obstacle in the way of Penal Reform."

Mannheim's analysis shows clearly that unless the public is increasingly made aware of these partly unconscious trends, the introduction of new measures alone will not guarantee their scientific application.

We shall have occasion later [1] to analyse from the psychological point of view the reasons why these old ideas have survived the scientific advances made during the last decades to the detriment not only of penological reform, but of all attempts to apply rational thought in the field of criminal research. For the present a few more examples will show how necessary it is to educate public opinion if the provisions of the new Criminal Justice Bill are to bring about a decisive change in the treatment of crime.

Since the introduction of the Probation of Offenders Act (1907) and its various amending Acts, and since special Juvenile Courts for children have been established, there has been ample opportunity for putting modern ideas into practice, at any rate as regards the young offender. Court statistics as well as the investigation by Elkin (6) show that the use which is being made of probation varies, not, as it should, with the type of offender, but with the practice of the different courts. No investigation has so far been carried out to show the results—whether successes or failures—of probation as compared with other methods of dealing with the offender, nor, as a rule, is the decision as to which method of treatment should be applied to any given individual based on scientific facts. The methods applied by J. Watson (22) and C. Mullins (19) are still exceptional. Usually sentences, such as fines, binding over, probation or institutional care, are graded according to the number and occasionally the severity of offences, rather than from a consideration of what

[1] Part III, Ch. I, p. 191 ff.

method would be most profitable to the particular child. It is not at all unusual to hear of cases of children under 9 years of age, who appear before a Juvenile Court, being put on probation because it is their first appearance in Court, although their environment is known to be so bad that no effort on the part of the probation officer could possibly prevent further contamination. Removal from home, even if to a foster-home and not to an institution, would seem too heavy a penalty for a first offence. The inference to be drawn from this example is obvious. The newer methods of treatment, probation for instance, have come into existence not as a new form of punishment but as a means of re-education. The way in which these methods are applied shows that they are still widely considered as milder forms of punishment rather than as methods of re-education which can only be made use of if they fit the individual offender and not merely the offence.

To take an example from another field. The term re-education or reformation of the offender implies that the method of treatment must be different from an ordinary educational process. There is some faulty development which will have to be put right before positive measures can be applied. It is only reasonable to demand that those who undertake this task should know something not only of ordinary methods of education, but of the forces which cause antisocial reactions and the methods by which these reactions can be changed into social ones. We should expect therefore those who have to deal directly with the offender, namely the probation officer, the staff of Approved Schools or Borstal Institutions, and others concerned, to have a very thorough training in the workings of the human mind, in addition to their legal and administrative knowledge. But this is not generally the case. Though emphasis is laid on the choice of the right persons, their training, at least so far as concerns knowledge of human behaviour, is far from adequate, and is certainly not uniform. It is not my intention to belittle the excellent work done by a number of these officers. They will themselves be the first to admit the difficulties under which they labour because they are insufficiently prepared for their specific task. And those workers who approach their work from a purely moral angle cannot but experience severe disappointment when faced with antisocial offenders for whom a moral code does not exist.

Endless examples could be given in illustration of the fact

that the legalization of new methods of treatment does not in itself produce radical reform.

The scientific knowledge which has brought about the change from retributive and deterrent punishment to the idea that the individual offender needs to be re-educated, is to be seen mainly in the facts brought forward in recent years bearing upon the motivation of human behaviour. The failure of the old methods, as Healy (13*a*) has pointed out, did not in itself lead to a rational modification of treatment.

Not only in the field of criminal research, but also in that of medicine, for instance, it is a long way from scientific discovery to practical application. As a rule social action lags behind scientific discoveries. In delinquency research we are confronted with a special difficulty. The old idea of retribution and vengeance which prevents progress is still active in the mind of the public. There are two methods of combating this : firstly, those tendencies which are usually unnoticed and which influence actions unconsciously must be brought to the fore, so that their disturbing influence can be recognized. Mannheim (17) has made one such attempt. Secondly, the scientific facts which have brought about the change in method embodied in the Criminal Justice Bill of 1939 must be brought repeatedly to public notice, until they become known to every person who is concerned directly or indirectly with the treatment especially of young offenders. It is to this second task that this book is mainly devoted.

CHAPTER II

THE PSYCHIATRIC APPROACH: OLD AND NEW METHODS

During the last century psychiatric research was inclined to maintain the existence of definite differences between the delinquent and the law-abiding citizen. At different times different theories were held as to the nature of the distinction, which was then considered to be the only factor in causing crime. According to the prevalent scientific trend of the moment, the shape of the skull and of the brain it enclosed, heredity, insanity, alcoholism, feeble-mindedness were each in turn for a decade or so considered to be responsible for producing criminals. The scientific methods of that time differed considerably from modern ways of approach, as the science of statistics and the use of control groups had not then been developed. In studying the literature of those days we are struck by the fact that a theory was framed first and afterwards applied to the criminal. As a result, one after another of these theories was discarded as new ideas became current. We know to-day that all those theories which ascribed the origin of criminal behaviour to one single cause, and to a tangible difference whether in mind or body between the criminal and the law-abiding citizen, were erroneous.

It was a change in method which brought about the fundamental change in psychiatric research on crime. Lombroso (16), still intent on finding fundamental differences between the race of criminals and the race of law-abiding citizens, stressed the necessity for studying the individual offender. Though the facts which he thought to establish have long been discarded (largely owing to the fundamental work of Goring (11)), his methodology paved the way for Healy's (12) fundamental work, *The Individual Offender*. The method of research which has led to our present-day knowledge insists on a thorough examination of the individual offender. Theories were tentatively formed only after the complete study of a large number of offenders and their comparison with suitable control groups, or after a psycho-analytical study, extending over months, of individual offenders. This modern research which is connected with the names of Healy and his collaborators, Burt, Aichhorn, Alexander, Staub and others, has shown beyond doubt that the differences in the psychological make-up of the delinquent and the non-delinquent are of a quantitative rather than of a qualitative kind.

CHAPTER III

THE PSYCHO-ANALYTIC APPROACH

The tendency, influenced by findings of psycho-analysis, to follow up the similarities between delinquents and non-delinquents instead of over-stressing their differences, has been a fruitful one.

To murder somebody whom one hates or to take possession of something which one wants is for the majority of normal people a fleeting desire felt on occasion when under emotional stress. Under certain environmental conditions, as in wartime, killing is not considered a crime. The fact that the number of people who even in wartime are unable to kill is so small allows us to assume that the impulse to kill is present in every law-abiding citizen, but under normal conditions does not lead to action. Further confirmation of this assumption is found in those individuals who, after living a blameless life, commit criminal actions either under great emotional stress or when in a state of clouded consciousness. In one particular form of mental illness, obsessional neurosis, the patient is tormented by thoughts and impulses of a highly antisocial kind, e.g., to kill his nearest relatives, to be cruel to his friends, to steal, and so on. Such persons usually have a high moral and ethical code, and would normally condemn such actions at least as much as would their average fellow-citizens.

The existence of such thoughts and impulses in the minds of socially adjusted human beings shows that the impulses which are put into action by the criminal are also present, though usually unnoticed, in the mind of the law-abiding citizen. Indeed, most people betray a knowledge of this fact when displaying righteous indignation at delinquent behaviour. Their reaction can be better understood on the basis of this common inclination towards antisocial behaviour which they have overcome and the delinquent has not. They are wrong in assuming that either the law-abiding citizen or the delinquent is able to alter at will his basic attitude towards the community.

Psycho-analytical research into criminal behaviour is concentrated primarily on the fact that the same antisocial impulses which are unconscious in the law-abiding citizen lead to action in the criminal, to the detriment of himself, and, in a lesser degree, of society. Psycho-analysts who interested themselves in the personality of the criminal (as for instance Freud himself and more exclusively Aichhorn and Alexander) had the advantage of starting their research with a knowledge of the workings of both the normal and the disturbed mind. Psycho-analysis had already shown that the actions of normal and still more obviously those of neurotic persons could be understood if their unconscious motivation was taken into account. It had discovered that the roots of unconscious tendencies which influence our actions go back to experiences of early childhood.

CHAPTER IV

THE SOCIOLOGICAL APPROACH

Sociological research takes as its starting-point the assumption that the character of the adult is moulded by his environment. This point of view has led to valuable results in criminal research. Sociologists discarded the old view of the " born criminal " and began to investigate the differences of environment of delinquents and non-delinquents. In common with the psychoanalysts they emphasize that the environment influences the individual from birth onwards, and their investigations are therefore concentrated on the young delinquent.

The most valuable contribution of sociological research, linked with the names of Healy and Burt who were pioneers in the field of delinquency, has been the emphasis on the multitude of environmental factors which work together in causing delinquency. The broken home, lack of discipline, bad companionship, lack of organization of leisure time, economic factors, to name only the most important items, are linked with the incidence of delinquency. Investigation of these factors, in conjunction with modern psychological research, has caused the shifting of emphasis from the punishment of the offender to the examination of the social conditions which have produced his antisocial personality. If any doubt remained as to the importance of environmental factors in the causation of delinquency, it was dispelled by Clifford Shaw (21) who, in a comparative study of twenty-one cities, showed that in each city the area of highest delinquency had the same characteristics.

But there are certain questions, very important from the point of view of prevention, which sociology has so far proved unable to solve. One reason for this is probably that there is no conformity in the various investigations indicating a significant correlation between each single factor and the incidence of delinquency, with the possible exception of the " broken home ". The correlations vary with the group of delinquents examined and the place where the investigation was undertaken. It is not as yet even certain that poverty always shows a significant correlation with the incidence of delinquency. This is confirmed by Healy's (13*a*) investigation. Healy (13*b*) showed that of two siblings growing up in the same environment one might become delinquent while the other did not, and he found the reason for this to lie in their emotional development rather than in their environment. That factors other than purely environmental ones must play a part in causation becomes clear also when we see that even in an environment where all the factors present have a high correlation with the incidence of delinquency yet only a minority of those exposed to them become delinquents in fact.

Those factors which in a recent statistical investigation (4) have been described as "susceptibility" to delinquency and which Aichhorn (1) called "the state of latent delinquency" are the special object of study in this book.

PART I

THE DEVELOPMENT TOWARDS SOCIAL ADAPTATION[1]

CHAPTER I

INTRODUCTION

It is exceptional for a criminal career to start late in life. Criminal statistics give the peak age for the first appearance in Court as between the ages of 15 and 17 years. Careful studies of the life-histories of delinquents at the time of their first Court appearance, however, prove that in a majority of cases delinquent acts or at least antisocial behaviour have been apparent before that time. Healy (13*a*) in his analysis of 187 cases found that the first offences began from one to five or even more years before action was taken. In my own experience, in the majority of delinquents of antisocial character, the first signs of antisocial behaviour appear between the ages of 7 and 9 years.

Here we come across an important problem. At this early age, many children commit minor offences who do not become delinquents later on. It is known that stealing is far more common in children of that age than court statistics indicate.

[1] Freud made his discoveries concerning the development of the child's emotional life by the psycho-analysis of neurotic adult patients. In 1909 he undertook the first analysis of a child (8*a*) which fully confirmed the facts hitherto set out. The method of child analysis has been developed from this time onwards and has made possible a more detailed study of the emotional content of the first years of life. Mainly owing to Anna Freud's work, many details have been made clearer and the development of the Ego has been more closely scrutinized (7*a*). Nothing in Freud's original conception has been fundamentally changed. Many of the original findings of Freud have been fully accepted by child psychology (as for instance the importance of the mother-child relationship, jealousy amongst siblings, infantile sexuality, and so on) though the author of these discoveries is not always quoted.

Within the last fifteen years M. Klein (15) and her followers have propounded a theory of mental development which deviates in fundamental principles from Freud's original theory, though it still makes use of Freudian terminology. The confusion arising out of this mixture of two fundamentally opposed theories (Freud's theory maintaining contact with biology, Kleinian theory disregarding the relationship between physical and mental development altogether) has been recently clarified by Glover (10).

The emotional development of the child as outlined in these pages has as its theoretical background Freud's original theory and such additions as are based on the principles of psycho-analysis (2, 7). This theory allows of an explanation of the facts as we find them in our clinical work with adult and child patients, and it is so far the only theory of mental life which satisfactorily explains the development towards antisocial behaviour.

It is not that children at this age do not know what they should and what they should not do. If they are of average intelligence they are aware that they are committing an offence for which they will be punished. They often do not like being naughty, but the temptation of the moment may prove too strong for them. Their conscience has not yet the firmness necessary to control their impulses under all circumstances. The equilibrium which governs the life of the adult has apparently not been reached at the age of 8, at which in this country criminal responsibility is assumed. We might say that children of this age are not yet fully socially adapted, although they have the intellectual knowledge of what lines their behaviour should follow if they are to be socially accepted.

BEHAVIOUR OF TODDLERS.

If we go back still further and observe toddlers in an environment in which they are allowed free expression of their impulses, the difference between the child's and the adult's social behaviour at that early age is much more pronounced, so much so that similarities are difficult to find. The most striking difference is certainly the variety of the toddler's actions and the intensity with which they are pursued while they last. A child engaged in playing with a toy may appear quite happy in his occupation until he sees another child with another toy which attracts his attention. Within a second we hear the screams of the second child who has been robbed of his possession ; a quarrel is in progress in which the other small occupants of the room join with obvious pleasure. The child who has taken away the toy and so started all this upheaval does not feel in the least guilty, but regards it as his right to take whatever he wants from any other child, nothing but the superior strength of the other preventing him from doing so. Unless they are under constant supervision, such children push and scratch and bite each other without any regard for the suffering of their victim, and the glee in their faces will convince even the superficial observer that they enjoy hurting another child with whom they will play happily a few minutes later. They may be very attached to the nurse so long as their desires are being fulfilled, but if they cannot get the toy they want, or if they are not fed when hungry, they will be angry and even show hatred towards the person by whom at other times they like to be cuddled. These small children love to play with dirt, they do not dislike sticky fingers, they do not mind wetting themselves or showing off their naked bodies. Feelings of shame, disgust or pity seem to be wholly absent; the toddlers are intent only on doing what gives them the greatest pleasure for the moment. And this pleasure is mostly gained by activities which, if present in the adult, would be classified as criminal, insane or perverse. Charming though small children may be at certain times, at others, and especially if many toddlers of the same age are together in a nursery, they give the impression of being little savages. They certainly are not socially adapted, for they have no regard for the desires of other people and do not submit of their own free will to demands made upon them. Looked at from another angle, we might say that they do not as yet show any signs of conscience. Their actions are governed solely by their impulses and by their desire to gain as much pleasure as possible and to avoid displeasure.

Familiarity with the behaviour of very small children tends to make us formulate the question in a different way from that with which we started, namely why some people are antisocial and others not. It seems really much more astonishing that so many of these little savages develop into socially adapted human beings than that some of them do not reach that stage. And it is even more astonishing that the taming of the antisocial impulses so freely expressed at this early age takes place in a comparatively short time: we have seen that a child of 8, even if not always able to do the expected thing, is already more or less socially adapted.

An understanding of the development towards social adaptation should be of considerable importance to those who are called to deal with human beings who have failed to achieve it. Such knowledge will also shed a new light on the influence of those environmental factors which predispose to antisocial development.

NEW FORMULATION OF PROBLEM.

The problem is really this: we have a small human being who is governed solely by his impulses, the satisfaction of which gives him pleasure. Many of these impulses are antisocial. After a few years we see that a majority of these toddlers have become socially adapted. A few remain who still show characteristics reminding one of the toddler, though intellectually they have reached the same stage as the adapted children. Surely the first step towards an understanding of these children should be to investigate what factors, environmental or otherwise, have brought about social adaptation in the majority.

This task is not as simple as it may appear at first sight. There is no possibility of conducting a controlled experiment with a child's impulses and emotions as there is when studying its intellectual growth. Not until the psycho-analytic method made it possible to study the unconscious (that buried part of the mind which reaches down into the early years of existence) could a comprehensible picture of the emotional development during the first years of life be obtained. Deep down in the unconscious these old antisocial impulses which we have seen expressed in the toddler are still alive, and influence the thoughts and actions of the adult. It was from the investigation into the unconscious motives of adults and from the study of the symptoms of neurotic persons that the first knowledge of the emotional development of the child and with it of the fate of these early antisocial instincts could be reconstructed. Since then, psycho-analytical observation of children of all ages has amply confirmed the first assumptions and has filled in gaps in our knowledge. The result, which was at first very astonishing to the investigator, has shown that the capacity of the small child for emotional experiences is far greater than was hitherto suspected, and that the modification of the primary antisocial impulses itself leads to character formation. Furthermore, it was seen that the way in which the primary impulses are modified is to a large extent influenced by environmental factors, though the processes involved proved to be very complicated.

If then we are going to try to understand how social adaptation is brought about, it will be necessary to follow up the whole of the emotional development of the child during the first years of life, with special stress on the modification of the primary antisocial impulses. This picture of the child's emotional development will enable us to point to those specific environmental factors which further a positive development, and to estimate the relative importance of those environmental conditions which show a positive correlation with the incidence of delinquency.

CHAPTER II

SOME PROBLEMS OF INSTINCT-THEORY

The impulses which we have seen expressed in the toddler are expressions of instinctive needs. Some theoretical considerations about the nature of instincts are therefore unavoidable as a basis for our investigations. There is controversy among psychologists as to the number of instincts which can be distinguished from one another. If the object of observation is the adult and if the method of observation is a behaviouristic or introspective one, and if, furthermore, the instinct is regarded as a purely psychological manifestation, any number of instinctive urges can be and have been assumed.

FREUD'S THEORY OF INSTINCTS.

Freud (8*c*) on the basis of his psycho-analytical experiences maintained that an instinct is a manifestation on the borderline between physiology and psychology. He defined the instinct as a stimulus arising inside the body as distinct from stimuli which arrive at our organs of perception from the outside. This difference of location carries with it intrinsic differences. If, for instance, a strong light falls on our eyes, we can avoid the disagreeable sensation by shutting them, that is, by flight. If a stimulus arises inside the body, it cannot be avoided by flight, and therefore continues to exert its influence, causing a rising tension which is experienced as a disagreeable sensation. This tension can be alleviated by an adequate action which brings about relief and is felt as satisfaction. Under certain circumstances, satisfaction can be delayed, but in the meantime the tension in the body is rising and the urge for gratification grows stronger. The satisfaction of the instinctive urge in relieving the tension is experienced as pleasure. This process can be clearly observed in all manifestations of the sexual instinct.

The source of an instinct is always a bodily organ, and this origination places the instinct in the field of physiology. The tension caused by the rising urge and the relaxation after satisfaction has been attained produce a measurable alteration in the balance of the autonomic nervous system. It is to this organic origin that the instinct owes its driving power. The feeling which accompanies the instinctive urge, namely the emotion, belongs to the realm of psychology. With this biological basis in mind, Freud adopted a dualistic theory of instincts. In studying neurotic individuals by the psycho-analytic method he found that he could reduce the number of instincts to two main groups, from which the very varied instinctive urges of the adult take their origin. These two groups of instincts, which he first described as the " self-preservative and sexual instinct " (8*c*), and later on formulated as the " life- and death-instinct " (8*d*), both seek satisfaction. As their aims are in opposition to each other, the individual has to find a satisfactory way of dealing with them. It is this struggle which constitutes the manifestations of life.

It is not the purpose of this book to go into any detail concerning the theories of instinct. It is sufficient to bear in mind that we start from the assumption that the instinctive urges in the small child belong to two groups, the life- and death-instincts, or, for practical purposes, the sexual and aggressive instincts. The sexual instincts are derivatives of the life-instinct and the aggressive instincts of the death-instinct.

FUSION OF INSTINCTS.

One more theoretical explanation will be necessary before we can understand the instinctive manifestations as we find them in the human being. Normally, in mental health, there is a fusion between the two primary instincts, the sexual and the aggressive. There is no instinctive urge which is entirely sexual or entirely aggressive. Even in sadism, where cruelty is certainly pronounced, the sexual element is unmistakable. In normal sexual intercourse, aggressive tendencies in the male are necessary and legitimate, and their absence, usually due to repression, may lead to impotence. There are stages in the instinctive development of the child when either the aggressive or the sexual tendencies are more pronounced, but the opposing instinct is always present. We shall therefore study the instinctive development of the child as a whole without paying too much attention to the division between the instinctive urges, except where the struggle between them and regard for the outside world leads to conflict.

CHAPTER III

THE MATURATION OF INSTINCTS (8*b*)

ORAL PHASE. The first activities of the newborn child in relationship to the outside world are little more than reflex activities. The infant's paramount need in his first days is to be fed and to be kept warm. As soon as the nipple or the bottle or, for that matter, any other object is brought in contact with the mucous membranes of the lips and mouth, the child begins to suck. No confirmation of any kind is yet available that the person who provides the food is of importance as such to the child. The child will cry when he feels uncomfortable, regardless of whether the discomfort is caused by cold or hunger, and will be satisfied as soon as his needs are fulfilled. During the first days and weeks, these needs are bodily needs only, paramount among them being hunger. But from the very beginning the child experiences a feeling of satisfaction and perhaps even of pleasure when being fed, when the warm stream of milk stimulates the mucous membrane of the mouth. Very soon, usually within the first six weeks of life, an activity starts which develops in conjunction with feeding. Between feeding times, and not only when urged by hunger, the baby starts to suck a part of his own body, usually the fingers and especially the thumb. The baby may first start sucking when hungry, but as he enjoys it will continue his sucking when not hungry and even immediately after being fed. The aim is not to get food into his mouth but to derive pleasure from this particular activity. This pleasure calls for repetition. Interference with the baby's activity arouses extreme displeasure, and discomfort, especially in the slightly older child, can be alleviated by sucking. Though arising apparently by chance, and combined with the function of taking in food, sucking very soon becomes one of the baby's most important activities. It is an instinctive urge. Its source is the mucous membrane of the mouth, its aim is the alleviation of tension by a rhythmical movement of lips and mouth, and its object is a part of the baby's own body. This activity, which is repeated merely for pleasure's sake, already bears in its structure a close resemblance to all those activities which arise out of the sexual instinct.

In these first months of life the mouth gains more and more

importance as the body zone from which the baby can derive pleasure. He uses it as an organ of recognition—everything is first put into the mouth at this stage—and slightly later, with the appearance of the teeth, it is an organ with which he can express aggression. We see that quite a number of the small child's activities are centred round, and arise out of, feelings experienced in the mouth. Owing to the importance of the mouth in the child's feeling and activities during the first year of life, we call this stage of instinctive development the *oral phase*, and the mouth the *erogenous zone* of this phase. At this stage satisfaction of instinctive urges can be derived from activities concerned with the child's own body. We call these *auto-erotic* activities. As the child's interest is still very largely centred around his own body and person, the child is, we say, *narcissistic* (8*e*).

ANAL-SADISTIC PHASE.

From the end of the first until roughly the middle of the third year the mouth loses much of its importance as an erogenous zone, and the organs of excretion come into the foreground as a body zone from which auto-erotic pleasure can be derived. Again we see that an instinctive activity becomes important in conjunction with a bodily function. During the first year of life excretory functions work more or less like reflex actions. It is at the time when control over the sphincters is being gained that the mucous membrane of the excretory organs becomes more sensitive, and the pleasure formerly derived from oral activities is now obtained in various ways from the mucous membrane of the excretory organs. Conditions now become more complicated, owing to the fact that in the meantime the child, as we shall see later, has developed an emotional relationship with the persons in his environment. In contrast to the instinctive activity of the first oral phase—sucking—auto-erotic activities centred round the anus are very often not observable to the outside world. They may consist in keeping back the excreta until they force their way out, which causes more pleasurable irritation to the mucous membrane than does expulsion at regular times, or sometimes in rhythmical irritations with the finger. What is more easily observable is the pleasure of the child when playing with his excreta or with any other kind of dirt. But as we already encounter at this stage the influences of the environment, which are opposed to this instinctive satisfaction, few of the auto-erotic activities of this phase, the *anal phase*, may actually be seen. The strength of the child's instinctive urges at this time may to some extent be assessed by the difficulties which he presents in training him for cleanliness, and by the fact that a large number of children do not achieve perfect control of their excretory organs until puberty.

Apart from these auto-erotic activities, there appear at this stage instinctive urges which are no longer centred around the baby's own body, but have as their object the people who surround the child, first and foremost the mother. By this time an emotional relationship has been established with the mother, and her presence and care and devotion are already an integral part of the child's life. While at the beginning of this relationship the child derived pleasure from being near the mother, from touching her body and being cuddled, at this second stage strong aggressive tendencies make their appearance. These will express themselves in anger or even hatred if wishes are not instantly fulfilled, and in the child's relationship to other children, especially those who are weaker, the tendency to hurt by biting, scratching, pushing, pulling the hair, and so on, is very pronounced. In a nursery where small toddlers are together, the pleasure one child derives from hurting another presents a difficult educational problem. At this time the child is already strong enough to hurt a smaller child, but is not far enough advanced in his emotional development to feel concern about the pain he may cause to the other. We recognize some of the antisocial impulses of the toddler which were described in the previous chapter. However, the wish to be hurt is just as strong as the wish to hurt, although this is much more difficult to ascertain by observation. Owing to the prevalence of these instinctive urges, namely the *sadistic* and *masochistic component instincts*, we call this phase of development the *anal-sadistic* one.

PHALLIC PHASE. Towards the middle of the third year, sometimes earlier, sometimes later, the child begins to be more interested in his genitals. The first indication is a tendency for him to exhibit his naked body, to show a marked interest in that of other little children, and, on the intellectual plane, to start wondering and sometimes asking questions about sex differences. To the onlooker the instinctive urges of this period are more clearly sexual than were those of the former phases, because the erogenous zone of this phase is the genitals, as it is with the adult. The auto-erotic activity of this period is masturbation. The instinctive urges directed towards the persons in the child's environment, parents and brothers and sisters, have now some similarity with the desires experienced in the love life of the adult. There is the tendency to possess the parent of the opposite sex, there is jealousy of the parent of the same sex, and there is jealousy, though at the same time comradeship, between the siblings, in their endeavour to be loved by the parents. The emotional life of the child at this period is very rich and deep, and on account of its importance in the development of the personality it will be discussed in greater detail in another chapter. Here we are concerned with the phases of development in the instincts alone, and in this respect it is important to note that although there are similarities between the instinctive urges and the sex life of the adult, there is still one great difference : children of either sex are interested in the male genital only, and regard it as the correct form of the genital. This misconception will prove to be responsible for the emotional conflicts which lead to the abandonment of the instinctive aims of this so-called *phallic stage* (8*f*).

SEXUAL CURIOSITY.

In the meantime the child's intellectual growth has proceeded rapidly, and preoccupation with the instinctive urges of the period directs his intellectual interests to a considerable extent. *Sexual curiosity* (8*f*) is very much in the foreground between the ages of 3 and 5, and it will depend on the attitude of the parents whether the child discusses some at least of his burning problems or whether sexual investigation goes on entirely in secret. Even if his questions are answered, the child's conception of sexual life is very different from the reality. From interest in the sex difference, which for the small child can never be completely cleared up, he proceeds to the problem where babies come from. This is interpreted in accordance with his emotional life at the time and in recollection of the former stages of instinctive development. Therefore we meet with some universal theories of birth, such as that one can have a baby by eating something specific ; or by kissing—a phantasy which can still be found in grown-up girls ; or that the child is born through the anus (an aperture well known to the child by reason of its former preoccupation with it) ; or that the child is born through the navel—certainly an attempt to deny the existence of the vagina (8*g*).

The child is also intensely interested in the parents' sexual life. Often, though by no means always, this interest is increased by actual observations. Here again, as the child cannot understand the function of the female genital, and in accordance with his own instinctive urges at this time, he interprets the parents' relationship as something sadistic, as an aggressive act on the part of the father against the mother or *vice versa*, and it is not unusual to find phantasies in which the parents' sexual life is connected with the lavatory or bathroom.

In this, the phallic phase, we find the instinctive urges already partly or wholly in opposition to the desires of the personality which in the meantime has been developing. The pattern is by no means so simple to explain as it was in the oral stage.

INSTINCTS IN LATENCY PERIOD.

After the fifth year of life, when the instinctive urges have reached a considerable strength and to a large extent have invaded the intellectual sphere as well, we can notice a slow but sure decline in the child's purely instinctive life. There are, as will be shown later, reasons in the emotional sphere why the child should give up desires which are then directed mainly towards the parents. But it seems that biologically also between the sixth year and puberty instinctive urges decrease. Theoretically, it is not impossible that this period, which we call the *latency period* (8*b*), is a product rather of civilization than of innate biological tendencies. However, we find that during this period, in our civilization at least, instinctive urges recede into the background with occasional sudden outbreaks, usually in the form of sexual games among children of roughly the same age.

INSTINCTS IN PUBERTY.

With the maturation of the sexual organs in puberty, the instinctive life comes once more to the fore. After the emotional upheaval of puberty the adult *genital instinct* emerges. The *component instincts*, which, as we have seen play a paramount part during the developmental stages, though still present, are now rather subdued and have come under the primacy of the genitals. Looking, to be looked at, sadistic and masochistic trends, the mouth as an erogenous zone—these still appear more or less pronounced as preliminaries to sexual intercourse. Until Freud made his discoveries it was commonly held that the sexual instinct first appeared in puberty. Freud's work, and ample observation of children since then, have offered proof that what we see at puberty is the product of a long development, and that the forms which the genital life of the individual will take after puberty are largely influenced by experiences in the emotional sphere during this long development.

PERVERSIONS.

The study of the development of the sexual and aggressive instincts in childhood has also given us a clue to the understanding of sexual abnormalities. The genital instinct is based on states of tension in the genital organs, its object is a person of the opposite sex, and its aim is intercourse. Formerly it was thought that the object and the aim of the sexual instinct were very closely connected with one another. We find, however, that only after puberty are the aim and object of the sexual instinct those of adult sexuality. During the stages of development, both aim and object change. The object may be the child's own body, in the early years for children of both sexes it is the mother, during a period in puberty it is usually a person of the same sex. The aim of the sexual instinct may be sucking, sadistic or masochistic practices, looking and being looked at. The sources of the instinct are originally the mucous membrane of the mouth and that of the excretory organs, until round about the third or fourth year the genital organs become the all-important erogenous zone. In studying sexual perversions, we find that they can easily be grouped under the headings of aberrations of the sexual instinct as to aim and object, and that they can be understood as developmental disturbances.[1]

SUMMARY.

To sum up: The genital sexuality of the adult is the product of a lengthy process of maturation. The sexual instinct passes through the oral, anal-sadistic and phallic phases before it reaches in puberty what we call the genital stage. Traces of the earlier stages of development can still be found mingled with genital sexuality, and they form the foundation for the sexual aberrations known as perversions. From birth up to roughly the fifth or sixth year, instinctive urges are strongly in the foreground. They recede into the background during the latency period and emerge after puberty as the adult genital instinct. The first stages of development, also called the *pregenital stages*, overlap to a certain extent, but it is fairly safe to say that, during the first year of life, oral instinctive urges are pronounced, during the second and third year anal-sadistic trends are more in the foreground, and from the third until the fifth year the phallic phase dominates the picture.

This development of the sexual and aggressive instinct is a biological one. How it can be helped or hindered by the child's environment, and the fate of those instinctive trends which cannot find a place within the adult genital instinct because they are antisocial or perverse, and the emotional counterpart of these instinctive trends will be discussed in the following chapters.

[1] Part II, Ch. VI, p. 153.

CHAPTER IV

THE MOTHER-CHILD RELATIONSHIP

In the preceding chapter the maturation of the instinctive life has been discussed as if the individual grew up in a vacuum, uninfluenced by his environment. This, of course, is by no means the case, but the child's relationship to the persons around him will be better understood if we bear in mind what instinctive urges the child wants to satisfy in his relationships at different stages of development. Before we proceed, therefore, to study the fate of the different instinctive urges, we shall form a clearer picture if we investigate the development of the very first and most intimate relationship in the child's life. Not only does this first relationship leave its imprint on the child's later personality, but it is also known that delinquents are persons who have been frustrated in their human relationships.

The relationship of the child to the mother develops slowly from the beginning of life. The majority of psycho-analysts, through experience gained from the psycho-analysis of adults and children, and through direct observation of babies from birth onwards, believe that during the first weeks and even months of life the relationship of the child to the mother is a rather simple one. The mother is the instrument which satisfies the child's bodily needs. Anyone who fulfils this function will arouse the same response in the child. A small group of psycho-analysts in this country, notably Mrs. M. Klein (15), has developed a theory of mental life which assumes that a rather complicated psychological relationship between the child and the mother comes into being immediately after birth. So far there are no scientific data available to support this theory ; on the contrary, the facts at our disposal tend much more to support the slow development of mental life on the basis of bodily needs.

MATERIALISTIC STAGE.

The baby, at first, is not able to distinguish between itself and the outside world. There is as yet no consciousness, and the infant probably begins to be aware of its own existence only when it is uncomfortable. It certainly cannot distinguish whether the discomfort is caused by its own hunger or by an outside agency. The baby reacts to both internal and external discomforts by extreme unhappiness, of which it makes the outside world aware by crying. When satisfied the infant falls asleep again, or, in other words, withdraws its attention from the world. Slowly, during the first weeks and months, the mother, especially in the case of breast-fed babies, becomes associated with the alleviation of pain and dissatisfaction. The first relationship of the child to the mother, therefore, is based on the satisfaction of material needs alone. The child's inability to alleviate its discomfort is responsible for this materialistic dependence on the mother or mother substitute. Anna Freud and D. Burlingham (2*a*) describe how separation from the mother at this stage is usually overcome in a day or two, except where it entails sudden weaning as well.

DEVELOPMENT OF EMOTION.

During the second half of the first year a change can be observed in the child's relationship to the mother.[1] Not that the child no longer wants to have his wishes fulfilled—this part of the relationship is still as important as ever—but he now seems clearly to realize that the mother is a person distinct from other people around him. He desires the mother's presence even if he feels no discomfort ; he wants to touch her, to fondle her breast, to smile at her, and so on. The child's eyes follow the mother when she leaves or enters the room and her presence elicits a glimmer of recognition. This mental unity which begins to be established at this time and which reaches its peak during the second year of life is probably intensified in breast-fed children who are in close contact with the mother's body. However, it is probably an exaggeration to assume that the child's relationship to the mother is different in quality in breast-fed and bottle-fed children. What matters more than the actual contact with the mother's breast is her loving or unloving attitude to the child.

It is probably true to say that the feelings of the child between the ages of 1 and 2 for his mother are akin to what we call love, and they are certainly as deep and lasting as anything the adult is able to feel. Various factors contribute to strengthen this relationship. There is the child's utter dependence on the mother as the person who prevents him from dying. There are the child's growing instinctive urges, now for the first time being directed against the outside world. And there is the fact that

[1] The child's relationship to the mother is at present the object of study in various research centres. R. Spitz, in two papers, " Hospitalism ", *The Psychoanalytic Study of the Child*, Vol. I, 1945, and " Anaclitic Depression ", ibid., Vol. II, 1946, has brought objective proof of the damage inflicted upon the child's development if this relationship is interrupted during the second half of the first year.

these instinctive urges, best described at this time as the wish to have the mother's body as near as possible, cannot wait for satisfaction, for they cause such a strong tension in the child that relief must be sought at once. At the early stage of this relationship, that is in the first half of the second year, the unity between mother and child is still perfect. The child's most imperative wish is to be fed and to have the mother near, and the mother is only too glad if the child eats well and is happy in her presence.

This intense feeling of love for the mother is accompanied by an equally strong fear on the part of the child lest the mother should leave him alone. The child has already learned to connect the disagreeable feeling of unsatisfied desires with the absence of the mother. On the other hand, he is not yet able to realize that the mother's absence may be only temporary. Each disappearance causes extreme unhappiness, only to be compared with an adult's grief for the death of a beloved person. For the child at this age, past and future do not exist ; only the present is real with its happiness or unhappiness. Anna Freud and D. Burlingham (2*a*) have collected very valuable material on the separation of the child from the mother at this stage of intense and happy relationship, and their deductions explain many symptoms which were observed in small children during the evacuation period in the Second World War.

DISTURBANCES OF MOTHER-CHILD RELATIONSHIP.

Unfortunately, this first love relationship of the child is not entirely satisfactory. For a time all goes well. Even the fact that the mother in return for her love has to make certain demands which diminish the child's instinctive pleasure can for a short while be endured. The child has to be weaned, he has to learn to be left alone for short periods, and his training in cleanliness begins. Owing to the fact that the mother's affection is of such paramount importance to the child, and, perhaps even more, that the fear of being left alone is so devastating, the child foregoes instinctive pleasure so that he may retain the mother's love and not be exposed to the fear of being left by himself. But soon, greater trials await this relationship. Another child may arrive, and the mother's attention will be more exclusively focused on the smaller infant. There may be older children who also have their share in the mother's love. There is the father who is felt as a disturbance in the unity between mother and child. This awareness of other individuals who are equally dependent on the mother and who share the baby's affection for her becomes more apparent to the child during the third year of life. We have seen that at this time aggressive tendencies are already rather strong, and the child will react to each disappointment with sudden rage or hatred. Though these feelings are strong while they last, they do not last very long, and love will prevail once more. It was thought at one time that it would be possible to bring up a child in such a way that he need not go through all these emotions of disappointment and hatred. This assumption, however, has proved to be erroneous. The child's relationship to the mother cannot remain an entirely happy one, because his demands on her are too great and his instinctive urges are antisocial. That is to say that nothing short of having the mother all the time without sharing her with anybody would satisfy the child, and nothing short of having all his instinctive desires fulfilled at once would guarantee his happiness at this stage. It would in fact mean that one would have to go on breast-feeding the child for years, let him remain dirty, let him torture smaller children and animals, and so on.

Though this relationship of the child to the mother is bound at times to be unhappy, and to cause disappointment, however loving the mother may be, her attitude and the way in which she sets about taming the child's instinctive urges will prove of great importance for the development of his character. The unhappiness caused by unsatisfied needs may be bearable or it may be unbearable. Therefore, although we cannot enable a child to grow up in complete happiness, we are very well able to turn disappointments into a valuable educational effort.

After the third year of life, the relationship towards the mother once more undergoes a change. The father and brothers and sisters have entered the field, and the child's instinctive urges are no longer exclusively centred around the mother. Before discussing this most important period of life we shall have to study more closely in what way, and by what means, the antisocial impulses of the child are modified.

CHAPTER V

ON THE MODIFICATION OF INSTINCTS

It cannot be sufficiently emphasized that all workers dealing with delinquents in any capacity ought to be aware of the fact that the antisocial urges they meet with in the delinquent are normal manifestations of the instinctive life of the small child, and that the preoccupation of delinquents with their desires and pleasures is equally manifest in the toddler. Unfortunately, it is necessary to stress this point, as officials are not infrequently met with who hold the opinion that the delinquent's impulses are "bad". Such impulses are neither bad nor good. Their presence in an unmodified form in the older child or adult is a sign that social adjustment has not taken place, and the reasons for this undesirable state of affairs have to be investigated and remedied. It might be expected that nowadays those who are professionally engaged in work on delinquency would be aware of this fact and therefore would not be satisfied by a purely moral approach without looking for a scientific basis for their convictions.

PLEASURE-PAIN PRINCIPLE.

In the preceding chapter it has been pointed out that the child, in order to keep the love of the mother and out of fear of being left alone, has to give up some of his instinctive urges. Actually there are two processes at work which in time bring about a modification of these urges. Some of them, such as taking pleasure in dirt, have to be given up on account of their antisocial nature. Others, such as the craving for the mother's presence, have to be toned down. The child has to learn that he cannot satisfy all his desires at once; he has to learn to wait. These instincts appear to be in the foreground at this stage, not only on account of their antisocial nature, but also because of a specific quality in the child's still undeveloped personality: as he cannot withstand the impulses which strive for satisfaction, he wants to satisfy his desires all the time, regardless of consequences which he is as yet unable to judge. In desiring pleasure and avoiding pain the child is governed by the *pleasure-pain principle.* So is the adult, but before satisfying his desires he takes into account the demands of society; those of the outside world, and of his own conscience. The adult is dominated by the *reality principle* (8*h*).

As the child is born into a civilized world, surrounded from the moment of birth onwards by people who have certain standards of behaviour, whatever those standards may be in any given society, the education in adjustment to reality may be said to start almost at birth. As far as our knowledge has progressed up till now it seems that the maturation of the instinctive drives is more or less universal, and probably independent of the surroundings, while the modification of instincts and subsequent emotional development are probably to a large extent conditioned by the particular environment to which the child belongs. Margaret Mead's (18*a*) work provides some interesting anthropological data which confirm this view. The modification of instinctive urges described in these pages refers to our Western civilization during the last few decades.

From the very beginning the child is kept waiting for food. Families differ in the strictness with which they adhere to scientific feeding times. But some waiting is usually involved. It is possible that during the first weeks and months of life strict adherence to feeding times will cause a conditioned reflex to be set up. Towards the end of the first year these conditioned reflexes are usually overcome by the child's imperative urge to get satisfaction at once. Then the necessary waiting for mealtimes causes a first clash between the wishes of the mother and those of the child. But the clash is not very severe. The mother, too, wishes the child to eat.

DISPLACEMENT OF LIBIDO.

We meet a different state of affairs at weaning time, especially if this falls in the second half of the first year. Then the child definitely wants to go on sucking the nipple. Sucking, at this stage, has much more significance than the mere obtaining of food, and the mother wants to substitute the bottle for the nipple. If weaning is done abruptly the child refuses food altogether for a shorter or longer period. In the end he has to give in. His dependence on the mother is too great and his hunger too imperative. Therefore, in order to relieve the increasing tension, the child has to learn to get satisfaction from a *substitute*. The way in which weaning is established amid this first clash of interests is of paramount importance. It is known that with the majority of children a slow process of weaning is much more satisfactory and leads to weaning being carried through almost unnoticed. This gives the child time to get accustomed to the bottle while he still has the breast at certain meals. His wishes are thus met, and it is recognized that he has to be guided slowly into other channels.

In the weaning process, where the child has to transfer his fondness from the breast to the bottle, we gain a first impression as to how an instinctive urge may be *displaced* on to *another object.* This does not entail a change in the instinctive urge itself, but merely a change of object. Often, however, it means that the child has to be satisfied with less instinctive pleasure than he could gain before. So far as weaning is concerned, the child also has to give up his close intimacy with the mother's body, a satisfaction which, as we have seen, is greatly cherished. This displacement of the instinctive urge, the displacement of " libido " as we call it if the urge is a sexual one, goes on all the time, and is used extensively in education, when a more social act is often substituted for a less social one. It should be borne in mind that in connection with this displacement the child has to give up a certain amount of instinctive pleasure.

Displacement is only one mechanism by which a certain modification of instinctive activity can be brought about, and it is a mechanism which from early on is brought into play by the environment. The force which drives the child to accept the substitute is the emotional relationship to the mother which towards the end of the first year is already fairly strong.

REACTION-FORMATION.

The next point where we can see a divergence of interests between the child and the adult is during the training in cleanliness. The situation now is different from what it was during the first year of life. The child's intelligence is growing, and his relationship to the mother is no longer so exclusively happy, owing to disappointments which have occurred earlier. He is still very dependent on the mother, but he also has some inkling of the power which he can exert by being troublesome. His instinctive urges at this time are very strong, and most of them have to disappear if he is to become socially adapted. The power of the child's instinctive desires at this period becomes apparent if we compare his behaviour when asked to give up something which provides instinctive pleasure with that he exhibits when discouraged from doing something he wants to do merely out of curiosity. All children, for instance, are interested in fire and would like to touch it. Some of them, as a matter of fact, probably the majority, abstain from doing so if told that it hurts and is dangerous. Others will do it once, and thereafter the recollection of the pain experienced will be enough to prevent a repetition of the act. Being dirty also has unpleasant results. The mother may show that she dislikes it, and may even use stronger means of showing her disgust. Nevertheless, the child, unless severely dealt with, will go on being dirty for quite a time.

Children at this age have already begun to imitate other children and adults. Table manners can be introduced by imitation only. But the fact that the small child is the only one in the family who still wets his knickers does not induce him to give up the habit. The process by which the pleasure in being dirty is changed into the adult attitude of wanting to be clean and of feeling disgust for dirt is a lengthy and more complicated one. The motive force which induces the child to forgo his pleasures is again his love for and fear of the mother.

The child of course very soon understands that the mother does not want him to be wet. In observing toddlers we can see how the child does not at first take much notice of this wish. In time he repeatedly sees pleasure and appreciation on the face of the mother if he has complied with her wishes, and disappointment if he has not done so. The child definitely wants to keep the mother's affection ; so slowly but surely he makes the mother's wish his own. He *identifies* himself with the mother's wishes and begins to fight his inner urges. There is a time before the child is really clean when he still occasionally satisfies his desire to be dirty, but immediately afterwards either disowns his action or calls himself naughty. Once control of the sphincters is obtained, the pleasure in the achievement itself helps towards stabilization. It is not unusual for a child a short time after he has become clean to show exaggerated disgust at the dirty habits of other children, as if he could not be quite certain of his own achievement unless he reacted violently against everything which might remind him of former and now unwanted pleasures.

What has happened in this process to the instinctive urge itself? It has apparently been replaced by the opposite tendency : instead of being dirty there appears the wish to be clean ; or instead of wanting to hurt the other child there is pity. It may be observed that the social wish is usually as strong as the original instinctive urge. The energy behind the original instinctive urge is used to subdue this impulse and to strengthen the opposing tendency. We call this mechanism of modification *reaction formation.* Cleanliness and the ability to pity other people are character traits. Here we have an example of how the modification of an instinctive urge leads to the building up of the character of the adult (8*i*).

There are many other instinctive trends belonging to the anal-sadistic stage which must be modified if the child is to become social. For instance, the child thinks that his fæces are something very precious, and not at all disgusting. They are his own products, belonging to his own body, and he invests them in his mind with all kinds of magical powers. This attitude, arising out of the child's instinctive urges at that time, has to disappear. He is required to part from his fæces at the mother's wish and to regard them as disgusting. The interest in the fæces, as a result of the training in cleanliness, is displaced to possessions of a different kind—to toys, clothes, and later on, to money. The strength of the child's attachment to his fæces can be gathered from the obstinacy with which he may react to the mother's wish to defæcate at given times and in a given place. Again, the original strength of these instinctive urges can be assessed by the strength of the energy displaced. We usually find the character traits of exaggerated cleanliness, closeness with money, and obstinacy combined in a given adult personality (8*j*).

So far we have seen two modifications of instinctive urges at work: displacement, which tends to tone down the pleasure gained by the substitution of a less pleasurable but still instinctive activity, and reaction formation, whereby the energy behind the original instinct is used to build up a reaction of the opposite kind. We see that so far as reaction formation is concerned energy is being used up continuously in order to keep the original instinct at bay, but this has a social aim. Cleanliness and pity, shame and disgust are qualities which are necessary in a social human being. Yet, as we shall presently see, this mechanism is not very economical so far as mental energy is concerned.

SUBLIMATION.

Perhaps there are other and more satisfactory ways of dealing with instinctive urges. A child may have a strong wish to hurt another child, but learn in time that the consequences of such acts are apt to be unpleasant. A little later he may be cruel to animals until this also is made impossible either by outward prohibition or by his realizing that the animal experiences pain too. So instead of pulling off spiders' legs, the little boy starts to take his toys to pieces, and this in time may lead him to investigate the working of mechanical toys and even, after having taken things to pieces, to put them together again. The instinct has been diverted from its original aim—

inflicting pain—to a new social aim, namely, investigation and construction. In this mechanism, which we call *sublimation* (8*c*), the greater part of the original impulse is used up in a social activity. This is certainly the most economic and socially useful method of modifying an instinct, and many of our activities have at their bases sublimated instinctive drives. This explains the fervour and tenacity with which we pursue certain activities as compared with others where we are less emotionally involved.

In this description of the mechanisms at work in displacement, reaction-formation and sublimation, it has been assumed that the child is given time to adjust his behaviour to his surroundings and that the fear of what would happen if he were to indulge in one or the other undesirable impulse is not overwhelming. Sudden disappointment or fears connected with instinctive gratification may bring about quite different results.

TURNING OF INSTINCT INTO OPPOSITE.

Let us again take as an example an aggressive urge, such as the wish to hurt the little brother. A sudden shock such as a blow from an adult may lead to the instinct becoming its opposite (8*c*). Satisfaction is now derived from being hurt instead of hurting, and little is gained in the building up of character.

REPRESSION.

But another way out may be found. The child who until this particular experience has been very aggressive may suddenly lose all his aggressive tendencies and at the same time become rather inactive. The aggressive tendencies have disappeared from his overt behaviour. But have they disappeared altogether? The same child may, for instance, years later " by accident " severely hurt his younger brother. These tendencies, although they have been excluded from the conscious personality of the child, have not disappeared—psychical energy cannot simply vanish from one day to another—but they have been *repressed into the unconscious* (8*k*) and will there remain in their original form. A vast amount of energy is necessary to keep these antisocial urges repressed, and both the energy behind the original instinctive drive and the energy used to keep this impulse in the unconscious are lost for further use. Furthermore, not only have the aggressive wishes themselves to disappear, but any activity which is in any way related to the old impulse has to go as well. Therefore, although the child will be easier to handle from now on, he has also lost a considerable part of his healthy, active drive. There is, of course, always the danger with repressed instinctive urges that one day they may break through against the will of the conscious personality either openly or in a disguised form.

REGRESSION. It has been observed during the wartime evacuation period that children who had hitherto been clean became dirty again when separated from their mothers. We have seen that the modification of instinctive drives at this stage is brought about by the relationship of the child to the mother, and the shock of sudden separation caused a *regression* (8*c*) of the instinctive energy back to a former level of development. The child has to have instinctive gratification. If he cannot get it at the higher level just attained he will regress to a former stage where he once before experienced satisfaction. A regression of instinctive energy to a former level of maturation may occur at any stage, and is usually caused by severe disappointment or acute fear. It is, of course, a very unsatisfactory way of dealing with impulses, as to a certain extent it causes an arrest in development. The level to which regression proceeds is by no means a matter of chance. On their way to maturation the instinctive urges meet with varying responses. If at any stage, say the anal-sadistic one, the child gets too much satisfaction, or if his desires at this phase are constantly frustrated, then some of the instinctive energy will be arrested at this phase. When later, on a higher level, gratification becomes impossible, the chances are that the instinctive energy will turn back to this old *fixation point*. It seems that a constant alternation between too much frustration and too much gratification at any given level is very apt to cause a fixation at that particular stage.

These are some of the mechanisms by which instinctive urges are modified. There are other mechanisms, some of which will be discussed in relation to case material, as it would lead us too far afield to go into greater detail at this stage.

INSTINCTIVE GRATIFICATION IN THE ADULT. Not all the instinctive urges to which expression is given during the stages of development described are transformed. Every human being has to have a certain amount of direct instinctive gratification, though there are wide variations amongst men in the relationship between direct and indirect or modified satisfaction. The instinctive urges of the phallic phase, which appear in puberty as the genital impulse, can and should largely find direct gratification in the sexual life of the adult, though to a certain extent and for certain periods of time sublimation of genital impulses is possible. Some remnants of the instinctive urges of the oral phase also remain more or less unaltered. Examples of these are for instance kissing as related to sexual activities, exhibitionistic tendencies, especially in the woman, and aggressive urges in the man. The bulk of the instinctive urges of the pregenital phases, being antisocial or perverse, have to disappear, and we have seen some of the mechanisms by which they are modified. Not all these mechanisms make their appearance at the beginning of life. Repression, for instance, presupposes that the personality of the child is already strong enough to keep an instinct under control, and this does not happen until the Ego is fairly well developed, say after the third year. Sublimation needs ability and the beginnings of a social sense, and does not come into action to any large extent before the fifth year. Displacement, on the contrary, arises from the beginning, and so does regression. Reaction formation appears first during the anal-sadistic phase.

In our civilization many of our instinctive urges are unable to find an outlet (8*e*). Though during the last few decades sexual repression has been lifted to a certain extent, the sexual urge cannot be gratified at the time when it makes its first appearance, nor should it be. But although the sexual urge can be gratified later on, our aggressive urges have to be modified to an ever-greater extent if community life is to become more satisfactory. I do not wish to enter more than is necessary into these complicated questions, but if we are to understand unbalanced human beings, of whom the delinquent is one, we cannot avoid being aware of the fact that the task of keeping one's instinctive urges in check is a singularly difficult one, in which failures are bound to occur. . The price of our culture, which makes this disappearance of direct instinctive urges necessary, is an increasing number of mentally disturbed persons.

CHOICE OF MECHANISM.

The situation would be less dangerous if it were possible either for the relatives or for the man himself to choose the mechanism by which his instinctive urges are modified. We shall see presently how the environment can help towards a more satisfactory solution. Nevertheless, every human being has repressions and reaction formations, mechanisms which, as we have seen, are uneconomical for the psychological make-up. Again we find that it is factors of quantity rather than quality which distinguish one personality from another. Repressions need not necessarily become a disturbing factor, and certain reaction formations such as cleanliness and pity are desirable character traits. Again even in the most disturbed personality we find some sublimations. To a certain extent, what mechanisms are mainly chosen for modification may be due to some innate quality. A person of high intelligence and great abilities will be better able to sublimate instinctive energy than will a mentally backward individual. But though these innate tendencies exist, and though we cannot deliberately choose the best mechanisms, the environment plays an important rôle in the fate of the instinctive urges, and the re-education of delinquents is impossible unless we can succeed in modifying their impulses in a satisfactory way.

Psycho-analytical research has been able to trace many more ramifications of instinctive urges into social activities than have been described here. Those who are specially interested in the subject should refer to the original papers and books (8*b*, *c*, *i*, *j*; 2*b*; 7*a*).

FACTORS INFLUENCING MODIFICATION.

The transformation of the original instinctive drives is an important factor in becoming social, equalled in importance only by the necessity for the child to be able to wait for satisfaction of his social desires. Many factors co-operate in allowing this twofold development to proceed satisfactorily. There is an innate tendency in the instinctive urges to progress to higher forms of development.[1] This biological tendency of the instincts makes it easier during the first years of life to offer substitutes to the child or to press for a modification of instinctive urges at a time when the next step in development is already near at hand. A child of 2 who is aggressive because he wants to hurt another child will not abstain from his aggressive acts when told that he causes the other child pain, for that is exactly what he wants to do. But six months later, when he is already able to feel pity, this explanation will lead to a transformation of the instinct.

NATURAL ENDOWMENTS.

The natural endowments of a child, the strength of his instinctive urges and innate intelligence will play a part in the choice of mechanisms, though this, of course, is not a conscious process.

These two factors, which we may call the constitutional factors, cannot be influenced by the outside world. But they only contribute towards and by no means constitute a satisfactory outcome.

The most potent factor in bringing about a modification of instinctive urges is the child's emotional relationship to the

[1] Part I, Ch. III.

MOTHER-CHILD-RELATIONSHIP.

mother. We have seen that at an early age when the child is not yet able to understand intellectually the necessity for social behaviour and when his own needs are still very imperative, the only motive for modifying his actions is the wish to please the mother and the fear of losing her affection. The training in cleanliness, for instance, which ends in the formation of character, occurs at a time when the relationship to the mother is for the child the only motive inducing him to give up his antisocial pleasures. The power which the mother has at her disposal during those first formative years is very great indeed, and much will depend on the way in which it is used.

EDUCATIONAL METHODS.

Of almost equal importance therefore are the educational methods used by the mother in bringing about the modifications of instincts. We have seen that the mechanisms employed are not equally economical so far as psychic energy is concerned. In sublimation nearly all the energy is diverted into socially useful channels. In repression all the energy is lost so far as the further building up of the personality is concerned. Repression, we have seen, usually occurs when the child is exposed to sudden shocks, either inflicted from the outside or caused by innate fear. It is at least possible to avoid shocks from the outside. If the nature and expression of the child's instinctive life is taken into account one imperative law can be deduced : the modification of instinctive urges, if it is to proceed satisfactorily, has to be given time. A certain amount of freedom of expression at the different levels of development should be allowed, and changes should not be brought about rapidly. It is quite true that one can succeed in getting a child to be clean very quickly if enough pressure and threats are used. But the effect of such methods on later character-development will be devastating. On the other hand, we have to guard against the opposite error of giving the child too much opportunity for gratifying instinctive urges which in the end will have to disappear. A child should be prevented from thumb-sucking during the day at the age of 2, but it will be better to provide adequate toys and other occupations than to put some bitter substance on the fingers.

In order to apply educational methods in such a way that they help and do not hinder the child's development, some knowledge of the different phases of instinctive development, of what is natural at a given age, seems to be necessary.

SOCIAL ENVIRONMENT

The whole of the social environment into which a child is born and in which he spends the first years of his life will naturally leave its imprint on the modifications of instinctive urges. In *Our Towns, a Close-Up* (20) we find ample material to prove that it is a mistake to hope for a satisfactory modification of instincts in an environment which makes cleanliness almost impossible. It will also be clear that in this environment the possibilities of sublimating urges are somewhat limited. The child's freedom of action, his toys, the possibility of living out certain conflicts in play, the time the mother can spend on each single offspring—all these are important items in the development of character. So of course are the actual personalities of the parents. If, for instance, the mother is unable on account of her own emotional difficulties to bear the expression of the child's instinctive urges, even an otherwise good social environment will not counteract the damage she will do.

These in short are the main factors involved in bringing about a satisfactory or unsatisfactory modification of the antisocial instinctive drives. With this knowledge it will be easier to understand the important emotional development which the child undergoes between the ages of 3 and 5 years.

CHAPTER VI

THE OEDIPUS CONFLICT

THE FATHER'S PART.

By the time the child is 3, his relationship with the mother has changed. The child is still very dependent and exacting, though he has already begun to realize that he cannot take exclusive possession of the mother, and the hostile feelings aroused by various disappointments have made the relationship a little less happy than it was a year earlier. Other persons in the environment have already begun to be important. The father, of course, plays a part in the child's life from the first. But as he is not the person who satisfies the child's material needs, his presence is at first, though agreeable, not necessary for the child's happiness. Anna Freud and D. Burlingham (2*b*) have made important observations on the rôle of the father in the early years of the child's life. To the child of 3, the father is already a very important figure ; he is admired for his strength and power and is a symbol of the outside world. Apart from the father there may be older or younger brothers and sisters with whom an emotional relationship is now being established.

The most far-reaching difference, however, compared with the age of 2, is based on the fact that the child's instinctive urges are now no longer exclusively directed towards the mother. Up to the third year the instinctive development of girl and of boy follows more or less the same paths. For both sexes the mother is the first love object. From this point onwards boys and girls develop differently as far as their instinctive life is concerned.

BOY'S ATTITUDE.

The little boy, up till now dependent on the mother, has adopted the same exacting attitude as the girl. Now there is a difference in the relationship. The boy begins to protect the mother, to display his strength in front of her, to imitate the father's behaviour and to talk about the time when he will be as big and as strong as the father. His exacting attitude to the mother changes ; he wants to be admired by her and to be treated in a more grown-up way. In other words, in many ways the little boy starts to behave like a lover. Often one hears boys of about 4 declare their intention to marry their mother when they are grown up. At the same time the relationship to the father also undergoes a change. Mingled with admiration and love there appears jealousy of the father on account of his relationship to the mother, and occasionally a very open attempt at rivalry.

GIRL'S ATTITUDE.

With the little girl something of the same kind happens, but with the difference that she will have to exchange her first love object, the mother, for the father, while for the boy his love object remains unchanged. The first sign that the girl is entering this new phase is her imitation of the mother. She starts to play with dolls and to mother them. She may like doing little jobs in the house, and she carries herself with more confidence. The child's admiration for the father, which may have been present before, now comes more into the foreground with the wish that the father should notice her. She shows off her dresses in front of him, she climbs on to his knees and very often meets with some response. It is well known that fathers generally prefer their daughters, and mothers their sons. Jealousy develops when the girl realizes the father's attachment to the mother. Owing to the fact that the child is still very dependent on the mother, this jealousy cannot be shown as openly as in the case of the boy. There is another shadow in the girl's life which makes this phase difficult for her. We said when discussing the maturation of instincts that in this, the phallic phase, the male genital only is acknowledged. The girl wonders why she is not a boy, and comes to the conclusion that there must be something wrong with her. Resentment is now added to jealousy, since the girl makes the mother responsible for her not having been born a boy.

Adults are inclined to laugh whenever the child shows these feelings openly at this stage. The attitude of the parents largely determines how often the feelings of the child at that age find expression in words. A child's statement that it wants to marry its parent when it grows up may seem funny to the adult, but it is in no wise funny for the child. The emotions experienced at this phase are very deep and strong, and perfectly comparable to those of an adult in love. It is not that the child is able to express in so many words what is going on within him. But there is this drive to take possession of the parent of the other sex, the fear born of jealousy of the parent of the same sex, who is at the same time still loved, and the impossibility of gaining any real gratification for these powerful urges.

The child may not have any real conception of what a sexual relationship is like, but as the auto-erotic activity of this phase is masturbation, he has some dim idea that it has something to do with the genitals. This is the time when sexual investigation [1] is at its height, and children frequently satisfy some of their curiosity by looking at each other or starting some kind of sexual game, imitating what they suppose their parents to do when they are alone. Children at this stage are really sexually excited, especially at bedtime, and they can relieve the tension by masturbation. The phantasies accompanying masturbation are *incestuous* and show something of the child's conception of sexual life. They very often contain sadistic elements, such as beating scenes, which are a disguised expression of the aggressive interpretation of intercourse. The masturbation of this period therefore becomes the centre of the child's infantile sexual life.

INFANTILE MASTURBATION.

PASSING OF THE OEDIPUS CONFLICT.

This first heterosexual love relationship of the child is doomed to failure, for physiological if for no other reasons. For the later emotional life of the adult much will depend on the way in which the emotional tangle of this period, which we call the *Oedipus phase* (8*m*), is resolved.

How does the child come to realize that he cannot satisfy his desires? There is first of all the fact of his small size as compared with the rival parent. Though the child, at this stage, pretends to be grown up, he of course realizes his weakness as compared with father or mother. As bodily strength is very impressive at this age, this realization cannot be postponed for ever.

FEAR OF CASTRATION.

A much more potent factor, however, is the fear aroused by the child's hostility towards the parent of the same sex. The child at this age is still very aggressive. If he hates a person, though that person may be loved and admired at other times, he wants the person to be out of the way. To be out of the way is for the child synonymous with being dead. The child, who still tends to believe that the parent is all-powerful and knows everything, believes that the father—if we take the little boy as an example—will guess his hostile feelings and will also know about his desires for the mother, and he expects his father to have the same aggressive tendencies against himself. He is afraid that the

[1] Part I, Ch. III, p. 20.

father might kill him or punish him in some dreadful way. The most dreadful punishment for the boy at this stage is to be robbed of his manliness, that is to be castrated. There may have been threats connected with his masturbation, which would make this punishment seem very natural to him. There may have, and in most cases has been, some observation of a little girl's genitals which would give realization to any vague threat or to the child's own feeling of guilt.

IDENTIFICATION.

The little boy is thus in an awkward position : there are his urges which are at times very pressing and make him wish to possess the mother. There is the fear that wishes of that kind will be punished by the father with the loss of the organ on which his manliness depends. In the long run the fear of having his body mutilated is stronger : the sexual desire for the mother has to be given up. Instead of wanting to possess the mother, the boy *identifies* himself with the father ; he wants to become like him, so that later on, when he is grown up, he can marry a woman like his mother. The boy is helped to this decision, which, incidentally, is never a conscious one, by his admiration and love for the father, which is there all the time and which also would have to suffer if he were to pursue his desire for the mother.

FATE OF INCESTUOUS DESIRES.

We have heard that instinctive urges cannot simply disappear. What happens to the impulses after this decision has been taken? The first thing is that the boy does not consciously want to know anything about his conflicts any longer. The conflicts, and with them some of the instinctive urges, are repressed, and the energy behind them is used to build up in the mind of the child the ideal figure of the father with whom the boy has identified himself. In this process these instinctive urges have lost their sexual character. Other impulses remain, but become inhibited in their aim. They constitute the tender feelings which the child later on will have towards his parents, being satisfied with friendliness and no longer clamouring for possession. The hostile tendencies, robbed of their object, become directed against the child's own person. They play an important part, as we shall see later, in the formation of conscience. Ideally, therefore, the impulses which constituted the Oedipus desires are modified in such a way that their energy is fully used for the further building up of the personality. In that case the Oedipus conflict as such is completely resolved.

NEUROTIC SOLUTIONS.

This, as we have said, would be the ideal solution, but it is doubtful whether it is ever fully attained. To mention some only of the other possibilities : the fear resulting from the incestuous desires may have been unusually strong, and increased by a sudden shock. In such a case the whole of the Oedipus desires may be repressed without there being time to direct the energy behind them into other channels. In this case the Oedipus conflict would not be resolved as described above, but would continue to exist in the unconscious. Every heterosexual tendency after puberty will be apt to arouse the old conflicts because the desires are still fixated on the first objects.

Or, the fear may be particularly strong on account of the actual personality of the father. If either the father is very severe or the desire for the mother is increased by the absence of the father who at the height of the Oedipus conflict suddenly appears (a situation very common in wartime), then the desire for the mother may be exchanged for a desire for the father. That is to say, in order not to be threatened by this frightening father the boy suddenly gives up the wish for the mother and seeks love and satisfaction from the father. This results in a passive and feminine attitude towards the father, which in turn has to be repressed because it would mean being like a woman and thus being castrated. One outcome of this solution may be manifest or latent homosexuality in later life, or antisocial behaviour.

Again, if the fear were very strong and the phallic organization for one reason or another very weak to begin with, so that every kind of satisfaction on this level seemed too dangerous, the libido might regress to a former level of development, usually the anal-sadistic one. The impulses belonging to this phase have in turn to be repressed on account of their sadistic nature. The result in adult life may be the outbreak of an obsessional neurosis or delinquency.

All kinds of variations on these possibilities may occur. As will be shown later, the outcome of this phase will become apparent after puberty and will influence decisively the love life of the adult.

SOLUTION OF CONFLICT IN GIRL.

The Oedipus conflict takes less vehement forms in the girl, though the change in the love object, as mentioned above, constitutes a severe difficulty which is often not completely overcome. As the girl has no male genital she cannot be afraid of losing it. We have seen how the realization of her deficiency, as she perceives it, increases her resentment and hostility against the mother. On the other hand her love for the mother and dependence on her are very strong. The girl's motive in giving up her sexual wishes for her father is the fear of losing the love of her mother without which she would be helpless. She ends this conflict by identifying herself with the mother in order to be able to have a lover like the father later on. The instinctive urges are modified in the same way and similar possibilities occur according to the strength of fear and feelings of guilt. With the girl, too, the conflict may end in an identification with the father instead of with the mother, which may lead to later homosexuality. Or the conflict may be repressed in its entirety so that the girl remains fixated to the Oedipus phase. This has often occurred in cases where all the later love objects are married men.

Children who have overcome the conflicts of the Oedipus phase tend to repress everything which might remind them of it. This means that every recollection of their instinctive wishes in that particular phase or before it is blotted out of consciousness. With it goes the memory of more harmless experiences, of places, persons, and so on. This is the reason why the majority of adults have no connected memories of their life before their fifth or sixth year. Occasionally this amnesia extends even to the seventh or eighth year. This *infantile amnesia* (8*b*) is also responsible for the fact that until Freud's discoveries, made by the psycho-analytical method, no scientific knowledge on infantile sexuality was available. Indeed, certain facts which it was difficult completely to overlook, such as infantile masturbation or sexual games between children, were regarded as anomalies and as having no place in normal development. This fact more than any other demonstrates the tendentious nature of this forgetting. The recollections of early childhood are not only passively forgotten, but are forced back from active memory and kept away from consciousness by an active force. Everything which might tend to bring this old conflict back into consciousness is kept away from the mind. It might be thought that children at that age simply have not yet the power to recollect and to store up in their memory to the same extent as adults. This is contradicted by the fact that these memories can be brought to consciousness again in the adult by the process of psycho-analysis,

INFANTILE AMNESIA.

and observation of children shows that their capacity to retain memories is considerable.

With this repression of the memories of the Oedipus phase, the child enters a new stage in his life where intellectual interests predominate. The most important step, however, taken in conjunction with the solution of the Oedipus conflict, is the growing independence of the child's ethical code in relation to that of his parents.

CHAPTER VII

THE FORMATION OF CONSCIENCE

INDEPENDENT ETHICAL CODE OF INDIVIDUAL.

The formation of an ethical code is one of the indispensable prerequisites of social adaptation. This ethical code, popularly called conscience, and in psycho-analytical nomenclature known as the *Super-Ego*, bears unmistakable traces of the ethical code prevalent in the environment of every individual. Ethical codes have not only changed in the course of time, but they differ at least to some slight degree in different groups of our present-day society. The ethical code of the public school man is different from the ethical code of the Cockney, though they have certain characteristics in common. This fact can be demonstrated more clearly in a country such as America, where communities of immigrants of different nationalities live together in close proximity, and where difficulties occur because children who have grown up in these communities have adopted the standards of their parents and so may often appear anti-social in an ordinary American environment (3).

It might be assumed that the ethical code is passively taken over by the child from the community in which he grows up. Though the influence of the environment on the formation of the conscience cannot be denied, yet on closer observation it will become apparent that the child's ethical code is very often either more or less severe than that of the parents, and in no way a mere copy of it. Furthermore, if it were a matter of passive adoption, it should not be difficult to change one's conscience from time to time under the influence of a new environment. But this is by no means the case. The Englishman, for instance, is renowned for keeping to his own ethical standards in whatever part of the world he may live. Ethically suitable environments have failed to produce an ethical code in delinquents. On the other hand, we find that some environments are apt to lead to changes in the conscience, as for instance certain group formations, while others fail to exert any influence on the ethical codes of people who come into contact with them.

The actual facts cannot be explained by a simple theory of adaptation to the ethical code of the environment. Another explanation, often given, that the conscience is inborn, fails to explain why no traces of it can be detected in the small child and why the ethical codes of various times and various environments exhibit dissimilarities as well as similarities.

Understanding of the structure of the conscience is, of course, essential to an understanding of the problems of social adaptation and antisocial behaviour. It has been stated above [1] that the difference between a child of 2 and one of 8 is a question of conscience. While the child of 2 judges his actions merely by pleasure and pain, a child of 8 already knows what is right and wrong, even if he is not always able to direct his actions in accordance with his knowledge. We shall therefore have to look into the formative years, between the ages of 2 and 8, in order to understand how conscience is formed.

IMITATION.

Children begin very early to imitate adults, to behave and speak as they do, to copy their table manners, and so on. This imitation is effective only where the child's interests are the same as those of the adult. It does not help, as we have seen, to educate children in cleanliness. It paves the way, however, for a further and more complicated mechanism in the adoption of the adult attitude. Anna Freud and D. Burlingham (*2b*) have made intensive studies of the nature of imitation in small children under nursery conditions.

IDENTIFICATION WITH DEMAND OF PARENT.

The next step has already been mentioned when discussing the training in cleanliness. Here, as we have seen, the interests of child and mother are opposed. Driven by love and fear, the child tries to make the mother's demands his own, against his own desires. He identifies himself, as we said, with the demand of the mother. This is more than imitation. The child does not intend to behave like the mother, but tries to have the same wishes as she has. We have seen that this identification with the mother's demands leads to the modification of the underlying impulse. This comes closer to the possession of a conscience, but it is not sufficient for what is needed in the adult. This identification with the mother's demands needs her presence, that is, it is effective only so long as the emotional relationship to the adult exists. We have seen that children who during the wartime evacuation period were separated from their mothers began to be dirty once more. The child becomes clean, not because he wants to be clean, but because the beloved person in his imme-

[1] Part I, Ch. I, p. 13.

diate surroundings desires it. This mechanism, of course, helps to a considerable extent in educating the child and in making him realize what he should and should not do. It also explains the similarity between his ethical code and that of his environment. At this stage, the child really adopts the demands of the parents. But he is, at the same time, entirely dependent on their presence, and will often do what he ought not, if the adult's back is turned. We can thus see that if no further development took place, the laws which society has instituted to guard the interests of the community would be observed only in the presence of a policeman.

With growing age and increasing intelligence the child will be better able to do what is desired of him even in the absence of the parents, but mainly in those instances where he already knows that yielding to his desire will cause immediate trouble.

IDENTIFICATION WITH AND INTERNALIZATION OF PARENT IMAGES.

The decisive step towards independence is taken at the end of the Oedipus phase, about the age of 5. We have described how the conflicts of the Oedipus period end in the identification of the child with the parent of the same sex, and, it may now be added, to a less obvious degree also with the parent of the opposite sex. This is no longer an identification with the demand of the one or other, it is the desire to become like the whole person of the adult. At the same time the parents cease to be love objects. They have, as it were, become internalized. They are present inside the child, watching over his actions all the time, whether they are there in reality or not. And, what is more, these internalized parent figures are the remnants of the Oedipus conflict. The child has to keep on good terms with them, or he will once more experience the fears and the feeling of guilt which belong to the emotional upheaval of this phase (8*n*).

We have seen that during the Oedipus phase the child is hostile towards the parent of the same sex. When the parent ceases to be the love object, these feelings can no longer find expression in the external world. These aggressive tendencies become directed inwards and are added to the Ideal Figure of the parent which the child has set up inside himself. The more hostile the child felt towards his father or mother, the more severely will the internalized parent, the conscience or Super-Ego, behave towards the forbidden desires of the child. It is often observed that children after the age of 5 or 6 feel extremely guilty about some small misdeed and expect punishment of a severity which their real parents would never have inflicted. This common observation can be explained by the addition of the child's own aggressive tendencies to the figures of the parents which now constitute the child's own ethical code.

The Ideal Figure which the child has set up inside himself bears, of course, a close resemblance to the real parents. But there are differences : we have just remarked that the conscience may be much more severe than the actual parents ever were, by reason of the addition of the child's own aggressiveness. Other differences may be explained by the fact that the child identifies himself with the parents as he sees them. Until the disappointments of the Oedipus phase, children regard their parents as all-powerful beings. They are so much stronger, they can do what they like, they know everything, they represent the vastness and grandeur of the whole of the external world which the child cannot yet master. The child's conscience is endowed with all these qualities, and this will remain the case even if his belief in the omnipotence of his parents is slowly lost.

FEELING OF GUILT.

It has been shown that during the height of the Oedipus conflict the child felt guilty towards the parents because of his hostile feelings and desires. The same feeling of guilt is now experienced if the child does not attain the standards set by his conscience. In other words, so long as the child, or for that matter, the adult lives up to the demands of his internalized parents, all is well, and he will not even be aware of this inner voice. As soon as there is a deviation from the expected standards the tension between the demands of the conscience and the wishes of the child's personality is perceived as a feeling of guilt. This feeling, as we all know, is extremely unpleasant, and urges the child without the presence of an adult to do the " right " thing.

As will be explained in a later chapter, the formation of conscience is not completed but only begun with the important identification at the end of the Oedipus phase. Later impressions will play a decisive part in the eventual formation of the Super-Ego.

This explanation of the formation of the conscience, developed by psycho-analytical insight into the structure of the personality and afterwards substantiated by observation of children, explains the variations of the conscience as described at the beginning of this chapter. It also explains why the ethical code of certain environments can be adopted and not that of others. If the environmental constellation is such that it represents parent figures, that is to say, if the individual concerned has a strong emotional contact with people in his environment, a process of identification on the lines of the earlier identification will be set in motion and with it a modification of the demands of the Super-Ego, provided the personality in question is mentally healthy (*80*).

To sum up : the formation of an independent ethical code, an independent conscience, is the product of the solution of the Oedipus conflict. The real personalities of the parents and the whole of the environment play an important part in the shaping of the conscience, though it is modified by the child's own instinctive tendencies and later identifications.

CHAPTER VIII

THE STRUCTURE OF THE PERSONALITY

With the solution of the Oedipus conflict and the subsequent formation of the conscience or Super-Ego, the structure of the personality as we find it in the adult has come into being. There will still be important changes in character, owing to experiences after the fifth year, but the foundations of the personality-structure have been laid, and the way in which the Oedipus conflict has been overcome decides to a certain extent whether or not the individual has the chance to remain mentally healthy.

SEPARATION OF EGO FROM ID.

We have followed the development of the child from pre-consciousness till the age of eight, when his mind shows a definite structure, consisting of the *Id*, the reservoir of instinctive energy ; the *Ego*, with which we consciously act ; and the *Super-Ego*, which controls both instincts and actions (8*n*).

To sum up briefly the development of these three regions of the mind : the new-born infant has as yet no consciousness. We have no means of describing what is going on in his mind ; we do not know whether there is anything going on. What we do know is that the baby feels urges, and gives expression to those urges by crying. When satisfied he again withdraws completely from the external world and sleeps. Slowly, as a result of the action of the various agencies of the external world and the growing maturation of the infant's senses, his perceptive powers and his intelligence, he learns to distinguish between his own body and the world outside, and thereupon consciousness comes into being. This occurs about the time of the development of speech, sometimes perhaps slightly earlier, as it is known that some children understand long before they learn to speak. Once the Ego has developed the mind is separated into two parts : the reservoir of the instinctive urges which in themselves are not conscious, and the Ego. The relationship between the two is very different from what it will be later on. The Ego is still extremely weak, consisting merely of an awareness of the self and of the mother, while the instinctive urges, as we have seen, are strong and are always able to find expression. This expression of instinctive urges gradually arouses the disapproval of the outside world. A conflict is thus caused in the Ego ; it has to choose whether it will immediately satisfy an instinctive urge at the cost of the resulting pain, or suffer the tension of the developing urge in the hope of getting a delayed satisfaction without feeling pain. The growing intelligence of the child, his growing perception of the world and his experiences help him slowly but surely to develop from the original pleasure-pain principle to the reality principle.[1] The modified instinctive urges help towards the strengthening of the conscious personality.

The difficulty during these early years is the fact that the instinctive urges, often opposing each other, each strive for satisfaction which is independent of the past and the future. The child of 3, for instance, will love one minute and hate the next. This love and hatred for the same person are not yet synthesized into a harmonious relationship of constant friendliness. We say that the small child is *ambivalent* (8*b*, *c*) in his feelings towards the persons in his surroundings.

AMBIVALENCE.

Roughly from the time when he is trained to be clean the child's Ego attempts at least occasionally to master and control the impulses arising out of the unconscious. During the height of the Oedipus conflict his instinctive urges find very little expression in the outside world. We have seen that anxiety and guilt about his aggressive feelings prevent the child from expressing impulses which arouse the disapproval of the parents.

ANXIETY.

The child probably begins to feel anxiety at a very early age. Anxiety is an inborn reaction towards danger. The first great danger which the child can perceive is that of being left alone by his mother. This danger exists for him not only when the mother is really absent, but also when she withdraws her attention from him. This situation is felt to be so dangerous because the child is then exposed to the rising tension caused by instinctive urges which cannot be satisfied. This tension causes anxiety, which is one of the most unpleasant emotions which can be experienced. Therefore the child will do everything in his power to avoid a recurrence of this unpleasant experience. In the beginning he usually has attacks of anxiety which overwhelm him completely. In time he learns to recognize the first sign of the approaching unpleasantness ; he experiences anxiety, as it were, in the form of a warning, and is able to take

FEAR OF LOSS OF LOVE.

[1] Part I, Ch. V, p. 27.

precautions. We already know the forms that some of these take. The child may repress an impulse just about to arise, or the impulse may be modified in one of the different ways we have discussed. Activities which may arouse a dangerous impulse, that is to say an impulse which will bring with it the disapproval of the powerful outside world, may be altogether inhibited. There are many more ways in which the child may avoid anxiety : the mechanisms employed will be economical if the threatened danger is not too overwhelming and if the child is not too often exposed to sudden shocks or, as we call them, *traumatic experiences.*

The anxiety aroused by the fear of being left alone, or the fear of the loss of the mother's love, conditions which for the child are synonymous, later gives way to fear of castration. We have seen that this anxiety leads to the resolution of the Oedipus conflict, that is, to the giving up of the child's most cherished desires. Again, the threatened danger is a real danger, the loss of manliness in the boy. For the small boy at least, this fear, as we have seen, is very real, being confirmed by the observation of the female genital. We have also learnt that the fear of castration, if too strong, will lead to a sudden repression of the Oedipus desires or even to regression to a lower level of development.

CASTRATION FEAR.

After the identification with the parents and the formation of the Super-Ego, anxiety is caused by the dangers which threaten from the disapproval of the conscience. As the Super-Ego contains the demands of society, which were represented by the parents, we call this anxiety *social anxiety*, and it will remain throughout life. It will lead to the fulfilment of the commands of the conscience.

SOCIAL ANXIETY.

Anxiety is the most powerful of the forces which drive the still weak Ego of the child to control his instinctive urges on the one hand and the outside world on the other. The child, as we know, is not always successful, and anxiety states in small children are so common that it is hardly possible to consider them as a sign of abnormality, unless they persist for too long a time. If, however, the early anxiety conditions, the fear of loss of love and of castration persist into the individual's adult life, they may form the basis of a neurotic illness.

It is not possible within the scope of this book to give more details of the theory of anxiety. Readers who are especially interested in the subject must consult specific works (8*b*, *p* ; 7*a*).

SUPER-EGO.

We have followed the division of the mind into the Id and the Ego, and have seen how the Ego is strengthened by the intellectual growth of the child on the one hand and by his mechanisms of defence against the forbidden instinctive urges on the other. The child has to face a conflict between his instinctive urges and the external world. After the formation of the conscience, the demands of the outside world are represented by the Super-Ego. We have seen that the tension caused by disagreement between the Ego and the Super-Ego is experienced as a feeling of guilt. The Ego now has to try to establish a balance between the demands of the Super-Ego and those of the Id. This is occasionally very difficult, especially if the Super-Ego is very severe and does not allow even those expressions of instinctive urges which would be tolerated by society. On the other hand, if an individual cannot obtain any direct instinctive gratification, or if what he does obtain is insufficient, there is the danger of some disturbance in the mental economy. Instincts cannot be abolished, and though they may be repressed in the unconscious, they have a strong driving force behind them. If they cannot obtain satisfaction in a direct way, they strive for it in a more hidden or disguised form. This may lead to the formation of symptoms and to a waste of mental energy, as more and more psychic energy will be needed to keep the intensifying impulses in the unconscious.[1]

ADAPTATION TO REALITY.

If the Ego is able to deal with the demands of the Id and the Super-Ego in such a way that enough instinctive energy can find direct satisfaction, then the individual is what we call mentally balanced or *adapted to reality*. Enough energy is left free for the activities of everyday life, and adaptation to changing environmental conditions will be possible, if the inner life goes on without continual conflicts on irrational grounds. Such an individual will feel happy and satisfied under ordinary circumstances and will find a rational way out of the difficulties presented by reality. Even the most balanced personality will experience times of stress. A love relationship may be unhappy through no fault of one's own, a beloved person may die, ambitions may be thwarted, there may be war, and so on. The difference between the mentally healthy and the unbalanced personality lies in the ability of the former, after a time of stress, to find a more or less satisfactory real or psychological solution.

[1] Part II, Ch. V(*b*), p. 117 ff.

SEVERITY OF SUPER-EGO.

Normally, one does not become aware of any division in one's mind. It has been stated repeatedly that the presence of the conscience becomes known to the individual if the Ego does not obey the demands of the Super-Ego. Everyone has probably had the unpleasant experience of feeling guilty about going to the pictures instead of working. There is one curious fact about the working of the Super-Ego. The more moral people are, the more guilty they usually feel. It might be supposed that anti-social persons would feel guilty, while those with a high ethical code need never do so. In fact the reverse is the case. How can this strange fact be explained? The child reacts to frustration of his instinctive urges by aggression. So does the adult. In an individual with a high ethical code this aggression cannot find an outlet in the external world, and is therefore turned against himself. Like the aggressive feelings of the Oedipus phase, these hostile tendencies are added to the conscience and make it behave more severely towards the Ego. This is the reason why people whose ethical code is strict suffer from an acute feeling of guilt, for they frustrate their instinctive urges more completely.

THE UNCONSCIOUS.

We never become directly aware of our unconscious. The unconscious, as we have said, contains our instinctive urges and our repressed memories. The Id is the vital part of the personality, the source of all energy, and also the part which is closest to the body. Instincts [1] are on the borderline between physiology and psychology. In the Id opposing instincts are close together, each striving for satisfaction. It depends on the Ego whether the instinct is allowed satisfaction, that is to say whether it may become conscious or must remain in the unconscious. Under certain conditions impulses may break through into the consciousness against the will of the Ego. Normally, this happens in dreams and in mistakes (8*q*, *r*). In abnormal mental states, unconscious tendencies find their way into the actions of everyday life in a disguised form.[2]

But it would be erroneous to imagine that our actions and thoughts are not constantly influenced by our instinctive urges and repressed memories. The unconscious, though we are not aware of it, being the vital and powerful part of the mind, influences whatever we do, say or think (8*s*). The conscious

[1] Part I, Ch. II, p. 15.

[2] Part II, Ch. V(*b*), p. 119 ff.

motives for our actions are only part of the story, and whatever decisions we make, the unconscious part of the mind is directing our actions. Case histories in Part II will illustrate this point in so far as mentally undeveloped personalities are concerned. The difference from the normal is one of quantity, and not of quality.

To sum up, after the decline of the Oedipus phase the structure of the personality emerges in the shape of the Id, the Ego and Super-Ego. If mental health is to be maintained the Ego must find a satisfactory solution for the demands of the Id, the Super-Ego and the external world. If this is achieved, the individual is adapted to reality and can cope with the changing situations in his environment without disturbance in his mental equilibrium.

CHAPTER IX

THE LATENCY PERIOD

With the solution of the Oedipus conflict the child enters a new period of his life as regards both his instinctive development and his outside activities.

EGO-DEVELOPMENT.

The beginning of school life marks a new and important epoch in the child's career. In contrast to his main interests during the first five years, which were centred around instinctive urges and their satisfaction, new scope is now given to the development of the child's intellect and character. School offers him the possibility of sublimating his instinctive urges in the intellectual sphere and in the realms of skill. We have seen that the child's instinctive life recedes into the background after the resolution of the Oedipus conflict. Later on, we shall discuss how many of his direct instinctive drives remain. Normally, however, there is instinctive energy free to be modified in the most useful way, by re-directing the instinctive urges into social channels. It may perhaps be doubtful whether activities such as reading, writing and doing sums, apart from using the child's intellectual powers, also make use of his instinctive urges in a modified form. The analysis of various disturbances of those intellectual functions during the first years of school life has shown without a doubt that the disturbance is very often due to the fact that the instinctive urges engaged in these activities are still fixated to their former aims, and therefore have to be inhibited. Modern education is trying to make use of the fact that it is the instinctive basis of intellectual activities which creates the interest without which teaching meets with no success. Hill (14), who employs the theory of sublimation extensively in his interesting work, has devised new textbooks to arouse the child's interest in intellectual subjects by making use of his instinctive preoccupations.

Occasionally we can observe how during the latency period sublimated instinctive urges may reinforce an intellectual ability and thus create a strong and lasting interest in a non-instinctive subject.

A little girl of 7 who had seemed to be very unhappy during the Oedipus period because of her sex, came home from school very excitedly one day. " Look, mummy," she said, " we learned long division in school to-day. Just look, it has got a tail and I can do it." From that day on, her interest in arithmetic grew. On being asked to organize the spare time in her form she started a club for doing arithmetic. About six months later, she asked her mother about the difference in sex and started the subject by wanting more exact information about where babies grew. While her mother was trying to explain to her the female genital in a way which the child could easily understand, with the help of diagrams, the little girl seemed quite uninterested. She took another piece of paper, wrote down a long division sum and showed it to her mother, saying " I can do that ! "

In order to become really good at the subject, this little girl had to be interested in mathematics as well as showing ability for it, and this interest persisted for many years.

This little girl had succeeded in sublimating her wish to become a boy into an intellectual achievement. The choice of the activity was probably based both on natural ability for the subject, and also on the observation that in her co-educational school boys were, on the whole, more interested in arithmetic than girls. The ability alone did not create the sustained interest. The girl had been good at sums since the age of 4, but this in itself did not make the activity as pleasurable as it became after the incident. This pleasure is necessary in pursuing intellectual activities with the zeal which leads to real achievement.

The more scope the normal child between the ages of 6 and 12 is given, the easier will it be to modify instinctive urges by the various mechanisms described.[1] The achievements gained by these new reaction-formations and sublimations, and by intellectual growth, tend to strengthen the Ego, and this enables it to gain better control over the instincts and to master anxiety more completely.

SUPER-EGO DEVELOPMENT.

Of equal importance for the mental development during this phase are factors, met with in school life, which bring about a further strengthening and widening of the Super-Ego. The child enters school at a time when his conscience is just beginning to form. The teacher represents for the child the authority whose demands must be obeyed and a pattern which must be imitated. The child identifies himself with the teacher—provided he is able to establish a good relationship with his pupils—on the basis of his Super-Ego. To the parents' image the image of the

[1] Part I, Ch. V.

teachers is now added, and the child's conscience becomes richer in content. A child of school age is not an empty book whose pages have still to be filled (2*b*). He has already had many experiences and has lived through the most important formative years. But the teacher nevertheless has a chance of being a decisive influence in the child's life. Though the child brings to his relationship with the teacher much that has been and still is living in his relationship with the mother, his relationship with the teacher is slightly different from that with the mother : he does not want from the teacher all the material and emotional comfort which he can still get at home. He wants the teacher on the side of his Super-Ego in order to be able more and more to live up to the standards of his own ideals. The relationship of the child with the teacher is based on intellectual achievement and the formation of the Super-Ego. It must not be forgotten that the child's inner struggle in this period is " to be good " and the help of the teacher is needed to strengthen the side of the " goodness ". This function of the teacher, of course, plays an important rôle in the social adaptation of the child, so that the teacher's personality and his knowledge of the emotional development of children at varying ages will determine whether he is able to give the help which theoretically he could render.

GROUP-FORMATION.

On entering school the child has to conform to life in a group. There are many children of the same age with whom he has to establish a relationship, and the teacher's attention is divided between many more children than was the mother's attention at home. This is one of the most difficult tasks with which the child is confronted ; his attitude will show whether he is socially adapted or not. Strictly speaking, school life is the second group into which the child enters. The first group was the family.

The child's relationship to the individual members of his family has already been discussed.[1] But apart from his complicated and changing relationship to father and mother there is an emotional tie which links all the members of one family together in one group against the world outside. The roots of this relationship usually go far back, to the time when the small child was aware for the first time that he had to share the mother's attention with brothers and sisters. The primary feeling of the small child in relation to the other members of the family is one of jealousy of this intrusion on the mother's affection. It has

[1] Part I, Ch. IV and VI.

been recognized during recent years that the child's first emotion towards the next infant is one of jealousy and hostility (8*b*). These aggressive tendencies are impulses against which the outside world reacts unfavourably. They have to be modified, and a bond is formed between the various children of one family by their common aim of being loved by the parents. So long as the parents' attention is equally divided between the children they can be happy together and identify themselves with each other in their common endeavour to please the parents or to form a league against them. Jealousies are reawakened if parents have favourites. The hatred which could be overcome by identification with the other child in the common bond to the parent then comes to the fore. So long as the child knows that the other child cannot have what he himself wants he is content. But the idea that the other child should get something from the parent which he himself has to do without is unendurable.

The identification of the children amongst themselves in their endeavour to gain the approval of the parents forms the basis for group-formation in general. As the adult, in order to be socially adapted, has to belong to many groups, religious, military, national, and so on, it will be seen that much depends on the way in which this first prototype of a group is built up (8*o*).

The child, on entering school, meets with the first group outside his home. He has been able to identify himself with the other children, especially so far as his Ego-activities are concerned, in order to gain the approval of the teacher. The teacher, as has been shown, represents the Super-Ego of the group, and as such can gain great influence over the character development of the children. Again, just treatment will further the consolidation of the crowd of children into a group which can easily be led.

FATE OF DIRECT INSTINCTIVE GRATIFICATION.

In the preceding pages the child's Ego- and Super-Ego-development during the latency period has been discussed. Though we have stated that the child's instinctive urges recede into the background during this period and therefore lend themselves to modification, this does not mean that direct instinctive gratification is no longer sought for and can be given up without a struggle. In order to complete this short survey of the child's emotional development during this period, the fate of the remaining instinctive urges must be followed up.

It has been stated that during the Oedipus phase masturbation, which is accompanied by open or disguised incestuous phantasies, becomes the centre of the whole of infantile sexuality.[1] After the attempt at solving the Oedipus conflict the child wants to give up masturbation, not so much on account of the actual sexual activity as on that of the accompanying phantasies. The bodily expression of sexuality, the masturbation, is now separated from the accompanying phantasies (7*c*). The masturbation can be stopped after a shorter or longer struggle. The phantasies become more and more disguised, and appear after a time as the well-known day-dreams of children of that age, very often concerned with hero-worship or ideas of greatness. Analysis of the day-dreams of the latency period invariably leads back to the old masturbation phantasies and to the Oedipus conflict. The tenacity with which children cling to their day-dreams and the pleasure they derive from them show their instinctive origin.

DAY-DREAMS.

Very often the period of instinctive quiescence is interrupted by outbreaks of sexual activity, either in the form of masturbation or in that of sexual games between two or more children. Such periods are usually accompanied by difficulties in education and are followed by severe feelings of guilt and a renewed struggle directed against instinctive gratification.

READING.

A less direct, but nevertheless extremely pleasurable instinctive gratification during the latency period is derived from reading. As I have been able to show (9), children's books contain phantasies corresponding with certain emotional phases in the child's life. The voluntary reading of children in the latency period serves exclusively for the satisfaction of instinctive needs and not for the acquisition of knowledge. The endeavour to influence the child's taste during this period in the direction of books which convey knowledge without containing the phantasies which would attract the child, fails. The reading of children at this age very often takes the place of the former masturbation ; it is an attempt on the part of the child to give up masturbation and substitute for it the gratification of living through the phantasies contained in the book. The observation of children at this stage shows that they react to the prohibition of reading at night in the same way as they did to the prohibition of masturbation, and the threats used by parents are often similar to those used in respect of the child's masturbation, especially in their emphasis on danger to health.

[1] Part I, Ch. VI, p. 40.

The child's voluntary reading, though still serving instinctive gratification, is a preparation for a later and very important sublimation, a fact with which educators should be familiar.

RELATIONSHIP TO PARENTS.

The most important change in the child's old emotional relationship to his parents occurs when he realizes that they are only human and have faults. This happens after identification with the parents at the end of the Oedipus phase when he has set up an ideal parent in his imagination. This insight into the fallibility of the parents is a very necessary step in development, as it will lead to the gradual loosening of old emotional ties and to the child's emotional independence.

This is not an easy step. The belief in the omnipotence of the parents dates from the time when the child still had the full attention of the mother, and had not yet experienced the disappointments of the Oedipus phase. Adults often think that their dependence on their parents ceased suddenly after some trivial incident, which showed that they were not all-knowing or all-powerful. These memories do not tell the whole story. They refer to incidents which usually happened at puberty and represented the end of a development which continued throughout the whole of the latency period.

FAMILY ROMANCE.

There is one almost universal day-dream which attempts to combine the old relationship to the parents with the struggle for independence. We must describe these day-dreams in greater detail, as the acting out of this phantasy plays an important part in the delinquent behaviour of a certain type of young offender.[1]

Children between the ages of 8 and 12 often imagine that they are not really the offspring of their parents. They believe that they were brought to their parents as small babies, and that their real parents are much more powerful and of a higher social standing than the parents they are living with. The phantasy is usually worked out in great detail, with emphasis on reunion with the imaginary parents. This phantasy, which is very pleasurable, forms the emotional basis of many children's books (9).

Freud (8*t*) called this phantasy the "family romance"; it contains openly expressed elements of the child's disappointment in his own parents. He does not want to belong to his parents any longer because he has already felt their criticism and endured painful disappointments. Chance remarks or actual experiences

[1] Part II, Ch. V(*b*), p. 148.

supply the colouring for this part of the phantasy. The phantasy parents, who are usually of a higher social standing, may be based on real experiences, but they invariably show characteristics of the parents as the child saw them in early life. The child can love these phantasy parents openly, which would be forbidden with the real parents on account of the incestuous nature of such feelings at the later age. The phantasy, therefore, both combines the old incestuous wishes with the new criticism, and is an attempt to separate from the parents. The child embellishes this romance with details regarding his emotional relationship with the parents and past events.

SUMMARY.

To sum up: during the latency period the child's Ego is strengthened by his intellectual growth and new achievements. Thus he is able to gain better control of the instinctive urges. The Super-Ego is enriched, especially through his relationship to his teachers. The family is the primary group formation; the child now becomes a member of a new and wider group—the school. The fight against the bodily expression of sexual urges, masturbation, is usually successful after many ups and downs. The incestuous phantasies accompanying masturbation are separated from the physical expression of the instinctive urges and find an outlet in the child's day-dreams, of which the family romance is the most universal.

The latency period is the time when those who later become criminals first show signs of antisocial behaviour.[1] A knowledge, therefore, of the normal child's emotional development will enable us to detect the difficulties of the antisocial child and to find an adequate remedy.[2]

[1] Part I, Ch. I, p. 11.
[2] Part III, Ch. VII.

CHAPTER X

PUBERTY

With the maturation of the sexual organs the instinctive urges, both sexual and aggressive, come again into the foreground.

In contrast to popular opinion, the sexual instinct does not originate at puberty, but has then already reached the stage of adult maturity.[1] The difficulties of puberty can be understood only if the development of the sexual instinct from birth until the resolution of the Oedipus conflict is considered.

We have said that during the latency period instinctive urges recede more or less into the background.[2] When at puberty the sexual instinct is again revived, the conflicts of the later Oedipus stage which have been more or less dormant during the latency period are also reawakened. Normal development in puberty will depend on the more or less efficient solution of the Oedipus conflict.

MASTURBATION. The first conflict facing the young boy or girl on the approach of puberty is connected with masturbation. Except in those rare cases where masturbation has been kept up throughout the latency period, the urge towards this auto-erotic sexual activity begins afresh at puberty. The adolescent has usually forgotten all about infantile masturbation [3] and feels this temptation now as a new experience. But the feelings of guilt aroused by the wish to masturbate still belong to the old phase where, as we have seen, masturbation had to be suppressed on account of the accompanying incestuous phantasies. Threats heard as a small child are remembered, and though an intelligent boy or girl could easily find out their irrational nature, yet owing to their connection with infantile sexuality they still keep their hold on the adolescent. The most universal fears connected with masturbation are those of losing one's intelligence, of going mad, of not being able to have children later on, of damaging the genitals, of looking pale and thus advertising one's hidden sexual activities. What makes boys and girls at that age listless and nervous is not the physical sexual activity but their worry and anxiety over the results of mastur-

[1] Part I, Ch. III, p. 21. [2] Part I, Ch. IX. p. 59.
[3] Part I, Ch. VI, p. 40.

bation. The struggle goes on for a long time, and, unlike the struggle of the latency period which is usually successful, with the reawakening of strong sexual urges in puberty it has no real chance to succeed. A certain amount of masturbation is normal in puberty. In our civilization this is the only safe sexual outlet for the adolescent. There is no need to encourage young boys and girls to masturbate, they feel the urge of themselves ; but there is some need for dispelling their irrational fears, which, as we have seen, are the remnants of the anxieties of the period of infantile masturbation. Knowledge of the common occurrence of masturbation at this stage will not do away altogether with the adolescent's feelings of guilt and struggle. But it will help him to overcome his old conflicts in a more satisfactory way.

This struggle and the accompanying phantasies which are derived from the old Oedipus phantasies go on until some kind of equilibrium is reached. Normally, this consists in a certain amount of masturbation with a weakening of the feelings of guilt and conflicts about it. In some cases it results in obsessional masturbation, in the compulsion to indulge in this activity all the time ; in others it leads to its complete suppression. Sometimes phases of obsessional masturbation may give way to phases of complete repression.

RELATIONSHIP TO PARENTS.

Apart from these auto-erotic sexual activities and the conflicts aroused by them, the sexual urges are now once more directed towards persons of the outside world. We have seen that the parents are the first love objects of the small child. With the solution of the Oedipus conflict the child tries to get away from the parents as objects of his instinctive desires, and we have followed up the growing separation from the parents throughout the latency period.[1] In puberty, with the revival of the remnants of the Oedipus conflict, the necessity for changing the love object becomes urgent, and its first signs are to be seen in the more or less open revolt against the authority of the parents. The firmer the fixation to the parents has been, the greater and more noisy will be the attempt to cut loose from home. The adolescent finds it helpful in this fight to degrade the image of his parents in phantasy and in reality. Parents who have maintained relations of friendliness and comradeship with their children are often disappointed when they realize that adolescents do not want equality with their parents. They want to stress the point that

[1] Part I, Ch. IX, p. 61.

they, the young generation, are much cleverer and much more energetic than their " old " parents are. Commonly, however, parents do not even offer equality, but try to treat their boys and girls like small children as long as possible. In this case there will be either open revolt or, if the fear of the parents and their punishments is too severe, the adolescent will find more hidden ways to demonstrate his contempt. This phase in which young boys and girls are normally somewhat " beyond control " is a necessary stage of development, and equilibrium will be reached after a shorter or longer period. Whether the outcome of this phase is friendliness and respect on both sides or an emotional break, will depend mainly on the parents' personality and their insight into the emotional conflicts of their children.

OBJECT CHOICE. The struggle against the old emotional ties with the parents is also somewhat relieved by the new object choice in puberty. Very often the first object of adoration at puberty is a homosexual one. This again is a remnant of the Oedipus phase, due in girls to their old instinctive desire for the mother and identification with the father, and in boys to the passive-feminine attitude and their admiration for the father. Usually, this homosexual phase does not lead to manifest homosexual activities except where opportunity arises, as in boarding schools. It may last for a longer or shorter period and its existence does not determine the later sexual activities of the individual.

Some time later a heterosexual object is normally chosen, still very much in line with the old infantile love objects. Boys of 16 or 17 fall in love with women much older than themselves, and girls with father figures. The amount of emotion put into these relationships is very great, but on the whole, owing to the fact that the objects resemble the parents, the relationship remains " platonic ". Sometimes the adolescents do not even know their heroes personally ; frequently they are figures taken out of books or from history.

Only towards the end of puberty is an object chosen which is more independent of the old emotional ties. This is the time when boys and girls find a first heterosexual love object in accordance with their age, and though this first relationship may still be an unhappy one, it shows that the way is open towards a normal sex life.

SUPER-EGO DEVELOPMENT. We have shown how the Super-Ego is enriched during the latency period and how the identification with teachers serves to strengthen the part of the child which wants to be "good". In puberty the general emotional upheaval caused by the revival of old conflicts shows itself also in the unstable command of the Super-Ego over the conscious personality. Times of the greatest severity, ascetic phases, alternate with times of indulgence in instinctive pleasure. The search for Ideal Figures goes on, and there is sometimes a conscious attempt to become like one of the heroes worshipped. The difficulty is that these heroes change very often during this period, so that the child's ethical standards are far from uniform.

EGO-DEVELOPMENT.

The same instability may be observed in all activities of the Ego. Scholastic attainments vary; usually there is a decline in attention and steadiness. Times of feverish activity, often centred round hobbies, alternate with times of passivity, self-centredness and moodiness. Some adolescents suddenly develop great abilities, such as artistic or philosophic talents. Very often these activities are short-lived, and of the multitude of boys and girls who write poetry in puberty only a few will retain these artistic gifts in adult life (*7a*). The emotional upheaval described above will clamour for expression wherever it can be found.

Altogether, it is no exaggeration to say that even in mentally healthy adolescents puberty resembles a mental illness, and it usually takes two to three years for the young boy and girl to find their balance. The more satisfactory the infantile sexual period has been, the shorter and quieter will be the emotional conflicts at puberty. Of course, experiences at puberty may still mean either mental health or illness. A boy who, as a result of his infantile conflicts, has strong homosexual tendencies may still develop more or less normally in adult life if the attempt at finding a heterosexual love object is not frustrated. Where the Oedipus conflict resulted in a severe infantile neurosis, the chances for a normal development after puberty are rather poor. There are many variations in development according to the outcome of the Oedipus phase, and the actual experiences in puberty. We shall discuss some individual varieties with the case histories in later chapters.

After the emotional upheaval of puberty the adult character emerges. External circumstances may considerably influence outward appearances, but the individual reaction to the fortunes of life is now definitely established.

CHAPTER XI

SUMMARY OF FACTORS LEADING TO SOCIAL ADAPTATION

The short survey of the development of the child's emotional life in the preceding chapters was intended to show which factors are responsible for the social adaptation of the individual.[1] It was argued that only a detailed knowledge of these factors would provide a chance of a true evaluation of those other factors, constitutional or environmental, which lead to antisocial behaviour. The necessity for stressing this point was shown to lie in the fact that sociological research, though often undertaken with meticulous care, is not yet in agreement as to which environmental factors are responsible for causing delinquent behaviour. The present investigation does not pretend to solve this question. It only maintains that the point of view taken in this book may offer more scope for further research.

It will be necessary to summarize briefly the most important stepping-stones in the development towards social adaptation.

I. The Child's Early Relationship to his Mother

The experiences during this very first relationship of the child to another human being are important for several reasons where later social adaptation is concerned.

(1) We have seen that the emotions which link the child to the mother are responsible for bringing about a modification of the originally antisocial instinctive urges.[2] If the power of the mother over the child at this early age is used in a rational way, the antisocial instinctive urges will be modified into socially acceptable attitudes and characteristics without too much loss of instinctive energy. Some of these modifications, like reaction formation and sublimation, once they are properly established, do not revert to the original instinctive trends except in severe mental illness. We have seen that these modified impulses become part of the individual's character. It has been stressed that these instinctive urges can be modified successfully only if the child's needs are understood and sufficient time is allowed for the original savage behaviour to change. That of course

[1] Part I, Ch. I, p. 13. [2] Ibid., Ch. V, p. 36.

involves extreme patience on the mother's side and excludes harsh and cruel treatment. This understanding and the time factor are of more consequence than may at first be realized. It means among other things that the child must be allowed to satisfy some of his antisocial impulses, which may be repugnant to the mother and a great nuisance in the home.

It has been shown [1] that the outcome, if other methods of education are adopted, may be less favourable. Sudden repression of instinctive urges brings with it the danger of an unmodified and still antisocial impulse breaking through in later life against the wishes of the individual.[2] We have shown how the child tries to gain control over his instinctive urges during the latency period and during puberty. But he cannot gain control over instincts which are excluded from consciousness and have remained in the unconscious in their original antisocial form. Furthermore, it has been stated how uneconomical this process of modification proves to be. Not only is energy constantly needed to hold the forbidden urge back in the unconscious, but there is also the tendency to keep at bay all activities which may be in any way connected with the unconscious impulse. All this energy which should be directed into social channels will be wasted, and the child's range of activities will be rather poor. This in turn limits his hope of gaining satisfaction of a socially permitted kind or of widening his achievements.

Too much repression of instinctive urges is often the result of harsh treatment making excessive use of the child's anxieties which, at this stage, consist in the fear of being left alone. Even greater danger can be expected from treatment which at certain times allows too much gratification of those instincts that eventually have to be modified and at other times uses harsh methods. This inconsistent treatment is seen, for instance, in the attitude of the mother who will satisfy her child's wish to suck for too long a time, will never leave him alone, will try to fulfil his every whim, but will be unable to bear the expression on his part of hostile feelings towards her. We have seen that hostile feelings form a part of the child's normal development just as much as do feelings of love. The immediate repression of aggression will do just as much harm as the frustration of friendliness. There is another possibility which is often met with in the families from which delinquents emerge : small children in overcrowded homes witness quarrels among adults and often even sexual scenes. We

[1] Part I, Ch. V. [2] Part II, Ch. V(*b*), p. 118.

have considered the child's aggressive phase of development and his sexual curiosity. By witnessing such scenes the child obtains too much nourishment for his instinctive pleasures, which in so far as they are aggressive have later to be modified. Naturally, therefore, such a state of affairs will make the child overexcited and will tend to exaggerate his own aggressive inclinations. The same children are usually severely punished for breaking a plate or for being a nuisance in the house in other ways. We therefore get an instinctive urge which for environmental reasons becomes too strong and at the same time an attitude towards this impulse which tends towards repression. The child's difficulty in mastering the situation is tremendous. He has to repress impulses which are constantly gratified by the surroundings. He is induced by his observation to indulge in phantasies of an aggressive nature, and on the other hand he is forced to be a model child and to maintain a standard of social behaviour which normally would be far in advance of his age.

(2) Equally important in the modification of instincts is the relationship with the mother. Closely connected with it is a steadily growing attachment to one person and the knowledge that the love and approval of this person are more important to the self than the immediate gratification of instinctive desires. We have said that at the beginning of life the baby is entirely narcissistic and learns only slowly to direct his desires and his emotions towards the outside world. We have also shown [1] that in the first years of life the balance between auto-erotic activities and the formation of an object relationship is gradually tipped towards the latter. The essential aim in social adaptation is the possibility of forming good object relationships. Most of the object relationships formed in later life are built on the pattern of the first experiences. If the relationship of the small child to the mother was satisfactory during the first years of life, later disappointments will have much less weight than if the first relationship was disturbed. One of the most important factors in this first object relationship, at least so far as the understanding of antisocial reactions is concerned, is the child's growing perception that it is more satisfactory to keep the mother's attention and to earn her love and approval than to fulfil his desires immediately. Within this relationship the child learns to wait for satisfaction. This [2] leads to the acceptance of the reality-principle instead of the original pleasure-pain principle.

[1] Part I, Ch. IV.

[2] Part I, Ch. V, p. 27.

Without this social adaptation is impossible. Our civilization is built up on the assumption that people are able to set their relationship to their fellow human beings above the gratification of their instinctive desires. This important step in development is first taken at a time when instinctive urges are very imperative, although the relationship to the mother is still more necessary than immediate gratification. Children who because of an unhappy relationship with their mother have not reached this stage of development will meet with the greatest difficulties later on. One feature which all delinquents have in common is their inability to postpone desires because they cannot form good relationships with the people in their surroundings, and this results in their excessive self-love.

Though a mother may cause disturbances in the child's development by her inconsiderate attitude, this danger is not so great as the actual separation of a child from his mother at an early age, especially if such separation occurs repeatedly. The absence of the mother and frequent change of mother-substitutes make the development of an object relationship on a sound basis impossible. The effect of separation from the mother at the varying stages of development has been studied by Anna Freud and D. Burlingham (2*a*), who give most illuminating descriptions of children who changed hands repeatedly during their third year of life.

II. The Oedipus Conflict

We have hinted [1] that the pattern of emotional relationships developed during the Oedipus phase will be important for the later love-life of the individual. As a matter of fact, it is not only the choice of a life partner which is influenced by infantile experiences. The attitude to people in authority, for instance, is closely related to the original relationship to the father, especially in men. This alone would make the Oedipus development one of the important stepping-stones in social adaptation, because the possibility of reacting in a friendly way to those above us, and at the same time of being able to hold our own against the opinions and actions of people in authority, is again one of the prerequisites of society as it should be. If the Oedipus conflict is resolved [2] it will end in the establishment of a friendly relationship with the father, and after the upheaval of puberty there will be the basis for equality between father and son. This

[1] Part I, Ch. VI, p. 42. [2] Ibid., p. 41.

outcome would be the most favourable for later social adaptation, especially so far as the attitude to authority and to those working under one's orders is concerned.

Unresolved conflicts originating in the Oedipus phase very often lead to neurotic illness in later life. Certain constellations, however, particularly if they are combined with disturbances which occurred in the earlier stages of development, are often found to contribute to antisocial behaviour.

We have described [1] how under certain conditions the fear connected with the expression of instinctive urges at the phallic phase leads to a regression of the libido to an earlier stage of development, usually the anal-sadistic phase. One of the conditions for this occurrence is a fixation of instinctive energy at this earlier phase. Here the relationship to the persons in the environment is a sado-masochistic one, and instinctive pleasure is experienced in the form of wishing to hurt and to be hurt. As will be shown later [2] on, this situation is very often one of the psychological foundations for antisocial behaviour.

Another result of the Oedipus phase has been described as the passive-feminine attitude of the boy towards his father. This attitude is dangerous because it entails the loss of masculinity. It has to be repressed, and the boy often has instead to defend himself against the occurrence of these tendencies by an attitude of forced aggressiveness and manliness, especially where persons in authority are concerned. Instincts, however, as we have seen, strive towards satisfaction, and the passive attitude may show itself in the dependence of the boy on slightly older, stronger, and often really aggressive and antisocial youngsters under whose influence he will be incited to actions which he would never dare to undertake on his own. This is a constellation which often leads to the formation of criminal gangs.

The psychological attitudes resulting from the Oedipus conflict are complicated, and can be understood only if the development up to the Oedipus phase is also taken into account. Pronounced difficulties in the Oedipus phase are often based on unsatisfactory development in the pregenital stages.

The satisfactory solution of the Oedipus conflict plays a part in social adaptation. Some of the reasons for this statement have been given above ; others will be added in case histories.

[1] Part I, Ch. V, p. 42.

[2] Part II, Ch. II.

III. Super-Ego Formation

Closely related to the solution of the Oedipus conflict and of the utmost importance for later social adaptation is the formation of conscience. We have already given some of the characteristics of the Super-Ego as it develops if an independent ethical code is formed.[1] We have shown that it is necessary for the child to identify himself with the parents at the end of the Oedipus phase, for otherwise his conscience will not become independent of the persons of the outside world. We have seen that there is one phase in the development of the Super-Ego where the child already identifies himself with the demands of the parents but still needs their presence, their approval and their punishments in order to do the right thing. It was explained at the time that the social result of such a state of affairs would be that everyone would do the socially accepted thing only in the presence of authority. One of the important factors leading towards social adaptation, therefore, is the independence of the conscience of the actual persons of the parents.

It has also been stated that the personalities of the parents with whom the child identifies himself will form the basis for his ethical code. If for instance the ethical code of the environment is a criminal one, conscience-formation may proceed normally, yet nevertheless the result will be antisocial behaviour. The child has taken to himself the criminal code of his parents.

Again it has to be emphasized that the development of the Super-Ego is influenced by the instinctive development of the earlier phases. Difficulties of a more severe kind in the pregenital and phallic phases will invariably be apparent in the structure of the Super-Ego. If there are only slight abnormalities in development, these influences on conscience-formation may be corrected by the forces which add to the content of the Super-Ego during the latency period.[2]

IV. Group Formation inside the Family

The first adaptation to social life occurs, as we have seen, inside the group which constitutes the family. There the child, driven by emotional factors, learns to respect the demands made on his parents by his brothers and sisters. If this group formation inside the family has developed satisfactorily—and this again is dependent on the instinctive development on the one hand and

[1] Part I, Ch. VII.

[2] Ibid., Ch. IX.

on the attitude of the parents on the other—it will not be difficult for the child to adapt himself to the next group when he first goes to school.

If, on the other hand, group formation inside the family has not proceeded satisfactorily, we shall expect to find the first difficulties, and also the first signs of antisocial behaviour, in the latency period.

BIBLIOGRAPHY—PART I

1. AICHHORN, A.: *Wayward Youth.* London, 1936.

2. BURLINGHAM, D., and FREUD, A.:
   (*a*) *Young Children in Wartime in a Residential War Nursery.* London, 1942, Allen & Unwin.
   (*b*) *Infants without Families.* London, 1943, Allen & Unwin.

3. CARR, J. L.: *Delinquency Control.* New York, 1941.

4. CARR-SAUNDERS, A. M., MANNHEIM, H., RHODES, E. C.: *Young Offenders: An Enquiry into Juvenile Delinquency.* Cambridge, 1942.

5. Criminal Justice Bill, 1938.
   Revised Criminal Justice Bill, 1939.

6. ELKIN, MISS W. A.: *English Juvenile Courts.* London, 1938.

7. FREUD, A.:
   (*a*) *The Ego and its Mechanisms of Defence.* London, 1936.
   (*b*) *Introduction to Psycho-analysis for Teachers.* New York and London, 1936.
   (*c*) *Sexualization and Sublimation.* Lecture, British Psycho-analytical Society, 1940. Unpublished.

8. FREUD, S.:
   (*a*) "Analysis of a Phobia in a 5-year-old Boy." *Coll. Pap*, III. 1925 (1909).
   (*b*) *Three Contributions to the Theory of Sexuality.* New York, 1910 (1905).
   (*c*) "Instincts and their Vicissitudes." *Coll. Pap.*, IV. 1925 (1915).
   (*d*) *Beyond the Pleasure-Principle.* London, 1922 (1920).
   (*e*) "On Narcissism: an Introduction." *Coll. Pap.*, IV. 1925 (1914).
   (*f*) "The Infantile Genital Organization of the Libido." *Coll. Pap.*, II. 1924 (1923).
   (*g*) "On the Sexual Theories of Children." *Coll. Pap.*, II. 1924 (1908).
   (*h*) "Formulations regarding the two Principles in Mental Functioning." *Coll. Pap.*, IV. 1925 (1911).
   (*i*) "Character and Anal Erotism." *Coll. Pap.*, II. 1924 (1908).
   (*j*) "On the Transformation of Instincts with especial Reference to Anal Erotism." *Coll. Pap.*, II. 1924 (1916).
   (*k*) "Repression." *Coll. Pap.*, IV. 1924 (1915).
   (*l*) *Civilization and its Discontent.* London, 1930.
   (*m*) "The Passing of the Oedipus Complex." *Coll. Pap.*, II. 1924 (1924).
   (*n*) *The Ego and the Id.* Int. Ps. Library Series, N. 12. 1927 (1923).
   (*o*) *Group Psychology and the Analysis of the Ego.* London, 1922 (1921).
   (*p*) *Inhibition, Symptom and Anxiety.* London, 1936.
   (*q*) *The Meaning of Dreams.* London, 1913 (1900).
   (*r*) *On the Psycho-pathology of Everyday Life.* London, 1914 (1904).
   (*s*) "The Unconscious." *Coll. Pap.*, IV. 1925 (1915).
   (*t*) "Der Familienroman der Neurotiker." *Ges. Schriften*, Bd. XII. (1909).

9. FRIEDLANDER, K.: "Children's Books and their Function in Latency and Pre-puberty." *American Imago*, 1941.

10. GLOVER, E.; "An Examination of the Kleinian System of Child Psychology": in *A Psychoanalytical Study of the Child.* New York, 1945.
11. GORING, CHARLES: *The English Convict, a Statistical Study.* London, 1913.
12. HEALY, W.: *The Individual Offender.* London, 1915.
13. HEALY, W., and BRONNER, A.:
    (*a*) *Delinquents and Criminals: Their Making and Unmaking.* New York, 1926.
    (*b*) *New Light on Delinquency and its Treatment.* New Haven, 1938.
14. HILL, J. C.:
    (*a*) *The Teacher in Training.* London, 1935.
    (*b*) *Dreams and Education.* London, 1926.
15. KLEIN, M.: *The Psycho-Analysis of Children.* London, 1932.
16. LOMBROSO, CESARE: *L'Uomo Delinquente.*
17. MANNHEIM, H.: *The Dilemma of Penal Reform.* London, 1940, Allen & Unwin.
18. MEAD, M.:
    (*a*) *Growing Up in New Guinea.*
    (*b*) *Coming of Age in Samoa.*
19. MULLINS, C.: *Crime and Psychology.* London, 1943.
20. *Our Towns, a Close-Up.* A Study made during 1939–42. O.U.P., 1943.
21. SHAW, C. R. and MCKAY, H. D.: *Juvenile Delinquency and Urban Areas.* Univ. of Chicago Press, 1942.
22. WATSON, J. A. F.: *The Child and the Magistrate.* London, 1942.

PART II

THE FAILURE OF SOCIAL ADAPTATION

CHAPTER I

INTRODUCTION

The legal conception of delinquency does not necessarily coincide with the psycho-pathological conception.

A person who appears in Court on a charge of manslaughter, committed while driving dangerously, need not in our sense be a delinquent in spite of his having committed a crime. A boy of 8 who stole a loaf of bread rather than die of starvation would be considered mentally healthy and not antisocial. Tommy B., one of Burt's (8) cases, had together with his little brother stolen eatables over a period of months. Both children were grossly undernourished. When brought into an environment where they had enough to eat they did not pilfer once, nor did they commit any other antisocial act over a period of ten years. Though these boys had offended against the law we should not call them delinquents.

From the psychiatric point of view, we speak of delinquent behaviour in all those cases where the offender's attitude towards society is such that it will eventually lead to a violation of the law. We should not hesitate to include cases which have not yet come before the Courts, nor should we hesitate to exclude from our lists such cases as those quoted above.

Though no statistics are available to show the percentage of delinquents in relation to non-delinquents in the psychiatric sense, the number of juvenile non-delinquents who come before the Courts seems to be very small.

The clinical descriptions which follow are solely confined to offenders who are delinquent from the psychiatric point of view.

CHAPTER II

ANTISOCIAL CHARACTER FORMATION

CASE I.

Billy was 7 years of age when he was sent to me for psycho-analytical treatment. His mother was seeking help because for the last two years the boy's behaviour had slowly changed until she found it quite impossible to manage him. He frequently played truant, did not come back in time when sent on an errand, used bad language when with his mother and Victorian grandmother, frequently exposed himself in front of grown-up people at home, and was cruel to animals and little children. When playing with older boys he alleged that they bullied him, but the mother suspected that he provoked them by his aggravating ways. He had not yet pilfered at home, though he used to extract money from all the members of the family by playing them up against each other, and by making use of the mother's fear that if she did not give him money when he asked for it he would steal. On several occasions he had wilfully damaged property, but this was done only when he was with older boys. What worried the mother most was that by no educational means at her disposal was she able to effect any change in his behaviour. On the contrary, the more she punished him the more unmanageable he grew.

SYMPTOMS.

HOME ENVIRONMENT AND EARLY UPBRINGING.

The boy came from an apparently good and very clean lower-middle-class home. The mother, who was 35 years of age at his birth, came of a higher social level than the slightly younger father, who was a working-man. Billy was the only child. The facts concerning his earlier life and upbringing were ascertained step by step during two years of psycho-analytical treatment. For a long time the mother was too suspicious to tell anything like the truth about the home situation.

The mother had been in love with another man, more of a social equal, and married the father only after her hope of marrying this other had been disappointed. Her relations, some of whom were quite well-to-do, did not approve of the marriage. Before it the father had lived for years with another woman. According to the mother's account this happened mainly because she did not consent to marry him sooner. The boy was born after two years of marriage. At that time the parents lived in a small house in a comparatively good district of London, and there was room enough for the boy to have a small bedroom of his own when he was about 2 years old. While the mother was pregnant, her sister, to whom she was very devoted, gave birth to a girl, and she herself was greatly disappointed when her own child, born six months later, was a boy. Even at this early stage the mother was not happy in her married life and looked down upon the father. She thought that she alone ought to bring up the boy, and the father was looked upon by her, and later by his son, as an outsider.

The mother was very concerned about the child's physical welfare and considered him delicate, though she also complained about his ravenous appetite when he was small. She still thought him very weak physically, though he was a well-built lad, extremely tall and strong for his age. There were no difficulties over the boy's training in cleanliness, which was accomplished very early. He was clean when only 18 months old, but he started to wet the bed again at the age of 4½ and continued to do so until he was 6½. Until about the age of 5 he was easily led, very good-natured, always looked very nice and clean, and to his mother there seemed nothing wrong with him except that he was a boy. The girl cousin always seemed to be brighter. When the boy was 4 the mother was finally alienated from her husband. When going for a walk with her son she met him with the woman with whom he had lived before they married. Taking the boy, she turned away from the father without giving any sign of recognition, and refused to speak to him afterwards. Through her own mother her husband explained to her that he had met the woman in the street and could not avoid talking to her for a few minutes. Though she had no reason to disbelieve this statement she was furiously jealous, and started to treat her husband even worse than before. Her husband's reaction to this behaviour was to break off sexual relations with her. About the same time intense air-raids began, the mother's mother and brother were bombed out, and she decided to go into a larger house and take them in. She had never contemplated having the boy evacuated, the thought of being separated from him never entered her mind, and she regularly went with him to the shelter while the father slept at home. When sleeping at home again, the boy shared a room with the mother and grandmother, while the father had a small room to himself.

The situation between the parents grew worse. The mother accused the father of visiting the pub too often, made him look small in front of everybody, and for long spells did not speak to him at all. There were periods of reconciliation, and for a short time during the treatment the parents lived together again. In the end, when the boy was 8½, the father left the house, at a time when the mother was working for a few hours a day at the house of the man next door, and she became more and more attached to this latter. She and the boy began to live more in the neighbour's house than in their own. Whether there was any intimate relationship between the mother and this man, who belonged to her own social class, could not be ascertained.

MOTHER'S PERSONALITY.

The mother herself was a very difficult woman: very tall, very stout, quite good-looking, and physically as well as mentally a striking personality. Her outstanding characteristics were her disdain for every sign of masculinity in the boy, her quarrelsomeness not only in her relationship with her husband but also with most other people around her, her absolute inability to take advice from anybody, her contempt for the school to which she sent the boy one year later than she should have done, her scorn, in short, for everyone whose opinion differed from her own or who wanted to exert any influence over her. She was certainly not a happy woman, and as her difficulties were due to her own conflicts no outside change could really influence her very much. Her difficulties became evident in her relationship with the boy. She was certainly devoted to him and could not bear to be separated from him for any length of time. She was very concerned about his physical welfare, though very characteristically she would worry when the boy was well, but would very often overlook the beginnings of a real illness.

INCONSISTENCY IN EDUCATION.

However, she still nursed her regret that the boy was not a girl, and frequently talked about this fact even in front of him. She was convinced that there was something wrong with the boy's brain, and discussed this idea fully with all sorts of people and also in his presence. She quarrelled with him as frequently as with other people. Her attempts at education consisted in constant nagging, but she was not able to refuse the boy anything he wanted. Although she was aware of his method of getting round her by whining, he succeeded every time. She always tried to forbid him to do everything he wanted to do, yet she was unable to keep to a " No " she had once uttered. This inconsistency showed itself in everything connected with the boy's life. So far as food and pocket-money were concerned she spoilt him ; on the other hand, there was no room for him to play inside the house, and he had no proper toys. The mother was very much upset that this lively boy of 8 would not play with a big toy horse which his father had given him. She was distressed that he would rather stay at home than go to school, but whenever it suited her she let him stay at home so that he might go out with her to buy clothes. She was worried about his staying out late at night, being afraid that he would not get enough sleep, yet she would take him to see friends or go to the pictures with him and not come home until eleven o'clock. She did not like him to play with other boys in the street because " that would make him rough ", and she refused to let him join the cubs or any other organization, consciously because she was afraid that he might catch an illness or come to some bodily harm ; unconsciously, certainly, because she was afraid that he might become too masculine. In the many discussions I had with her she would oppose any manly activity, but would complain bitterly that the boy whined so much and seemed to be afraid of older boys. During the period between his fourth and eighth year, when the relationship with the father was so bad, she constantly frightened the boy by telling him that she would leave both him and his father ; on the other hand she was furious when the father threatened the same thing. The boy, of course, understood the situation and took bribes from both father and mother to be on one or the other side. He obtained quite a lot of money in this way.

It was only after some time and with difficulty that the facts about the home life and the mother's attitude towards the boy could be ascertained, so that most likely, if the boy had come before a Court, the home would have been considered a good one and the mother to be very concerned about the boy's welfare, which—consciously—she was.

BILLY'S PERSONALITY.

Billy, tall, strong, good-looking in a slightly effeminate way, was of normal intelligence (I.Q. 100) but very backward in school. At the age of 8½ he could not read or write properly, but was quite good at sums. At the first meeting, at the age of 7, he was rather shy, seemed easily frightened, and did not want to be left alone with me in the room. But very soon he was his usual self, friendly so long as he could do exactly what he wanted, cheeky in his answers, witty and charming, and at bottom entirely uncommunicative. He had no insight into the fact that his behaviour was in any way unusual or that he had any difficulties. That is by no means rare in children, but children who have neurotic symptoms suffer and can easily be convinced that the doctor can help them to get rid of their anxieties or conflicts. This boy did not suffer. He was very happy so long as he could get his own way. When prevented from achieving his aim he became defiant, angry and vicious. He quickly understood that what was wanted of him was that he should talk about his life, his friends, his activities, and so on, and equally quickly he became determined to do nothing of the kind and, if possible, not to talk at all. This attitude was very pronounced for a few weeks during the treatment, when he had transferred his anti-social attitude completely to the consulting-room. He would come late whenever it suited him, very often putting in an appearance only for five minutes. When there he wanted to play games, but would decline to talk. Or he would start wandering about the room and doing the few things which he knew could not be permitted even in my consulting-room, such as lighting paper at the electric fire, damaging furniture, and tearing my curtains. Before attempting this he had already tried to find out my reaction to his throwing toys about or jumping on the couch or throwing chairs on the floor. Whenever he did a thing like this he looked at me sideways when he thought I was not observing him. Plainly he wanted to start a quarrel, and went out of his way to provoke a prohibition against which he could rebel. When he did talk at such times it was in order to try to cause difficulties between his mother and myself.

LACK OF FEELINGS OF GUILT.

The most striking factor in this behaviour was his absolute lack of feeling of guilt. Although he knew exactly when he was late and that I was waiting for him he merely enjoyed the situation. The only thing he was afraid of was that his mother might hear about it and that he would be smacked. But this fear was not strong enough to prevent him from strolling about in the street for as long as he chose. He could not understand my remaining friendly; it clearly puzzled him, but it did not make him feel guilty or deter him. When I confronted him at one time during the treatment with questions about his sexual activities at home, especially his desire to exhibit himself, he did not like it, but did not feel ashamed of it. He boasted how he could shock grown-up people by his behaviour. He talked quite openly of his hatred for his father and the way he made him pay for every little service he did him, demanding payment, for instance, for getting him his slippers at night. There were times during the treatment when he and other boys stole fruit from neighbouring gardens, and he also joined them in looting bombed houses. He knew that it would be disastrous if a policeman saw him, and was careful not to be found out. But the action itself he regarded as quite justifiable. He would describe to me how he tortured his cat and sometimes smaller children without the slightest concern for their suffering, but he would be furious if the cat or the dog or another child tried to hurt him in return. On the other hand he was proud to show me any little cut or bruise when he happened to hurt himself. He would also be very angry if his mother punished him, and he could not see any justification for it. He was quite indifferent to the fact that his mother was waiting for some bread which she had asked him to fetch, and he did not come home with it for several hours. Towards the end of the two years of treatment he once remarked that it would have been better if he had not stayed out the day before, because then he would have been allowed to go out the next day. This remark was the first sign of a feeling of responsibility for his own actions. He was then nearly 9 years of age; normally such a reaction might be expected from a child of 5.

LACK OF INTERESTS.

Billy was uninterested in nearly all school subjects, nor did he care to know anything about plants, animals, mechanical things, or the world in general. He had not much feeling for words, partly because he could not yet read. But even children who cannot read are, at this age, usually very interested to learn how things work and to know what is going on in the world. He was intensely interested in aeroplanes, but could only distinguish fighters from bombers, and he did not know which countries were at war with each other.

PLEASURE IN FIGHTING.

He had, as became clear during the treatment, one only interest: fighting and watching other people fight. This interest showed itself in all his activities and phantasies. Whenever he started to play with any kind of material, he always finished up with a fight. There was nothing elaborate in the way he set about it. He arranged two parties and flung them at each other until each side was hurt.

His sadistic phantasies received ample nourishment from the signs of destruction he saw around him, and air-raids were for him very enjoyable occurrences. He loved the crash of bombs, and enjoyed frightening the people in the shelter by interpreting each noise as a near miss. He would provoke quarrels with his friends in school, with his teachers, and with his mother. I have already described how he tried to provoke quarrels with me. All his energy was taken up by his phantasies and by such actual fighting as he could provoke. This was the only thing which gave him real pleasure, and he pursued the satisfaction of this pleasure for all he was worth.

This is a very typical story of early antisocial behaviour. On studying case histories of older delinquents carefully, it will be found that in the majority of cases similar difficulties had occurred in the home when the child began to go to school. At this age, when for the first time the child has to adapt himself to society outside the family circle, it can easily be seen whether the foundations for social adaptation have been successfully laid. Billy had not reached this stage, and was therefore a nuisance. People were angry with him and punished him, but they did not succeed in this way in adjusting him. The more he was punished the more unmanageable he became.

What is the difference between his mental development and that of a socially adapted child of his age?

BILLY'S CHARACTER-DEVELOPMENT.

Detailed comparison of his instinctive life, his Ego- and Super-Ego-development, with that of the norm is possible because the psycho-analytic process brought to light the unconscious as well as the conscious motivation of his behaviour.

(1) *Instinctive development*

Between the ages of 7 and 9 the child is, as we have seen, in the latency period, and sexual activities recede into the background, except for an occasional relapse. Billy, on the other hand, had begun to exhibit himself during the latency period. He had not only continually sought direct instinctive gratification, but a gratification of an unusual kind if we consider the stage of development that he should have reached. Boys at the age of 3 occasionally exhibit themselves, but this sexual activity should long ago have been overcome by the shame which is normally developed against this instinctive drive.

Taking into account Billy's phantasies, to which he seemed

fixated to an unusual degree, a further difference from the normal development can be detected. We have seen that the masturbation phantasies of the Oedipus phase become transformed into the day-dreams of the latency period. These day-dreams are greatly varied and are coloured by the child's daily experiences, and the instinctive background is usually very much disguised. Billy's day-dreams were uniform and crude. They represented a fight between two people, both of whom got hurt in the end, and they invaded his life and activities to such a degree that nothing else had any attraction for him. The analysis revealed that this phantasy represented the boy's idea of intercourse. Certain observations which he had made during the time when his parents still lived together, before his fourth year, and the parents' actual behaviour, led him to interpret intercourse as an aggressive act in which one or both partners are hurt.

This phantasy, together with his exhibitionistic tendencies and his relationship towards the people of his environment, showed that he had not reached the phallic phase, but that, partially at least, his libido had regressed to the anal-sadistic level, where the component instincts of hurting and being hurt are most pronounced.

To sum up: Billy's instinctive development was different from that of the average child in the latency period in so far as direct instinctive gratification continued without any break and without any struggle, conscious or unconscious; and the libido had partially regressed to the anal-sadistic level.

(2) *Ego-development*

The disturbance of the instinctive life naturally brings with it disturbances in the Ego-development. We have seen that a child of about 5 tends to be governed by the reality- instead of by the pleasure-principle, and that during the latency period the reality-principle becomes firmly established. There were certain spheres in Billy's life where he also seemed to conform to reality. He was very good at extracting money from the members of his family. He was also skilful in not being caught when being mischievous outside his home. But so far as his impulses were concerned he was still very much ruled by the pleasure-principle. He was compelled to gratify any impulse immediately, even if punishment followed. The satisfaction of his wishes was much more important to him than his relationship to people; his environment, including the demands of the people he loved, was forgotten, and nothing existed in his mind but the urge to alleviate the tension caused by the unsatisfied instinct, a state of affairs which we have seen to be prevalent in children up to about the third year of life.

Billy's poor record at school, his lack of knowledge and achievement were also caused by the failure of the Ego to conform to the reality-principle. His instinctive energy was not guided along socially accepted channels—in other words, it was not sublimated ; each impulse, if permitted by the Ego to arise, strove for and received immediate gratification. Not all his instinctive urges came to the surface. Many desires connected with the Oedipus conflict were, as will be described later, repressed. They found some outlet in regression to his exhibitionistic activities and to his phantasies, but they were not transformed into social activities. By observing Billy's attitude when trying to read, two important phases could be distinguished : his extreme pleasure when he succeeded in reading a word and was admired for it, and his extreme displeasure and inability to continue if he came up against a word which was unfamiliar to him ; it was impossible to induce him to tackle the difficulty. The first attitude shows an attempt at sublimating his exhibitionistic tendencies ; he enjoyed showing off—exhibiting—his intellectual ability instead of his genitals. The second attitude shows why this attempt at sublimation could not really succeed, at least not with the usual methods of teaching : his inability to read a word caused a displeasure which could not be overcome for the sake of later pleasure, as he could not wait for satisfaction ; he had to succeed at once or he gave up. The process of learning, which includes the ability to endure a certain amount of displeasure, could not therefore take place.

There was difficulty in forming new sublimations ; moreover, some reaction-formations which are usually established in earlier years did not function properly, thus showing that the disturbance did not date from the latency period but could be traced back to the first years of life when instincts begin to be modified.

As already mentioned, no other interests or hobbies apart from school subjects appeared until towards the end of treatment. Billy was not interested in games or in collecting things, activities common among boys of his age. Mechanical toys did not appeal to him, and the fashionable interest in aircraft which leads other boys to distinguish all the different types and to gain knowledge of the working or piloting of aeroplanes did not go with him beyond imagining one aircraft crashing into another.

As a result his Ego remained weak and could not control his instinctive urges. Billy's intellectual capacities alone did not help him to be interested in his school work. Without the impetus which is derived from the instinct, attainments remain far below the intellectual potentialities.

(3) *Super-Ego-development*

We have seen that during the latency period the Super-Ego is broadened by identification with persons in authority, especially teachers. This is expressed in the actual feelings and emotions of the child by the conscious wish to do the right thing and by severe feelings of guilt if instinctive urges are gratified contrary to the wish of the conscious personality.

Billy certainly did not come up to these standards. As a matter of fact it was rather difficult to find any signs of conscience in him. He certainly did not feel guilty about his misdemeanours, and there was no inner voice in him which warned him against the fulfilment of his forbidden desires. He showed fear on certain occasions, not on account of his own ethical code, but when he was likely to be punished. Intellectually, he knew what was right or wrong, but somehow he did not apply the knowledge in his actions.

The religious instruction of children in the latency period leads to a strengthening of their conscience. With Billy, though he went to Sunday School, even this did not work. He mentioned God only when we talked about how certain things are made ; when he did not know the answer he would invariably reply that Jesus made these things and he therefore need not bother to know about them ; he made use of his religious training when it suited his own ends.

We have described this identification which makes the ethical code of the child independent of that of the parents as an important step in Super-Ego-formation,—a process which ought to be completed during the latency period. Billy had not taken this step. His attitude towards right or wrong was still dictated by the persons in his environment, and he postponed desires only when forced to do so by his mother or some other person in authority. But it goes even further than that. We said that in this process of identification the instinctive urges which formerly aimed at possession of the parent are desexualized and exhausted in setting up the Ideal Figure in the child's mind. Billy's relationship to the people around him still had a sexual quality. His quarrels with his mother were pleasurable for him, and whenever possible he provoked prohibitions in order to rebel against them. So instead of an ethical code which tends to become independent, we meet with a situation where conscience is still represented by the actual persons of the parents, and the fulfilment of demands imposed by the parents is turned into a game from which the boy derives instinctive gratification.

The retarded formation of the Super-Ego explains why ordinary methods of education suitable to Billy's age did not work with him at all. Education during the latency period makes use of the child's Super-Ego ; it appeals to his " better feelings ". Not so with Billy. Demands made upon him did not meet with a response. They were merely a part of his emotional relationship to the person concerned and would be used by him in whatever way promised the greatest amount of instinctive gratification.

BILLY'S OBJECT-RELATIONSHIPS.

This disturbance in the structure of the personality will manifest itself also in Billy's object-relationships.

(1) We should expect a boy of that age to make attempts to become more independent of his mother, and to impress her with his manliness and adult ways. Billy, on the contrary, still clung to his mother like a much smaller child. He was furious if she did not attend to his food at the right time ; he wanted her at night before he went to sleep. She gave him his bath every night ; when bullied by other boys he came running home, crying, and asking his mother to protect him. When he was at school one summer during the holiday—at a time when he was under treatment—he induced his mother to fetch him home after a few days. This dependence upon the mother did not make him obey her ; his emotional relationship to her was marked by constant quarrels. We have seen that a partial regression to the anal-sadistic level had taken place. In this phase of development the most pronounced instinctive urge is to hurt and to be hurt, and his quarrelsomeness satisfied this need. By provoking his mother to punish him and by opposing her wishes all the time, Billy expressed his love for his mother. A more grown-up way of demonstrating his feelings was not open to him.

(2) Billy's relationship to his father could be understood only after long analytical treatment. Consciously he hated his father and went out of his way to demonstrate his contempt for him.

Behind this hostile attitude was hidden a strong attachment of which he was entirely unaware. It was displaced and showed itself in his admiration for soldiers, especially airmen, for whom he would wait in the street and attract their attention so that they would talk to him and often give him money. In such encounters he was not cheeky and aggressive as he was with his mother ; he was shy, passive, friendly and open to any suggestion they made to him. He behaved in the same way with older boys whom he met in the park. He had to do what they told him and acted for a time as if he were under a spell. This kind of relationship appeared only with chance acquaintances and with various boys at school. But it showed something of the nature of his unconscious passive attachment to his father, and it explained his exaggerated fear when there was any suggestion of his being taken away by his father. This passive attachment to the father was warded off by his consciously hostile attitude towards him. It was only towards the end of the treatment that he was able to form a more or less normal relationship with the man next door, who clearly was a father figure for him. He was then able to be friendly, to take his advice, to obey his orders and even to wish to have the same occupation when grown up.

(3) Billy's relationship to persons outside the family circle was a repetition of his relationship with his parents. Outstanding in every relationship was his urge to quarrel, to hurt and to be hurt so far as children were concerned. His teachers he defied in the same way as he defied his mother ; he quarrelled with girls, especially his cousin ; he quarrelled with boys when they were of the same age ; he bullied the smaller ones and was very much under the influence of a few of the bigger ones. Naturally, therefore, his schoolfellows did not like him and often called him silly.

CAUSES OF DISTURBANCE.

What had caused this disturbance in Billy, a child of normal intelligence, splendid physique and fair general abilities ?

According to our scheme [1] we shall look for the first disturbing factor in the child's early relationship with his mother. The development of this relationship was largely dependent on the mother's personality and on her attitude towards the child.

MOTHER-CHILD-RELATIONSHIP.

Billy's mother was from the very beginning divided in her feelings towards the boy. On the one hand she was very possessive ; she gave him

[1] Part I, Ch. XI.

excellent physical care and she did not leave him too much alone. On the other hand she was disappointed that he was not a girl. Whatever that meant for her unconsciously, it expressed itself in hostile feelings towards the child. Very small children are so close to their mother that they feel her emotions even if these are not openly expressed. As soon as the boy could understand spoken language he had ample opportunity of hearing expressions of the mother's hostility towards him : the girl cousin was upheld as a shining example ; a picture of the boy at 18 months old was shown to me in front of him with the remark, " Doesn't he look like a little girl ? " The mother would also reprimand the boy in front of everyone and discuss his silly and naughty ways.

For a small child the withdrawal of the mother's love is a severe shock, resembling that of her going away altogether. A boy who had been treated like Billy would feel this particularly strongly on account of the mother's exaggerated attention and love at other times.

The mother's ambivalent attitude was equally unsatisfactory in relation to the modification of instinctive urges. Some she satisfied too well and for too long ; others she repressed too early and too quickly. Billy's greed was always satisfied. On the other hand, she was very severe about his training in cleanliness, but she submitted to the child's wish that she should accompany him to the lavatory and clean him until he was 8 years of age. The boy's conscious wish in this direction shows that he derived pleasure from this procedure on the anal-sadistic level. The boy was too often frustrated on the one hand and over-indulged on the other on the anal-sadistic level of instinctive development. These conditions predispose to a fixation to that particular stage.

Apart from this disturbance in the modification of instincts, the inconsistency of the mother's attitude, which was pronounced in all her dealings with the boy, prevented him from learning the necessity of waiting for satisfaction if he wanted to keep her love and attention. This, we have seen, is the basis on which the evolution from the pleasure- to the reality-principle is made possible.

OEDIPUS PHASE. With these disturbances in the early stages of development the boy entered the Oedipus phase. Before the age of 4 he had already had ample opportunity of witnessing sexual scenes between the parents. The analysis showed that there was no clear distinction in his mind between quarrels and sexual scenes. There was one outstanding assumption about the outcome of the intimate relationship between the parents: he was convinced that one of the partners got hurt and usually he thought it was the father. His drawings from the time when this unconscious material slowly appeared depicted men with one leg or one arm lacking, or with wounds on one of the extremities. Occasionally, however, there was the idea that the woman got hurt too. It will be remembered that his fighting phantasies, which embodied his ideas about intercourse, ended very often with both parties being killed.

Owing to this sadistic interpretation of intercourse and the phantasy of the man being hurt—an idea which was constantly confirmed by his mother's hostile attitude towards the father—the adoption of the male rôle seemed to the little boy very dangerous. Added to this was the mother's contempt for men and the idea which must have arisen in him that she would love him more if he were a girl. On the other hand, his instinctive urges towards the mother were very strong, and from his recollections it became clear that he started to masturbate but was immediately rebuked by his grandmother, who told him that she would cut off his sexual organ. This confirmed his unconscious idea about the danger of wishing for the possession of the mother, and the Oedipus conflict was repressed as soon as it made its appearance. It has been stated that the disagreement between mother and father took place when the boy was about 4 years of age, and that from this time onwards he first shared a bunk with his mother in a shelter and afterwards slept in a small bed beside her own, creeping into her bed whenever possible on the pretext that he was afraid. This environmental situation increased his Oedipus wishes, which he had already unconsciously perceived to be dangerous because they would cost him his masculinity. This fear, as we have seen, normally plays the decisive rôle in the solution of the Oedipus conflict, but in Billy's case where the instinctive urges were so strong and partly unmodified it did not lead to the normal solution. He could not identify himself with the father for two reasons: it would cost him the affection of his mother, and it would mean the loss of his masculinity on the basis of his phantasy about intercourse. So identification took place with the mother, and his instinctive desires were directed towards the father, only to be instantly repressed again, because this solution also would endanger his genital organs. There was no way in which his phallic desires could find an outlet; even in his everyday activities the mother was set against any real boyish desire of his, and his natural sexual curiosity was instantly repressed. But he had to have instinctive gratification, and a part of his libido regressed to a phase where he could get ample satisfaction, especially in his relationship to the mother ; to the anal-sadistic level where a fixation had already taken place. So he began to quarrel with his mother and to be cruel to animals and, as his mother put it, " all his nice, clean ways were gone ".

SUPER-EGO-FORMATION.

This solution of the Oedipus conflict in conjunction with the disturbances in instinctive development led to the imperfect building up of his Super-Ego. The regression to an earlier instinctive level permitted the boy so much instinctive gratification that insufficient libidinal energy was free for the building up of the Ideal figures of the parents within himself. He did identify himself, with the mother more pronouncedly than with the father, but this identification was never really desexualized. There was no need to turn his aggression inward, a process which, as we have seen, helps considerably towards the stabilization of the conscience, as he could still express it in his sado-masochistic relationship with the people of his environment. To obey or not to obey the demands of his parents became, as we have seen, a sexualized game with the actual parents and not a demand of his internalized parent figures.

This is the story of Billy. Billy is not, as it might appear after this lengthy exposition, an exceptionally unpleasant or exceptionally disturbed boy. He is a good-looking, lively youngster who from his seventh year has shown signs of antisocial behaviour in a very typical way, but in so moderate a form that he had not come under the notice of the authorities. But before the treatment and for a long time during it he was " beyond the control " of his mother. His story has been told at such length not because he is a particularly interesting case, but because he illustrated the typical antisocial character formation.

ANTISOCIAL CHARACTER TRAITS.

What is the outstanding feature of Billy's character ? First and foremost it is the urge to satisfy his desires at once, at all costs and regardless of results. This urge is so strong that it overshadows his relationship to the persons of his environment. Immediately a desire was aroused he would forget that the person who prevented him from obtaining satisfaction was of importance to him or that the disapproval of this person might afterwards prove to be unpleasant. The people of his environment are of importance so long as they gratify his wishes, and his positive feelings towards them are forgotten if they prevent him from getting immediate satisfaction. He can then only feel hatred. Though this materialistic relationship of the child to the mother is normal in very small children, if it persist in the older child, and if it is extended to people outside the family circle, it creates the difficulties described in detail in Billy's case.

This character trait, often described as selfishness, has at its basis the failure to evolve from the pleasure-principle to the reality-principle. It is to be found in the majority of delinquents, regardless of their difference in type, and it forms one of the most formidable obstacles to treatment, either social or psychotherapeutic, because treatment as well as education is based on the establishment of a good object relationship. Aichhorn (2), too, has drawn attention to this specific character trait of the delinquent.

Not all the delinquent's desires are in themselves antisocial. Some normal desires become antisocial only by their urgency, leading the child to satisfy them at the wrong time and in the wrong place. Most children, for instance, like to wander about in the park. The child who plays truant does this during school hours, the healthy child before or after them. In our society, an older child or an adult who cannot wait for the satisfaction of his normal desires impresses us as being antisocial.

However, many of the delinquent's impulses are antisocial in themselves. They are, as we have seen, the unmodified desires of the small child. The fact that insufficient instinctive energy has been withdrawn from these primitive impulses by way of modification explains why they appear with such overwhelming strength.

Instincts, we have seen, strive for satisfaction, whether they are socially acceptable or not. The instinctive urges of the delinquent behave no differently in this respect from the impulses of the law-abiding citizen. It is the Ego which decides which of the impulses can find their way into action, and the Ego is guided in this decision by the demands of reality and by the voice of the Super-Ego. The Ego of the offender is still governed by the pleasure-principle, so that when the instinctive urge arises reality ceases to exist. This weakness in the Ego is further enhanced by the lack of sublimations and reaction-formations which prevent it from being strengthened. The impulses, including the antisocial ones, cannot be controlled by this weak Ego, which does not get sufficient support from the side of the Super-Ego. The conscience of the delinquent has not yet become independent. If the persons in authority are absent there is no power, no driving force behind the intellectual knowledge of right and wrong. The intellectual powers alone are not a sufficient incentive to acquire knowledge; in the same way the intellectual judgment of what is considered right and wrong without instinctive power behind it does not carry much weight against the force of the increasing instinctive tension.

ANTISOCIAL CHARACTER FORMATION.

Three factors, therefore, contribute to this character formation which manifests itself in the inability to withstand a desire regardless of the results: the strength of unmodified instinctive urges, the weakness of the Ego, and the lack of independence of the Super-Ego. These three factors are, as we have seen, interrelated; the lack of early modification of instinctive energy plays an important part in the weakness of the Ego and in the disturbance of the formation of the Super-Ego.

If the child enters the latency period with this antisocial character formation it need not necessarily develop into a delinquent. But this character formation constitutes a "susceptibility" to delinquent reactions, and the future of the child's social attitude depends on many constitutional and environmental factors. Aichhorn (2) speaks of a state of "latent delinquency" and maintains that there is no "manifest" delinquency unless a deformation of character has existed beforehand. I have drawn attention elsewhere (13*b*) to the conclusions of the authors of *Young Offenders* (3) that in interpreting their statistical data it appears that there must be a "susceptibility" to delinquency, and that in those children in whom this state exists, certain environmental factors may lead to delinquency.

SUMMARY.

To sum up: the antisocial character formation shows the structure of a mind where instinctive urges remain unmodified and therefore appear in great strength, where the Ego, still under the dominance of the pleasure-principle and not supported by an independent Super-Ego, is too weak to gain control over the onrush of demands arising in the Id. This character formation is at the basis of the condition which Aichhorn calls the state of "latent delinquency" and it will depend on the various factors exerting their influence in the latency period and puberty, whether delinquent behaviour becomes manifest or not.

CHAPTER III

ANALYSIS OF ENVIRONMENTAL FACTORS

(a) Introduction

In Billy's case we have been able to follow up step by step the influence of environmental factors in disturbing the development of social adjustment. The psycho-analytical method of research allows us to study the interaction of the environment—represented in the first instance by the parents—and inner psychic factors in great detail, although in a small number of cases only. It would be misleading to use the cases of delinquent behaviour examined by psycho-analysis as a basis for statistics. Cases of antisocial behaviour which have undergone psycho-analytical treatment do not constitute a representative sample of juvenile delinquency in general. There are too many extraneous factors in the decision whether the offender shall have this kind of treatment. Some of these factors will be discussed in the chapter on psycho-analytical treatment. We cannot therefore hope to estimate in figures the significance of different types of environmental influence simply by examining cases in great detail. However, a comparison of psycho-analytical with sociological findings may throw some light on the more general problems of causation.

Before making this comparison it will be well to distinguish between those primary factors which lead to the formation of the antisocial character, and the other factors which are likely to change latent into manifest delinquency.

We have shown that the future delinquent enters the latency period with a disturbance in the structure of his mind which we have described as an antisocial character formation. The factors which lead to this specific character development we shall call *primary factors*.

Experiences during the latency period may help to correct the disturbance, in which case the child may never show overt antisocial behaviour, or may exhibit only slight manifestations which disappear before or shortly after puberty. It is also possible that no antisocial behaviour may occur during the latency period, but that a shorter or longer period of disturbance under the emotional stress of puberty may give way to a more or less normal development later on. On the other hand, the experiences of the latency period—as in Billy's case—may consolidate the character formation as it emerged at the age of 6 and then lead to continuous delinquent behaviour, beginning to some extent during the latency period and becoming more open during and after puberty. The factors which tend to consolidate the antisocial character formation and which are added to the still potent primary factors we shall call *secondary factors*.

In my opinion it is very important to try to distinguish between these primary and secondary factors if we are to build up a rational scheme for the prevention of crime. For instance, to attach the same importance to the use of leisure as one does to the constitution of the family would lead to the entirely erroneous idea that the extension of club facilities would have the same effect on the incidence of delinquency as economic changes, which would give mothers time and energy to bring up their children more satisfactorily. Equally important is the distinction between cause and effect. The low educational standard reached by antisocial children is due to unmodified instinctive energy. We should therefore not be astonished at the results of statistical enquiries which show that the school attainments of delinquents do not reach the standard of those of a control group (9). To draw the conclusion from such results that a change of school alone would modify the delinquent behaviour would lead to disappointment : the antisocial attitude has to be influenced, and with success in this, school attainments will improve.

The contribution of psycho-analytical findings to sociological research lies in the analysis of the primary and secondary environmental factors causing delinquency, and in distinguishing causal influences from manifestations which are themselves the effect of antisocial development.

(*b*) Primary Factors

The primary factors which lead to antisocial behaviour are to be found in the relationship of the mother, and later on of the father, to the child and in those other emotional factors which constitute early family life. Environmental factors such as poverty, unemployment, bad housing, and to a certain extent overcrowding, indirectly exert their influence up to about the fifth or sixth year of the child's life by disturbing the mother's relationship with the child. It is therefore understandable that a disturbance in the parents', especially the mother's, personality, without the influence of adverse economic conditions, may have the same effect on the development of the structure of the child's mind as bad environmental conditions which prevent the mother from giving the child sufficient attention in the widest sense ; on the other hand a good relationship to the mother may counteract bad environmental conditions. This explains why even under very bad economic conditions only certain individuals and not others become delinquent.

In Billy's case we had an example of a home situation which exerted an undesirable influence chiefly on account of the parents' personalities, especially the mother's ambivalent attitude towards the child. Sociological influences were of course not excluded. The mother's wish that the boy should not play in the street, which prevented a natural outlet for his boyishness, was certainly influenced by her middle-class prejudices. Again, her attitude towards the father, which had a devastating influence on Billy's character, was to a certain extent biased by her better social standing. But these factors alone without the deep disturbance in the mother's personality would probably not have had so far-reaching an effect.

ESTABLISHMENT OF OBJECT RELATIONSHIP.

We have described the establishment of a firm object relationship between the child and the mother as a factor of great importance in the development of social adjustment. Billy's relationship to his mother was disturbed by the mother's ambivalent attitude. The withdrawal of the mother's attention, arising from her negative feelings, arouses severe anxiety in the child and leads to constant interruptions and disturbances in his growing attachment. The same disturbance might be caused by environmental factors not dependent on the mother's personality. She may not have time to give the child enough attention ; this often happens in large families under economic stress ; or the child may be repeatedly separated from her for shorter or longer periods during the first five years of life. Anna Freud's and D. Burlingham's (*7a, b*) observations in a residential nursery have given us valuable material, showing disturbances in the formation of an object relationship when the child is either separated from the mother or has never been looked after by any single person for any length of time.

It would be interesting to see whether statistical investigations into the causes of delinquency confirm the theory that a disturbed mother-child relationship during the first five years of life is a significant factor.

STATISTICAL DATA.

So far as I am aware no investigation has been undertaken, directed to establish exactly this fact, although the importance of the early family situation in causing delinquency is recognized by some authors. Burt (8), for instance, states that the " commonest and the most disastrous conditions are those that centre about the family life ". The authors of *Young Offenders* have made an extensive enquiry into the various types of homes from which their delinquents come as compared with those of the control group. Families with only one parent are separately grouped, but the data apply to children from 7 to 16, and nothing is known about conditions during the first five years of life. The importance of the " broken home " in the causation of delinquency emerges from statistics in *Young Offenders* (9) as well as from those in *Juvenile Delinquency* (5), and more especially from Burt's (8) investigation. Burt finds that " defective family relationships are more than twice as numerous among the delinquent as among the non-delinquent ". In Healy's statistics (16*a*), too, defective home conditions are shown to play an important part in causation, but, of course, the " broken home " includes factors other than the mother-child relationship. Norwood East (10*b*) found that provided " the parents were absent at the age of 14 or after, their presence or absence at the age of 5 made no significant difference to the frequency of multiple convictions " (p. 96). This fact might be taken as denying the importance of the child's early relationship with its parents as compared with the relationship at puberty. But for an investigation like ours, where emphasis is laid not merely on the presence or absence of parents but also on the type of relationship which exists in the home, such data are inconclusive.

We must therefore conclude that statistical investigations cannot be used to support the statement that the first object relationship of the child is an important factor in social adaptation, and the disturbance of it a significant one in the causation of antisocial behaviour. Not that those investigations which touch on the problem contradict this idea, but that only an investigation undertaken for this particular purpose could either prove or disprove our contentions. Such an investigation would be a difficult task, for it would have to include not only those cases in which the child was actually separated from the mother or in which several persons were concerned in its early upbringing, but also those where, as with Billy, the mother's attitude prevented the development of a normal relationship. But on the other hand, this would be an investigation based on the primary psychological needs of the growing child.[1]

CASE MATERIAL. It is not difficult to quote from the case material concerning delinquents many instances where this first relationship had been severely disturbed for one reason or another. Field workers are familiar with the fact that on closer investigation such a disturbance almost invariably comes to the surface. The experiences of the first wartime evacuation period also point to the importance of the uninterrupted mother-child relationship for the development of social adaptation. But apart from the last example, which in a way might be regarded as an unintentional experiment on a grand scale, observations of individual workers, thorough though they might be, would not satisfy the statistician, who would want to know whether similar conditions were not found among socially adapted children also. The research which does most to prove that the first object relationship is of such paramount importance is to be found in Healy and Bronner's (17*b*) *New Light on Delinquency*, where it is shown that of two siblings growing up in the same environment the one who has not become delinquent has been able to form a good relationship with the mother or with another person in the family.

An investigation on a broad basis, inquiring into the details of the mother-child relationship during the first five years in delinquents and in a control group, preferably of neurotic children, would have to do more than merely establish the fact that this relationship is of great importance. Few modern research workers would deny this fact in any case. But the number of analytically investigated cases of antisocial character formation is as yet too small to allow us to say with certainty which type of disturbance of the early mother-child relationship leads to antisocial behaviour and which to the development of a neurosis, and whether any such specific factor can be found in the mother-child relationship alone apart from the influence of other equally important factors in social adaptation. The solution of this problem will have to wait for future research.

As the second important factor leading to social adaptation

[1] The first statistical proof of the significance of early separation from the mother in causing delinquent behaviour has been recently brought by J. Bowlby, *44 Juvenile Thieves, their Characters and Home Life*, London, 1946.

we have noted the satisfactory modification of the primary instinctive urges of the small child. We have shown that his modification is dependent on the child's emotional relationship with the mother, so that in most cases disturbances in one sphere will react unfavourably upon the other.

MODIFICATION OF INSTINCTS.

In Billy's case the mother's inconsistent attitude towards the child's instinctive urges was to a large extent based on her own conflicts. It led to a disturbance in the modification of instincts mainly because some instincts did not get enough satisfaction while others were gratified too lavishly and for too long a time. A similar disturbance may be caused by factors which, while influencing the mother, do not arise from an inner psychic disturbance. If a mother has a child every year and has the burden of the household in addition to the care of the children, she will have neither time nor patience to deal satisfactorily with the instinctive manifestations of the child. Much as she may want to train the child properly, it will not be humanly possible for her to take, for instance, three to four months over the child's training in cleanliness and to be patient if lapses occur over and over again. Also in an overcrowded home some of the instinctive urges which have to be modified are usually very roughly dealt with if the child gives expression to them—aggressive impulses for instance—while they are freely expressed among the adults with whom the child shares the room.[1]

Statistical investigations point to certain prevailing factors in the delinquent's environment which either produce an unsatisfactory modification of instincts or altogether prevent it.

Living too close to adults, and sharing a bed with them or with another child, has a definite influence on the instinctive urges. Burt (8) found a high correlation between overcrowding and juvenile delinquency, but a much lower correlation when he compared his delinquent group with the control group taken from the same environment. Nevertheless, overcrowding was more common among the delinquents. Rhodes (9) concludes that there is relatively more overcrowding in the delinquent than in the control group, while Bagot (5) found that among Liverpool delinquents overcrowding is probably one of the principal causative factors in delinquency, though he believes that the importance of overcrowding is due not so much to its psychological effect as to the fact that it drives the children into

[1] Part I, Ch. XI, p. 68 ff.

the streets at night. It is certainly true that overcrowding exerts an influence in more than one direction, but during the early years of life its effect on the growing mind will be outstanding.

We may confirm this by examining statistical figures dealing with the question of discipline. We have discussed the importance of the parents' attitude towards the manifestations of instincts during the first years of life. This attitude or the behaviour arising from it is synonymous with discipline. The statistical figures available refer to much older children, but we cannot go far wrong in assuming that in many cases the attitude of the parents towards the child has remained more or less the same from early years.

Burt (8) states that of all the conditions listed as causes " the group showing the closest connection with crime consists of those that may be summed up under the head of defective discipline. Such features are encountered five times as often with delinquents as with non-delinquent children ". Among the variations of defective discipline Burt states that " most frequent of all, and most disastrous, is the union of licence and severity within the same home, perhaps in the person of the same capricious parent ". Bagot (5) finds the want of " calm and consistent discipline " prominent among the causes of delinquency, occurring in about 49 per cent. of cases in first offenders, and in about 71 per cent. in recidivists. Healy (16*a*) stresses the importance of this factor in his enumeration of causes.

It may be considered significant that there is a similarity between statistical and psychological data as to the importance of " defective discipline " in causing delinquent behaviour. Though my own data are not statistically conclusive in any way, I have never found the same degree of inconsistency in the handling of primitive instinctive drives in the history of neurotic patients as I invariably find in the histories of delinquents. In my opinion this is the specific factor responsible for the development of antisocial character formation instead of neurotic disturbances (13*a*). Both Aichhorn (2) and Alexander (4) emphasize this constant alternation between frustration and gratification of early instinctive drives in the cases which they have fully investigated.

OEDIPUS CONFLICT AND SUPER-EGO FORMATION.

Further factors in the development of social adaptation consist in the vanquishing of the Oedipus conflict and in the formation of the Super-Ego, both of which are influenced by previous events. If the child enters the Oedipus phase in an already disturbed condition the outcome will be less satisfactory than if the first steps of development have been successful. From the environmental point of view, the character traits of both parents, their relationship to each other and the general atmosphere of the home play an even more important part than before. There is no need to go more fully into statistical findings on this point, as nearly all investigators find a relatively high correlation between the "broken home", the "vicious home", and a "bad home atmosphere", and the incidence of delinquency, although, except for Bagot's investigations, the correlation is not overwhelmingly high. This may be so for several reasons: first, if a large number of cases have to be investigated, the time spent on each single case cannot be very great, and trained observers are not always available to probe deeper into the emotional background of a family. Secondly, conditions in the home may be different at the time of the investigation from what they were during the first years of the child's life. Moreover, it is the combination of various factors and not any single factor which leads to maladjustment. And it is the relationship of the child to the persons of its environment rather than the actual environment itself which causes the damage. Even in a "broken home" a child may form a very satisfactory relationship with its mother, and though the absence of the father will leave its mark on the child's mind, this need not predispose to delinquency. On the other hand, as was shown in Billy's case, a home may really be a "broken home" without giving that impression, if it is visited only casually. This, as will be shown in other case histories, forms a great obstacle to arriving at exact statistical investigations so far as the home atmosphere is concerned.

The attempt to prove the importance of primary factors leading to delinquency from statistical data has not been too successful. It has to be borne in mind that none of these investigations sets out to prove or disprove the exact points emphasized here. The data relating to the investigation which comes nearest to the problem here raised, namely that into defective discipline, seem fully to prove the importance of these factors in causing delinquent behaviour.

This attempt at a comparison has nevertheless been made in order to show the close interaction between what are usually distinguished as environmental and psychological factors. Environmental factors, with very few exceptions, exert their influence by acting in one way or another on the mind of the person concerned, more indirectly in early childhood than later. In fact, in a problem such as delinquency these two factors cannot very well be investigated separately. Early environmental influences leave their mark on the mind of the child, and later ones fall on a mind already moulded. On the other hand there is no mental conflict which is not rooted in environmental factors as well as in purely psychological ones. In this connection it is important to draw attention once more to the conclusions reached in *Young Offenders* (9). This investigation was originally planned in conjunction with a " psychological " investigation, but the latter for various reasons could not be undertaken. The authors, however, on the basis of their carefully conducted but purely environmental investigations, come to the conclusion that without the assumption of a " susceptibility " to delinquency, in other words, a psychological tendency which predisposes an individual to be affected by certain adverse environmental conditions, their data could be interpreted only incompletely. This assumption, derived from a starting-point different from that on which this book is based, confirms more than any single statistical investigation the thesis that adverse environmental conditions will, after the age of 6, lead to antisocial behaviour only if a state of " latent " delinquency or antisocial character formation has previously existed.

INTERACTION OF PSYCHOLOGICAL AND ENVIRONMENTAL FACTORS.

Environmental factors may lead to the formation of an antisocial character. But it is not only the environment which causes this : it is the interaction between the environment, represented during the early years by the personality of the parents, and the child's instinctive urges.

INHERITANCE.

It would lead us too far afield to go into all the theories regarding the importance of inheritance in the causation of delinquency. The work of Healy and Burt proves that criminality as such is not inherited, and both authors emphasize that only a more general factor is inheritable, namely a tendency to instability. Psycho-analytical experience regarding the problem of inheritance runs on similar lines. There is no doubt that there are individual differences in the strength of instinctive urges which can be observed even during the first weeks of life. In some children innate impulses may be so strong or so imperative that not even partial satisfaction would be sufficient. This may lead to disturbances even under good environmental conditions and with sensible parents. Moreover, we have reason to believe that the extent to which an individual is able to sublimate instinctive urges is dependent on constitutional, that is inherited factors. This in turn may play a part in social maladjustment. In any given case it is usually extremely difficult to decide which manifestations are due to constitutional and which to environmental factors. It is all the more difficult to disentangle these two series of factors as they interact from the beginning. For instance, the child's pronounced greed may lead to an exaggerated reaction on the part of the mother ; or strong anal-erotic tendencies in the child may lead the mother to pay too much attention to the child's desires at this stage of development, either in a positive or a negative way, and so lead to a fixation point. In examining such a child at the age of 10 it may seem as if the mother's incorrect attitude were the sole basis for a disturbance, while it may have been, to some extent, a reaction to the child's desires.

The decision as to which factors are constitutional and which environmental is of theoretical rather than of practical interest. It is those traits which have been caused by environmental circumstances that we can modify later on, and the attempt at modification of behaviour will have to be made in all but desperate cases.

In discussing the primary factors which lead to delinquency we have to remember that these factors shape a mind endowed with certain inherited qualities and that it is the interaction of environmental and constitutional factors which brings about the variety of reactions.

SUMMARY. To sum up, the primary factors leading to antisocial behaviour are represented by the attitude of the parents towards the child during the first five or six years of life. This attitude may be due mainly to the structure of their own personality or mainly to the pressure which a bad environment exerts upon them. These primary factors may lead to the development of an antisocial character formation, and the degree of disturbance may vary from a slight tendency to antisocial behaviour to an already fixated behaviour of that kind. But it is maintained that, without this character development, later environmental influences will not lead to the manifestation of antisocial behaviour. The child's inherited endowments may tend either to enhance or to minimize undesirable environmental influences.

(c) Secondary Factors

Environmental factors which influence the child during the latency period and puberty have been statistically investigated for their respective correlation with the incidence of delinquency. Companionship, progress in school, use of leisure, and conditions of work have all been examined in detail, and it has been found that some environmental factors akin to these categories have a positive correlation with the incidence of delinquency. The manner of correlation varies very much in different investigations. The cinema, the display of goods in department stores, the proximity of places of amusement, the lack of club facilities, and bad companionship have by some investigators been given a prominent place in causing delinquent behaviour, while others, especially Burt who combines sociological with psychological research, and recently Bagot, warn us against putting too much emphasis on factors of this kind. Such a warning is very justified. It is much easier to provide the growing youth with facilities for occupying his leisure time than to remedy the deeper reasons for his antisocial reactions.

These environmental factors, however, are undoubtedly connected with the incidence of delinquency, although less directly than would appear at first sight. We have mentioned that the bad school records of delinquents are the effect of their antisocial character formation, as has been described in detail in Billy's case. It is not unlikely that the irregular club attendance of delinquents in districts which have facilities for it is also due to their difficulty in conforming to community life. Probation officers often express their disappointment that their efforts to get their boys into clubs have met with no success. To take another example: Healy (16*a*) found that the influence of bad companionship was a single factor in causing delinquency in 34 per cent. of his cases—surely a very impressive figure—while Burt (8) gives the figure as 18 per cent. and at the same time doubts whether this bad influence would have exerted such power on a healthy mind.

I think it will clarify the situation if we examine the whole problem on the basis of the child's emotional development during the latency period and during puberty. We have said that the primary environmental factors lead to the formation of the antisocial character with which the child then enters the outside world. It has to be borne in mind that in the majority of cases these primary factors continue to exert their undesirable influence, certainly during the latency period, and often during puberty also. The youngsters usually stay at home at least until they start work and very often much later, and the home atmosphere, unless drastic changes have occurred, tends to stabilize the disturbance which it originally created.

SCHOOL VERSUS STREET.

Normally, the child on entering school is exposed to environmental influences which help him to gain control over his undesirable impulses in several ways ; by a strengthening of the Ego through intellectual achievements, by a strengthening of the Super-Ego through new identification, and by the necessity of conforming to community life which leads to identification with persons of the same age on the basis of a common task.[1] In the normal child all these processes go on unconsciously and unnoticed, but that they have been successfully achieved is seen in the child's adaptation to reality : he comes to regard school as his duty in the same way as the grown-up regards work—as a necessity.

The child who has successfully undergone the emotional development of the first five or six years of life enters school with a mind capable of benefiting by its opportunities. The child in this phase of development wishes to be good and clever and is grateful for any help given him in that direction. In a child with an antisocial character formation the situation is different. He does not wish to be good, he has very little energy left to interest himself in school subjects, he is still so prone to fits of jealousy that community life offers little pleasure, and he cannot bear having to postpone the fulfilment of his wishes. His school life therefore offers very little satisfaction and many frustrations, and he is badly equipped to stand disappointments. No wonder that the results are less satisfactory than with non-delinquent children. The displeasure experienced at the beginning of school life very often starts a vicious circle. Owing to the frustration of his daily life the child is driven to satisfy his antisocial desires —the only way in which he can gain pleasure. He may start to play truant, and the return from the pleasures of the street to school will become harder and harder. Had he been able to shine in school at the very start there might have been a chance of satisfying at least his wish to show off, and antisocial children have this desire more strongly than normal children. But the lack of interest caused by the unsatisfactory modification of

[1] Part I, Ch. IX, p. 59.

instinctive urges often makes it impossible to be really good at any one subject. The results are a bad scholastic record and bad behaviour in school—conditions which have been shown to be more prevalent among delinquent children than among a control group.

If the environment outside the school were still more unpleasant than the school, the child would probably become happier in school ; we have seen that children with an antisocial character formation are still ruled by the pleasure-principle. Such a situation is difficult to imagine, but there are various degrees of pleasure offered outside the school. The greater the attraction of activities unconnected with school the smaller the chance of adaptation to normal life. The temptations offered to the child in the way of amusement and antisocial activities may therefore be regarded as secondary factors leading to delinquent behaviour. In connection with the disappointments of school they may lead to manifest delinquency, and it may then appear as if the display of goods in department stores or access to the cinema have originally caused the antisocial reaction. Very important conclusions may be drawn from the fact that the child with an antisocial character formation does not find enough satisfaction in school life, a state of affairs which eventually will drive him into antisocial behaviour. These conclusions will be discussed in Part III. But it should be realized that there are degrees and shades of disturbance, and there is no line of demarcation at this stage between the normal and the antisocial child. With some children very little will be needed to make latent delinquency manifest, while with others a slight change in their environment may be sufficient to help them to develop further in a normal way. In order to clarify the situation extreme cases have to be illustrated.

BAD COMPANIONSHIP.

What about the influence of bad companions? Let us again start with an example from Billy's history. During his treatment he committed some offences, one of which involved the mother in difficulties. Under the influence of some older boys he stole fruit from a neighbouring orchard with them, he was present when they damaged a house, and he went with them into a bombed house and stole some books. He never did anything of the kind when he was alone. He certainly was not the leader of the gang. So the idea might arise that these delinquent acts were committed only under the influence of these bad companions. In this case, owing to the fact that Billy had been under analysis during this period, we are in a position to explain his behaviour on the basis of his conscious and unconscious motives, and to see how far his companions were responsible for his delinquent act. To be more precise: would Billy have committed a delinquent act if he had not met boys of that kind?

Billy's passive attitude towards older boys has been described as being based on his repressed passive attitude towards his father. In the relationship with his real father this attitude was too dangerous to be maintained and was replaced by open hostility. But as his passivity towards men had the driving force of an instinctive urge behind it, it had to be gratified somehow. It appeared on the one hand in his admiration for airmen and on the other in his passive attachment to certain older boys. This passivity, derived from his relationship to his father, increased his suggestibility towards these boys, whom he would obey as if spellbound, an attitude quite different from his other object relationships. Naturally, therefore, it was very easy for these boys to get him to do forbidden things. This again might mean that the delinquent actions did not arise out of Billy's character. But it was Billy, and he alone, who chose these friends. He did not feel the same attraction towards the socially adapted boys with whom he came into contact—and there were far more of them in Billy's environment—as he felt towards the ruffians. No, Billy was attracted by this type of boy only because such boys behaved as he wished to behave: their aggressiveness impressed him as being manly.

Thus again we come to the conclusion that so far as the effect of bad companions is concerned, there are several factors at work, not all of them purely environmental. There is the passive attitude derived from the unsatisfactory solution of the Oedipus conflict; there is the attraction of antisocial behaviour, based on Billy's character formation. And there is the opportunity of meeting boys of that type, which is an environmental factor. We can therefore say that the prevalence of rough boys in a neighbourhood increases the temptation and is therefore another secondary factor likely to change latent into manifest delinquency, but it is not a causative factor in delinquent behaviour.

UNEMPLOYMENT.

To take an example from the life of older boys. It has been stated that unemployment or uncongenial employment on first leaving school increases the incidence of delinquency and may therefore be regarded as a causative factor. That unsatisfactory working conditions are related to the outbreak of delinquent behaviour cannot be denied. But again the situation is not so simple as it may appear. Let us assume that a boy with an antisocial character formation who may not yet have committed any delinquent act enters puberty and experiences the usual emotional upheaval of that time. He may feel more unsettled than a healthy boy because of the fact that all his unsolved conflicts which have been more or less quiescent during the latency period come to the fore again. Thus he leaves school and finds himself in a job which does not satisfy any of his inclinations. Unlike the balanced boy he will not be able to bear unpleasantness in order to do his duty or gain some advantage later on. Such a boy cannot wait for months and in the meantime experience frustrations every day. He must have satisfaction at once, and this desire will be strengthened by the fact that in an unsuitable job none of his instinctive energy will find a way into socially accepted channels. He will most probably get out of the job, try another one, find it equally unsatisfactory, and with this history will find it more and more difficult to secure a satisfactory position. The road to antisocial behaviour is open : his companions are earning money, and he wants to have money too. Or he may feel a grudge against his employers, whom he accuses of treating him badly, and then find satisfaction in committing aggressive acts.

It is also possible that the boy with the antisocial character formation may have difficulty in securing a job at all. Then the road to delinquency might be even shorter. Such boys cannot bear waiting, and if money cannot be earned in a social way, it has to be forthcoming from somewhere else. Or again, their grievance against society arouses their aggression and allows them to behave antisocially.

Uncongenial work and unemployment, then, are secondary factors which, when imposed on young people with an antisocial character formation, will give rise to antisocial behaviour. They do not cause delinquency, but they are certainly important factors in increasing its incidence. If such factors are present to any large extent, the boy with a slight antisocial character formation is given no chance to go straight and become more balanced after puberty.

CHAPTER IV

THE COMMON OFFENDER

The burglar who earns his living by robbing people of their property, and other inhabitants of prisons who spend the greater part of their lives behind bars, were all young once. When they were young, before they earned their livelihood by criminal acts, most of them were exactly like that quite attractive rascal, Billy. Lombroso (22) studied these criminals in adult life, when their attitude towards society had already been fixated for many years and there was no longer any other occupation open to them. He called these offenders " born criminals ", and believed that they represented a subnormal type, a return to " primitive man ". Even then Lombroso emphasized the similarity between certain aspects of the mind of the born criminal and that of the child, such as its predominant concern with the present moment, the lack of inhibition, the fact that temporary motives drive out or paralyse past experiences or considerations for the future.

The common offender, according to East and Hubert (11), constitutes 80 per cent. of the prison population. Nowadays the conception of the " born criminal " is no longer tenable. Such offenders are now supposed to be mentally normal, that is to say, they show no sign of mental deficiency, psychosis, neurosis or organic illness of the brain. When seen in adult life, and on superficial investigation, the impression may be gained that they have chosen the life of criminality of their own free will.

If seen when they are young, and if full investigation is made, the picture is different, the outstanding feature being that the material gain derived from antisocial behaviour is not very obvious. But even so early they show an accumulation of undesirable character traits. One moment they promise to do what is asked of them but the next moment act differently. They lie without giving an impression of insincerity. They are more easily disappointed than are other young people of the same age, and they react to each frustration by an increase of antisocial behaviour. They live for pleasure's sake only, and seem to have a much better life than young people who are socially adapted.

COMMON CHARACTER TRAITS.

But this is not really so, and in the end they suffer much more than society suffers from them. Psychologically their behaviour is due to the fact that they are still dominated by the pleasure- instead of the reality-principle, and that the gratification of their desires is more important to them than any object relationship. They are narcissistic and emotionally infantile, unable to stand any tension, while their desires and their grasp of reality in so far as it serves the gratification of their desires are already those of an adult.

These young offenders are also very hostile towards their elders and society in general. A sado-masochistic relationship to the parents, due to a partial or full regression to the anal-sadistic phase as described in Billy's case, is rarely absent in the common offender. This relationship is later transferred to society in general, and though the hostility may be open or hidden it is never absent. The "grudge against society", a feeling met with in so many offenders, has this kind of object relationship as its basis. In the course of an antisocial career the offender has probably had many experiences which would seem to substantiate his complaints. The attitude of society towards the offender will be discussed in a later chapter,[1] when it will be seen that there is ample reason for dissatisfaction. But it has to be borne in mind that the offender, by establishing a sado-masochistic relationship with the people of his environment, provokes the very attitude he meets with.

TYPICAL CHARACTER FORMATION AS UNDERLYING CAUSE.

These common offenders have an antisocial character formation. In some cases, the disturbance is so pronounced that even a slight provocation will arouse antisocial reactions; in other cases only severe provocation will cause delinquent behaviour. This provocation may be purely environmental, as for instance bad economic conditions, or it may be psychological, as for instance a mental conflict. But the offender deals with internal or external stress in the same way; by acting impulsively, irrespective of results to himself or to the environment. In the majority of cases the provocation is to be seen in a frustration of some kind, and the answer is therefore a hostile act against the environment which has imposed the frustration.

The antisocial reactions themselves are not very numerous: playing truant, running away from home, stealing, breaking and

[1] Part III, Ch. I.

entering in the older boy, waywardness and perhaps prostitution in the young girl. The immediate cause for one or another antisocial reaction may occasionally be very obvious. Removal of this cause, be it environmental or psychological, may help for a short time. But it does not really influence the underlying antisocial character formation, and new frustration or a new conflict will again provoke the antisocial reaction instead of normal behaviour. This factor is unfortunately very often overlooked. Stealing, for instance, is often found to be caused by a lack of affection on the mother's side. In a child of over 7 years increased attention from the mother or another person of the environment will not in itself be a safeguard against a repetition of the offence. If a child of that age reacts to frustration in this particular way he is likely to have an antisocial character formation, and much more extensive measures will be necessary to remedy this. Healy (16*b*), when discussing mental conflict as the cause of antisocial behaviour, gives a wealth of case histories illustrating the emotional stress which was the immediate cause of the delinquent behaviour. Prominent among such conflicts were jealousies between siblings, sexual difficulties of one kind or another, and rebellion against the parents during puberty. The experiences of these boys and girls can also be found in the histories of neurotic or normal individuals; they are in no way specific experiences. The majority of human beings live through times of severe emotional stress when they are young, especially during puberty, and such conflicts are often caused by unhappy experiences inside or outside the home. A minority of these young people become delinquent; some become neurotic, others remain mentally healthy. If a youth has an antisocial character formation he may become a delinquent under emotional stress. In my view, the conflicts described by Healy were the immediate but not the ultimate cause of delinquent behaviour.

TYPICAL DEVELOPMENT.

As a rule emotional stress during puberty does not cause antisocial behaviour in boys and girls who have previously shown no sign of their antisocial character formation. On careful investigation former delinquent acts will be found, perhaps undetected. Very often a period of "unruly behaviour" precedes the actual delinquency. If the antisocial character formation is at all pronounced it will manifest itself first at the beginning of the latency period, at the age of 6 or 7, in the impossibility of conforming to ordinary methods of discipline suitable for this age. Children are "beyond the control" of their parents; Billy was a typical example of the failure of ordinary methods of discipline to control behaviour, and we have seen that this was due to the lack of Super-Ego development inherent in faulty character development.

The overt form of delinquent behaviour following this period of unruliness is to a certain extent influenced by external circumstances. Playing truant may become infectious, and so may the theft of motor-cars. But the usual development of antisocial behaviour proceeds in boys from playing truant and pilfering at home to stealing outside the home and breaking and entering. Girls play truant less often, but pilfering is a common occurrence, while during puberty staying away from home slowly leads to prostitution.

Boys and girls whose antisocial behaviour is caused solely by their antisocial character formation present easily recognizable types.

THE AGGRESSIVE YOUTH (AICHHORN).

Aichhorn (2) has made a special study of a type of young offender whom he calls the "aggressive youth". He was able to study the reactions of a number of these boys while they were living in an institution under his care. By way of a therapeutic experiment he proved that his conception of their character structure was correct.[1] This type is well known to all field workers on account of the unusual obstacles these boys present in the way of any reformative effort if their special peculiarities are not taken into account. In addition to the usual signs of an antisocial character formation, these young men have an open hatred of everybody in authority, an utter disregard for the property of other persons and an entire lack of consideration for any other human being. Their cruelty is remarkable, and so is their provocative attitude when challenged. In the childhood histories of this type of offender Aichhorn found in every single case gross disturbances of the early family setting and an abundance of primary environmental factors leading to the antisocial character formation. The cause of this pronounced cruelty and provocative attitude is to be found in the regression of the libido to the anal-sadistic phase of development. As has been shown, a certain degree of regression is somewhat typical of the antisocial character development in general, but in this type the regression is very pronounced and predominant.

[1] Also Part III, Ch. V (*a*) p. 240 ff.

THE "WAYWARD GIRL".

In recent years girls who enter on an "immoral life" at the age of 14 or even earlier have come to present a difficult problem for parents and authorities alike. Not that this type of girl was unknown before the war, but under the external circumstances of increased opportunity their number has increased to a disquieting degree, and it has been recognized that the available methods of treatment are inadequate. On superficial enquiry it may appear as if the problem were one of environmental factors only. But in every case of this kind which has come to my notice, signs of an antisocial character formation have been present before puberty, and there was not one without a disturbance in the early family setting.

CASE 2.

Susan is a very typical example of a "wayward girl". She was a good-looking platinum blonde of 18 who for the last two years had been living with a countless number of soldiers, usually of the officer class. In none of the many jobs in which she started had she stayed longer than a few days, even if the work she was doing had been chosen by herself. She was put on probation for an offence connected with her identity card, and though very pleasant and friendly towards the probation officer did not fulfil any of the requirements of probation. No friendliness, no understanding, no discussions on the effects of her way of life (she had already been in hospital once with venereal disease), made the slightest impression on her, though she was of superior intelligence.

Susan was the eldest of two girls brought up by their grandparents. It could never be ascertained what had happened to the father or why the children were not brought up by their mother. The grandmother was already nearing 70 when Susan was a small child, and though very fond of the girl, she had never been able to control her. When Susan was 9 her grandmother was crippled in an accident; from that time onwards Susan ran completely wild, played truant and refused to come in at night. She was committed to an Approved School when she was 11 as being "in need of care and protection", and stayed there until she was 15. Her character was described as "bad and inclined to be immoral". She absconded from the domestic job in which she was placed on her release, and as a result was sent to a strict Catholic convent. She seems to have been on friendly terms with the Mother Superior there, and occasionally wrote to her later on, from a fictitious address, that she was going to give up her

" wild " life and return to the convent. While still in the convent she wrote stories about her amorous life—at that time existing in phantasy only—and took care that these writings should be found after she had left. On leaving the convent three months after the expiration of her licence from the Approved School she joined the A.T.S., but was discharged after five months for continual absenteeism ; and since then she had been living a life of prostitution.

These two types of offenders represent extremes, as do the children in *Branch Street* (24). They are examples of a development where a marked antisocial character formation was enhanced during the latency period and puberty by environmental and psychological factors. The difference between these extremes and the child who presents behaviour problems is one of quantity and not of quality. Even normally the Ego's control of the instincts during the latency period and the emotional upheaval of puberty is not perfect, so that mild antisocial reactions may occur occasionally in a child who will be able to achieve social adaptations in the end. In order to be able to assess the degree of the disturbance, not only the single offence but all the various aspects of the child's life have to be thoroughly examined. This problem, as well as the ways in which environmental factors can assist in creating a favourable outcome, will be more thoroughly discussed later.[1]

[1] Part III, Ch. II and VII.

CHAPTER V

NEUROTIC MANIFESTATIONS

(*a*) Introduction

DEFINITION OF NEUROSIS.

Neuroses are illnesses of the mind which lead to the development of so-called psychogenic symptoms. Irrational fears, such for instance as of crossing an open space, paralysis of a limb without an organic basis, compulsions such as washing one's hands incessantly, even the layman knows to be due to a disorder of the mind and not of the body. The personalities of individuals who produce symptoms of this kind are not very different from those of normal people ; more especially, neurotic individuals are with very few exceptions law-abiding citizens, and even the obsessional neurotic whose symptoms often reveal extremely hostile thoughts against other human beings, displays in his actual behaviour a strong and often exaggerated social conscience.

On the other hand, the attention of psycho-analysts has been drawn to the investigation of criminal behaviour in cases where the offender's delinquent actions showed in their structure a great similarity to neurotic symptoms, and it was with these cases that the first attempts at psycho-analytic treatment were undertaken.

THE NEUROTIC AND THE DELINQUENT SYMPTOM.

A neurotic symptom is the outcome of an unconscious mental conflict, and unless the unconscious material is revealed the symptom appears to the person afflicted with it and to the onlooker to be entirely meaningless. In the same way, certain delinquent acts can be understood only if their unconscious motivation is unearthed. It has been found that there is no fundamental difference between unconscious conflicts underlying neurotic symptom formation and unconscious conflicts causing those delinquent actions which we might call " delinquent symptoms ". (4, 13*a*).

Aichhorn (2), Alexander (4), Healy (4) and recently R. D. Gillespie (14) have drawn attention to the fact that it is not yet known why one individual becomes neurotic while another becomes delinquent. These authors suggest that severe early deprivations predispose towards the latter development.

I have tried to show that the reason why one individual is

satisfied with a substitute gratification in phantasy—the neurotic symptom—while another must procure the substitute gratification in action—the delinquent symptom—is a difference in character formation. The character formation of the neurotic is either normal as in the hysterical patient, or shows a Super-Ego of abnormal severity, as in the obsessional neurotic. The delinquent, as has been shown, has an antisocial character formation.[1] The specific factor in the causation of the antisocial character formation is probably the constant alternation of too much frustration and too much gratification of primitive instinctive drives (13*a*). This specific factor will be especially pronounced under the conditions which the authors previously cited describe as those of " early deprivations ".

If an individual with an antisocial character formation suffers from the pressure of unconscious conflicts it is probable that a delinquent and not a neurotic sympton will appear, if symptom formation occurs at all (see Case 3) ; or under the stress of unconscious conflicts a hitherto concealed disturbance in character formation may come to the fore and manifest itself in delinquent behaviour (see Case 4).

The percentage of young offenders in whose delinquent behaviour neurotic manifestations play a part is rather high. The combination of antisocial character formation with neurotic illness does not result in a uniform picture. There are only a few well-defined types, such as the kleptomaniac, the impostor, or the " criminal from a sense of guilt ". It is much more usual to find that antisocial behaviour is influenced by neurotic tendencies ; the addition of neurotic symptoms to the antisocial character formation varies in quantity. These variations account for the manifold picture encountered in studying antisocial actions.

In order to understand the motives in the case histories which follow, some problems of symptom formation must be discussed in more detail.

(*b*) The Return of Repressed Impulses

We have described how, during the early stages of development, many instinctive desires and conflicts arising from them have to be repressed, since they are incompatible with the demands of the outside world and later of the Ego and Super-Ego. The mechanism of repression is not a desirable one because energy is constantly needed to keep these instinctive urges from

[1] Part II, Ch. II.

becoming conscious ; moreover the repressed impulses are inaccessible to further modification. This is a waste on two counts. Nevertheless, even the most normal human being has repressed certain desires and conflicts. It is their quantity and not their quality which distinguishes the normal from the abnormal.

Instinctive urges are invested with energy which drives them constantly to find an outlet in action ; therefore more and more energy has to be used to keep the undesirable impulse repressed. Situations may arise where the power of the repressed drive becomes stronger than the inhibiting forces of the Ego and Super-Ego. The repressed impulse will then return. Some of the typical mechanisms by which repressed desires find gratification contrary to the conscious intention of the individual will be here described.

FAULTY ACTS.

A little girl had been very jealous of her younger brother, born when she was 3 years of age. The jealousy and envy of the brother had to be completely and quickly repressed. Three years later another child, this time a girl, was born, and the elder sister's reaction was friendly from the start. She mothered the baby, and in doing so on one occasion lifted her out of a chair and let her fall to the ground. The baby was afterwards very ill and the older sister was torn by remorse. Some weeks later milk was short in the house, and the mother asked the elder sister to look after the baby's feed and to be careful. The otherwise skilful girl, trying to be careful, spilt the whole of the milk, and was now afraid that the baby would have to starve. She again cried with mortification. Some months later, she quarrelled with her elder brother while they were close to the small sister, so that the baby was again thrown on the floor and had concussion. The grief of the older girl was so intense that the mother feared she might become ill if the younger sister did not recover.

Three such accidents cannot be ascribed to chance. The girl had not the slightest conscious intention of harming her sister, whom she adored. Why, then, the acute feelings of guilt? Do we not gain the impression that there was deliberate intention behind these careless acts? Emotions, though they may seem unreasonable, are a much truer guide to the state of our mind than are our conscious thoughts. The girl's feelings of guilt were justified, because there was an intention to kill behind her actions. This intention was unconscious. It was originally a desire to make away with the younger brother. The birth of the little sister revived this old conflict. The girl at first succeeded in repressing her jealousy, helped by the fact that the newcomer was a girl, and her conscious attitude appeared to be a reaction formation.[1] She was friendly from the very beginning, and showed an exaggerated love for the small baby. None of the normal signs of jealousy at the birth of a younger child could be detected. This showed that the fear of arousing the old conflict must have been very strong, so that every fresh desire akin to the former had to be repressed even before it became conscious. With this new addition to the old repressed urges the power of the unconscious desires became too strong : they broke through against the will of the conscious personality, and in such a way that the child could not possibly prevent it. They did not arise in the child's mind as a conscious thought, but they managed to find their outlet in action before becoming conscious. Faulty acts of this kind need not always be so dramatic and dangerous as in this case. Much broken china may be laid to the account of the repressed hostility of the servant towards her mistress, and many forgotten appointments can be explained on this basis.

One way therefore for a repressed instinctive desire to find gratification is for it to break out into action in its original form and against the conscious intention of the person concerned.

It is a general rule that a danger point for the eruption of the repressed impulse arises if the experience which caused the original desire is repeated, that is to say, if a second or third or fourth repression has to take place. We see also that the desire to kill has become independent of the person against whom it was originally directed : it is the sister and not the brother who is threatened by the faulty act. In the unconscious the impulse can be gratified in a distorted form as well. Both these conclusions are important for the understanding of neurotic illness.

THE PHOBIC MECHANISM.

A little boy, at the height of his Oedipus conflict, suddenly develops a fear of going into the street.[2] It is discovered that he is not afraid of the street itself but of the danger of meeting a horse. He is afraid of horses because he imagines that they intend to bite him. If not

[1] Part I, Ch. V, p. 29.

[2] It is not possible in this context to follow up the details of an analysis of a phobic symptom. I shall therefore only repeat a few of the relevant facts from a phobic symptom in a child analysed by S. Freud (12 *a*).

forced to go out he is perfectly happy and not otherwise disturbed. This is a phobia ; it is common as a passing symptom in childhood and constitutes one type of neurotic illness in adults.

The repressed conflict at the basis of the little boy's symptom was his Oedipus desire. The understanding of the symptom will again be helped by an investigation into his unconscious emotional state. The boy is afraid that a horse might bite him. The emotions, as we said, do not lie, and we can understand the fear when we realize that the horse represents the little boy's father, and to be bitten by it was the retaliation expected for the boy's desires towards his mother. The anxiety was displaced from the father to an animal. The horse was chosen because the father used to play a game with the boy in which he pretended to be a horse.

The fear of meeting a horse was very unpleasant. But by displacing the fear from the father to an animal the object which aroused the fear could now be avoided : it would be impossible for the boy to avoid the sight of his father, and still more impossible for him to avoid the fear of his own conscience. If the boy does not go into the street, where he might meet a horse, all is well ; there is no longer any fear, and therefore no danger of the Oedipus desires as such arising in his consciousness. This gain on the instinctive side is offset by the fact that the phobia causes the inhibition of an important Ego function.

The strange picture of the illness is caused by the fact that the laws of the unconscious are different from those of our conscious thinking : a person is replaced by an animal, which has a remote connection with the original object. Very often the displacement goes even further ; the fear or other emotion may be displaced to an object representing the original person or part of the person in a symbolic form only.

This phobic mechanism is much more complicated than the breaking through of an unaltered impulse, but it achieves more successfully the aim of the neurotic illness : that of disguising completely the meaning of the underlying desires.

THE HYSTERICAL MECHANISM.

A girl, after having been kissed for the first time, suddenly develops dysphagia (difficulty in swallowing). She has in addition the feeling that something is sticking in her throat. There is no organic cause for the complaint ; examination discloses that it is an hysterical symptom. So far good results have been achieved by starting the investigation with the conscious emotion related to the disturbance. But this girl does not display any emotion ; she is on the contrary prepared to endure the symptom and feels indifferent towards it. Yet it is strange that a symptom of this severity, which makes eating, drinking and swallowing a major problem, should not be felt as very unpleasant. On further investigation we find that together with the symptom an unpleasant emotion has made its appearance. The girl, since her first sexual experience, feels disgust on imagining any kind of intimacy with a man and has lost all desire for marriage. This is an emotion which we should not expect. It would be much more natural for a young girl to enjoy being kissed and to look forward to being married. Such were this girl's feelings before her sexual experience. The assumption is therefore justified that the first sexual experience of being kissed aroused a desire which had to be repressed because it was akin to an already repressed desire. The repressed desire belonged to the Oedipus conflict, and contained sexual wishes towards the father. As the girl was still fixated to her original love object, any intimacy with a man was likely to arouse the old forbidden desires. Normal sexual desires also had therefore to be avoided. The girl succeeded ; from this time onwards she felt disgust for any intimacy with a man, and this was a most efficient safeguard against the wish for a sexual relationship. But she succeeded only by developing a hysterical symptom at the same time. On analysing this symptom we find that the girl is now preoccupied with her mouth and throat from morning till night. The act of swallowing, which normally is a reflex activity of which we are not consciously aware, has become a process demanding constant attention. From the girl's analytical history, which brought into consciousness many repressed recollections, it appeared that as a small child she had watched perverse sexual activities between her parents in which the mouth played an important part. At that time she had phantasies that babies are conceived by eating apples, an idea which shows that the mouth still had for this girl the significance of an erogenous zone. The sexual activity which aroused the hysterical symptom was kissing, and it was apparently so forbidden because it touched on the Oedipus wish which unconsciously, for this girl, was still connected with sexual activities of the mouth. The symptom enabled her to be preoccupied with her mouth from morning to night, but this preoccupation was no longer pleasurable. The symptom, therefore, serves as a compromise between the old instinctive urge, stored in the unconscious as a perverse phantasy, and the punishment for indulging in the forbidden desire. The two emotions, the pleasure and the punishment, cancelled each other out, and the result was emotional indifference towards the symptom. It is important to realize that here, in a hysterical symptom, the psychological conflict caused a functional disturbance. The girl does not pretend not to be able to swallow ; she really cannot swallow. The innervation of her throat no longer functions properly. In what way this step from the mind to the body takes place we do not know. It is probably due to a displacement of energy. But it is characteristic of the hysterical illness that almost any organic symptom can be imitated.

In the conscious mind, emotions cannot cancel one another out as occurred in this symptom formation ; moreover, it is also possible for the unconscious to express the instinctive urge and the feeling of guilt in one single act, the symptom. The neurotic symptom is generally a compromise between the instinctive urges arising in the Id and the suppressing forces belonging to the Ego and Super-Ego (12*c*).

THE OBSESSIONAL MECHANISM.

A boy of 16 developed a fear of coming into contact with dirt or germs. He began to wash his hands incessantly, he could stay only in certain rooms or walk through certain streets which he considered to be clean, and he could eat only food brought to him by his father or sister. Any alteration of these strange conditions of living caused acute states of anxiety.

Shortly before the outbreak of this obsessional neurosis the boy was extremely worried about his desire to masturbate. The accompanying phantasies were of a sado-masochistic nature, and indicated a regression to the anal-sadistic phase of libidinal development. According to this he regarded masturbation as a " dirty " activity likely to endanger his health.

With the outbreak of the illness the desire to masturbate for a time disappeared. The symptom had the character of punishment—threatening contamination with dirt or illness—and of atonement : if the described conditions of existence, which made life nearly unbearable, were rigidly observed, anxiety could be warded off.

But there are already indications that the instinctive urges have found a way in the symptom-formation as well—if only in a symbolic form : by washing his hands incessantly the young man behaved as if he had satisfied his desire to masturbate. At a later stage in his illness the character of punishment and atonement of the symptom was more and more replaced by a disguised satisfaction of instinctive urges. He began masturbating again in an obsessional way—incessantly and without gaining sexual gratification—but also without experiencing a sense of guilt.

These examples illustrate, in a simplified form, some of the mechanisms of neurotic symptom formation.

In the first example, the repressed impulse finds expression in action, though the gratification is already to some extent a substitute gratification: the hated child was not the sister but the brother. But in all the other examples the gratification was no longer achieved by impulsive actions but by a substitute satisfaction in phantasy.

The breaking out of the impulse into action—which is the prototype of the delinquent symptom—is made possible by a weakness in Ego and Super-Ego formation. In all the other cases, the repressing forces emanating from Ego and Super-Ego are strong enough to keep the impulse away from action. This difference in character formation, as already mentioned, accounts for the fact that the compromise between the unconscious desire and the repressing forces is sometimes a delinquent symptom, while in all the other cases it is a neurotic one.

The apparent strangeness of certain symptoms is due to the difference in quality between psychological processes governing the conscious and the unconscious mind, differences which explain not only neurotic symptom formation but also the strange dreams of the normal individual (12*c*, *d*, *e*).

To sum up: if for some reason a repressed instinctive urge becomes too strong it has to find a way to gratify itself. As the repressing force, emanating from the Ego and Super-Ego, is still at work, this gratification can be achieved only in a disguised form, unrecognizable by the conscious mind. The symptom represents the compromise between the desire and the repressing forces.

(1) A Kleptomanic Symptom

CASE 3: THE SYMPTOM.

Mary was just 10 years of age when she was sent one day to get some groceries for her mother. After giving her order to the shop assistant she saw in front of her a display of chocolate cigars. Looking up, she found that the assistant's back was turned, and suddenly the child's arm shot forward and she took two of the sweets. She did not hide them, but was standing quite still with the cigars in her hand when the assistant turned round and saw her. The assistant, who knew the girl and her mother very well, asked her in a harsh voice about the sweets. The child could not answer, got a good scolding, and was told that her mother would hear about her disgusting behaviour. With which words the assistant took back the sweets, and the girl went out of the shop as if in a dream. Half an hour later she met a friend of hers in the park and related the incident to her in a completely new version. With annoyance and in a defiant tone she related how she had taken the two chocolate cigars only in order to ask the price, and the woman in the shop had accused her of stealing. After she had relieved her mind by this narrative she forgot the incident, which never reached her mother's ears, until its significance became known many years later when she underwent psycho-analytical treatment for training purposes. She was then a very respected member of society, followed a profession, was married and had children.

Let us suppose that this girl had come before a court on this charge of stealing. Her attitude towards the people who questioned her would have been typical. She would have denied the deed, been sulky, and when confronted with the truth could not have offered any explanation. She had enough money on her to buy the sweets, and she did not particularly like chocolate, a fact which could have been confirmed by members of her family.

PREVIOUS HISTORY.

As in the majority of cases, former little thefts could be elicited. The girl had for years frequently taken money from her mother's purse without ever being found out. She usually bought school equipment with it. Some weeks before this incident she had been a member of a gang of children, boys and girls of her own age, who were pilfering in shops. This stealing had been going on for a few weeks when one of the children talked at home and it was stopped. Mary excelled in this gang by the very audacity with which she stole and the skilfulness with which she could hide things, but it was not she who had started the pilfering. Apart from this stealing and the fact that she did not get on too well with other children, being often involved in quarrels, there were no other difficulties. Mary was well above the average in intelligence, very well adjusted in school, and known to be very ambitious. At the age of 10 she already had definite plans for her future: she wanted to go to college.

DIFFERENCE FROM COMMON ANTISOCIAL BEHAVIOUR.

This case, taken at this stage at its face value, is a typical example of incipient delinquency: stealing starts at home, slowly develops into stealing outside the house, as a member of a gang and later alone. Only if it is realized that the reason for a delinquent act may not be apparent at first sight will further information be sought. There were some inconsistencies in the last act of stealing which reveal what was unconscious in the girl herself: first of all, she stole a kind of sweet of which she was not very fond and which she was able to buy; secondly, the fact that so clever a girl as Mary, who had already had some experience in stealing, should be so stupid as to be caught.

This then is the story of Mary's stealing: she came from a good middle-class home, which at first sight seemed very satisfactory. There were two brothers, one older and one younger, neither of whom had committed any antisocial act. Both parents seemed fond of their children. Again, as in Billy's case, outward appearances were very deceptive. This very good middle-class home was all but a "broken home" so far as the atmosphere for the children was concerned. The mother was mentally rather disturbed. She suffered from phases of depression, and at other periods was very elated. Her attitude towards life and the children was very different during these phases. When depressed she was always at home, took everything which happened very seriously, and nagged at the children. When elated she would go out a good deal, without returning in time for meals, so that the children would occasionally be late for afternoon school, and there would be constant quarrels between the parents. As with most people who have a mental disturbance of this kind, the mother was very self-centred. Though she would devote her whole time to the children when they were small and be very concerned about their physical welfare, she had no conception of what was going on in their minds. She was proud of her children because she had produced them, and she wanted them to be constantly acknowledging how much she did for them. She openly preferred the youngest son; next to her heart came the oldest boy. But she very often told other people in front of Mary that she had wanted her first child to be a girl, and so was very glad when

RELATIONSHIP TO MOTHER.

Mary was born. At the same time she was disappointed because Mary at first had no hair, and later her hair never grew long enough to plait. The same ambivalence which Mary's mother showed towards the girl's sex was expressed in her attitude to her education. She satisfied the child's greed very fully at times, while at others she suddenly issued strong prohibitions against her taking certain kinds of food. This attitude caused a disturbance in the child's eating between the ages of 2 and 3—a disturbance which afterwards gave way to rather pronounced greed. Mary, when small, was greatly attached to her mother, and was probably very jealous when the younger brother was born. She was then 3 years of age. This attachment, within which the child experienced grave disappointments caused not only by the birth of the brother but by the constant changes in the mother's attitude, showed outwardly only slight alteration when she began to go to school. But certain reactions in the latency period showed that this relationship to the mother was by no means only a positive one. When separated from the mother for short periods between the ages of 6 and 9 the child, who at that time was by no means tied to her mother's apron strings, would suddenly be overcome by a strong longing for the mother and a strong feeling of guilt for her disobedience at times when the mother was at home. For since the age of 5 Mary had become rather disobedient and difficult to handle on account of her pigheadedness. This longing for the mother when she was away bore no relationship to her behaviour when she was present, and it became clear that the feelings of guilt were due to unconscious hostile impulses which the child could in part express unknowingly through her disobedience. The absence of the mother was unconsciously perceived by her as being due to her own hostility.

Unlike the mother, the father openly preferred Mary. In the frequent quarrels between the parents in the children's presence, Mary was constantly torn between loyalty to her mother and admiration and love for her father. This conflict was increased by the fact that the parents used the children, especially Mary, as instruments of their own emotions. If, for instance, the father went out after a quarrel the mother would send Mary to fetch him back. If Mary was especially naughty she was told that she was exactly like her father. At other times, however, there was a reconciliation between the parents, and they would be demonstratively affectionate to each other in front of Mary, who then felt "out of it".

LATENCY PERIOD.

By the age of 6 Mary already felt very unhappy at home, especially as she knew that her friends had parents who did not quarrel. This unpleasantness in the home, Mary's superior intelligence and her ambition to know things and to be able to read and write like her elder brother, whom she admired, and of whom she was jealous, led to her interest and excellent adjustment in school. There she was socially adapted, but she was rather antisocial at home, having started to quarrel with her brothers and to be disobedient. At school Mary was able to satisfy her ambitions. But she was not happy. She did not get on well with the teacher of her class, and was constantly jealous of a cousin of hers who usually had better marks and was a greater favourite of the teacher's. Mary, as already mentioned, did not get on too well with other children, mainly on account of her easily aroused jealousy and ambition.

During these first school years, Mary, apart from being slightly beyond control at home, had started to steal money from her mother's purse. The stealing in the gang occurred shortly before Mary and the other children, who were all in the same class, were to leave their elementary school. As we have said, the stealing became known, though the children got off rather lightly. One of the mothers discussed the matter with them and left it at that. Mary's own mother never heard of it. The leader of the gang was Mary's cousin, the girl who was known in school as being so good and trustworthy, and Mary took a certain delight in knowing that at least she was not so bad as her cousin : she would never have started such a thing on her own. After the whole business was finished, Mary suddenly started to feel guilty about it, and was terrified that her mother would be told. The summer holidays came, and Mary was looking forward very much to going to a secondary school next term and so fulfilling her ambition to become as clever as the older brother.

Then something happened which quite upset Mary's balance. An older cousin, a girl of 18, was accused of having repeatedly stolen sums of money from members of her tennis club. She did not come before the court, but the matter was known all over the small town ; the girl was expelled from the club and had to leave her home. This cousin had known about the stealing gang, and Mary was terrified lest now, after being punished so much more severely for her own stealing, she should tell everyone about Mary's misdeeds. The result of this, Mary thought, would be that she would not be accepted for secondary school and all her ambitions would come to nothing. She felt more and more guilty about her actions and got into a real state of anxiety. She did not dare to talk to anyone about her worries. In the midst of this conflict Mary stole again, this time alone, and so unskilfully that she was found out. It is rather strange that this action should have arisen out of the conflict about the former stealing, and still more astonishing that she should steal from a shop where the children had formerly tried to pilfer and did not succeed because the assistant seemed to suspect them. Another factor was equally difficult to understand : the shop assistant was very friendly with Mary's mother, and we have seen that Mary was terrified lest her mother might hear about her anti-social actions. But apparently this last act of stealing served a useful purpose : all Mary's feelings of guilt and her anxieties suddenly vanished, the only feeling left in connection with this incident being indignation that the shop assistant should accuse her. Even that disappeared after a few days, and she was now looking forward to starting school without feeling any further conflict.

THE CONSCIOUS CONFLICT.

The most striking difference between Mary's former stealing and her last delinquent act is the fact that she consciously approved of her actions in the beginning, but was consciously opposed to the stealing of the chocolate cigars. In the latter case her conscious personality was suddenly overcome by a strong impulse which she was unable to keep in check. Moreover, the whole thing happened so quickly that the girl did not know at all why she did it. There is a queer reversal of feelings : we have seen that she felt very guilty before she stole the chocolate cigars, and that her feelings were completely relieved by the action and its result. Actually we might say that it was the feeling of guilt which drove her to commit another delinquent act.

THE UNCONSCIOUS CONFLICT.

The explanation of this apparently simple act of stealing is not satisfactory if the conscious actions and thoughts alone are considered. Indeed, the child's action is inexplicable unless unconscious factors are taken into account. The best starting-point for an investigation will be the attempt to understand the emotions which the child actually felt. We have seen that her feeling of guilt started after the stealing gang had been dissolved. At that time no real punishment was inflicted upon the children. Mary had been accustomed to treatment of a different kind at home. Her mother was very harsh at times and did not mind smacking Mary if she did something naughty. The mother never learned about the antisocial act, and so the well-known reaction did not supervene. So Mary suddenly felt that she herself did not approve of what she had done. Her conscience took a step towards becoming more independent, and she felt guilty. Her guilt feeling increased to an intolerable strength when she learned about the severe punishment of the older cousin. That is what ought to have happened to herself. And in her phantasy she imagined that the one thing she had set her heart upon, namely, being as clever as the older brother, would be taken away from her: she would not be admitted to a secondary school, and it was all her own fault. If she had been conscious of the explanation just given, all would have been well: she could have gone to her mother and confessed to her. But that was not possible; she had no idea where her guilt feeling and anxiety really came from, and, as we shall see presently, she could not confide in her mother because her hostility towards her mother was really at the bottom of the whole unconscious conflict. But the feeling of guilt had to be relieved, for the tension was unbearable. Mary stole, this time with the intention of being caught and punished. Having been scolded harshly after the sweets were taken away from her she felt happy again. Her guilt feeling was relieved, for she had been punished. She would not at this juncture have consciously chosen this way out, which might have brought her into even greater trouble: but she did not think. The impulse found a way into action against her conscious wishes.

This explains why Mary stole so unskilfully that she was caught. But it does not explain why she had to steal at all, or why she stole a sweet which she did not like to eat.

We have seen that Mary had for years been stealing money from her mother's purse. We have also seen that her relationship to her mother was not a very happy one. There was a strong early attachment, but her love for the mother had to undergo severe trials. The mother preferred the boys; and, as we have learnt,[1] it is quite natural for a small girl to wish to be a boy even if the mother's attitude is less biased. In addition to this open preference the mother emphasized that it was she

[1] Part I, Ch. VI.

who had wished to have a girl. So apparently it was the mother's fault that Mary was born as a girl—without plaits. This feeling, in addition to her jealousy of the mother during the Oedipus phase—which was rather emphasized in the girl owing to the father's support of it—evoked in Mary a strong hostility to her mother, for which she found expression in her disobedience and in her stealing from the mother's purse. Perhaps even this early stealing was of a somewhat symbolic nature : by stealing the money she at the same time wanted to take from the mother by force what she had not given freely ; affection, and perhaps the means of being a boy. Many little girls have the same unfulfilled desires. Not all of them steal. Mary expressed her desire in this particular way because her impulses were very strong, her Ego was comparatively weak, at least where certain instinctive urges were concerned, and her Super-Ego was not yet independent : a condition in the structure of the mind which we have described as antisocial character formation. So the impulse could find a way into action.

CHARACTER FORMATION.

It has been emphasized that Mary's feelings of guilt had begun when she realized what would happen if her mother heard about her actions. This was not so rational as appears at first sight. Mary's mother, who could be very severe if the child were disobedient, would certainly have taken her side and would have believed that the other children led her astray. To the outside world Mary's mother often stated that her children were better than all the other children because she had borne them and brought them up. But Mary could not stop to think about this, because she knew about the former stealing, which was a hostile act against the mother. This unconscious knowledge forced her to atone for her misdeeds in the peculiar way we have described : she stole again, from a person who was a friend of her mother and of the same age, a person whom she knew to be severe, and consequently she obtained her punishment. Now she need feel guilty no longer. The whole unconscious conflict which had lasted for so long a time was expressed in a symbolic form in this one compulsive act of stealing : the hostility against the mother, the pilfering of something she wanted very badly—affection and the means of being a boy—the returning of the cigars and the punishment. The stealing, the symptom as we might call it, serves two ends : it gives some satisfaction, in a symbolic form, to the instinctive urge, and it satisfies the demands of the Super-Ego for punishment. It is, like every symptom, a compromise.

Had Mary had a different character structure her unconscious conflict might have been expressed in an entirely different way. It would certainly not have led her to commit an antisocial act.

This case is a good example of the mixture of antisocial and neurotic behaviour. The antisocial character formation of this girl was mitigated by several factors : owing to her superior intelligence and her unhappiness at home she was able to adjust herself to school life. She had also been able to sublimate some of her instinctive urges in a satisfactory way ; she was able to express her wish to be like her brother in intellectual ambition. Though this ambition disturbed her relationship with other children during the latency period it was a great help in strengthening her Ego. We have seen the progress in her Super-Ego development ; when the gang's stealing went unpunished it led her to assume the responsibility for her own actions. The neurotic stealing was Mary's last antisocial act. She became a balanced and responsible personality. As will be shown in a later chapter,[1] the environment which provided her with ample opportunities to sublimate her instinctive urges played an important part in this satisfactory development.

KLEPTOMANIA.

In Mary's case there is a psychological difference between her stealing with the gang, to which she submitted on account of her antisocial character formation, and her last act of stealing, which was prompted by an unconscious conflict. While in the former instance she was aware of what she was doing, going into a shop with the intention of pilfering something, in the latter she acted under a compulsion. In Mary's case this symptom appeared only once, while in the mental disturbance called kleptomania such obsessional acts are repeated again and again. This disturbance is very rare, and for the trained observer it is easy to diagnose. The mechanism of this obsessional stealing is very similar to that described in Mary's case : the stealing is the result of an unconscious conflict and represents a symbolic gratification of the underlying impulse, while the punishment which usually follows such an antisocial act gratifies the feeling of guilt. As in Mary's case, full investigation in a case of this kind usually reveals the underlying antisocial character disturbance, though this disturbance may not

[1] Part III, Ch. V (*a*), p. 244.

have been too obvious and may not have led to antisocial acts until the neurotic conflict came to the fore.

For the layman the first indication of the neurotic nature of antisocial behaviour of this kind, which, by the way, is even more rare in young offenders than in adults, is the inexplicable way in which the offence is usually committed. We have already seen in Mary's case that there were discrepancies in her last act of stealing which should move us to further investigation. But they were not very obvious and might have been overlooked. It is more striking when, for instance, a wealthy woman repeatedly steals articles of no value from a department store.

(2) A Symptom in Puberty

If an offender's life and actions have been otherwise blameless and the relation of the antisocial act to them is not clear, the magistrate or probation officer will nowadays ask for a psychiatric examination. But a compulsion to steal is by no means the only kind of antisocial act in which unconscious mental conflicts may manifest themselves. In the majority of cases the antisocial behaviour caused by neurotic mechanisms may reveal the underlying mental conflict only when closely and carefully examined.

CASE 4: THE DELINQUENT ACT.

A short case may illustrate this point. Peter was 15 when he came before the court on the rather serious charge of embezzlement. He had taken a Post Office savings book. This book fell out of the pocket of one of his fellow workers who had gone home, and Peter picked it up, intending to return it the next morning when the factory opened. The next day he was sacked for being repeatedly late, and to hide this fact he kept the book. He did not mention at home that he had lost his job, but instead lived on the money for about five weeks. He took fifteen pounds in all, until at one post office it was noticed that his signature in no way resembled the signature in the book; this aroused suspicion, and the whole story came to light.

The boy came from a good middle-class home. He had one sister, two years younger than himself, who had never been difficult, and a baby sister of 6 months. Peter had so far never committed any antisocial act, but he had had a bad report from the headmaster of his last school. He apparently had not worked much for his last two terms, and his headmaster complained about his general conduct, but no definite charge was made against him. He had left school six months before he committed his delinquent act and had been working in the office of a factory. For the last two years he had been a member of the Sea Cadets, and was thought by his officer to be one of the steadiest and most promising lads under his supervision. He wanted to go to sea as an engineer, but could not start training until he was 16. Therefore his father found him a job for the intervening year and a half. He hated this job because it meant sitting in an office all day. He was very often late, and was quite glad when he was dismissed. During the five weeks when he was out of work he left home at the usual time and walked through the streets, often going to the pictures. He took three pounds from the post office each week, paying his usual thirty-two shillings at home for his keep and keeping the rest for himself.

From this history we might get the impression that the boy took the money in order to have a good time, that he was lazy, and that the opportunity offered him by finding the savings book showed him an easy way out of his difficulties. We might moreover form the impression that there was nothing wrong with the boy except that he was morally weak. His actions seemed to be well considered, and there certainly were not, at first sight at any rate, the same inconsistencies as we have seen in Mary's case.

FURTHER INVESTIGATIONS.

The investigation in this case could not go very deep for extraneous reasons, but enough facts came to light to indicate that the case was not so simple as might have been expected from the original history.

The home from which the boy came was a good one. The father was a magistrate, a very strong personality ; he was severe, but greatly interested in children and their problems. Until the boy was about 12 the father would take him out to play football with him and his friends in their free time. The mother was a kind and friendly woman, very fond of the boy, and in need of his affection, which he gave her more freely than her daughter. Peter was on very good terms with his sister, and latterly the two children would often form a common front against the parents.

Peter's childhood was uneventful. He was always very healthy and physically strong, and he had no outstanding educational difficulties except that he was stubborn if forced to do something. But it was quite easy to persuade him in a friendly way. He had been evacuated for a year and a half, behaving well when away from home, but wishing very much to return. Both parents are quite certain that he never pilfered at home except that occasionally he took food from the larder without asking. In his home this was not considered a crime. During the last year he had been very restless, moody and generally unsettled.

When Peter was 13½ he was told that his mother was going to have a baby. At first he reacted rather unfavourably to this disclosure, which was made to him by his father. But when the father was away during the mother's pregnancy he behaved most considerately, going to his mother's bedside during air raids and holding her hand (though otherwise he would not wake up if there was an alert), missing school when she felt ill, helping her at home, and in short assuming a very grown-up, protective attitude towards her which was different from his usual boyish behaviour. When his father returned after a fortnight he again became more aloof. Shortly after the birth of the baby he started to adopt it as if it were his own. He would take it up when it cried, carry it about and spend his free time looking after his little sister.

His bad behaviour in school followed the time when he was first told about the mother's pregnancy. From the boy's own story it became apparent that he disliked his masters, especially the headmaster, and used every opportunity of showing them that he was not afraid of them. This defiant attitude led after some time to his being accused of everything which went wrong in his class. Sometimes it was actually his fault, but even when it was not, as was more often the case, he took no pains to convince his teachers that he was not guilty. At that time his interests were diverted from school to his activities in the Sea Cadets, and he was intent only on being able to start his career as soon as possible, which would at the same time mean leaving home.

THE CONSCIOUS CONFLICT.

The boy was very tall and very good-looking, with superior intelligence (I.Q. 135), and he had little to say about his delinquent act. His explanation was that he did not want his father to know that he had been dismissed; he was afraid that he would despise him as a failure. He did not belittle the affair, and when seen for the first time was convinced that as a punishment his father would forbid him to continue as a Sea Cadet, a fear entirely without foundation.

Psychologically the most striking feature was his defiance of authority concealed behind a superficial friendliness. He showed no open signs of rebellion, but it was not difficult to discover his hostility towards the father. He himself could not quite understand his feelings. On the one hand he realized that his father had always been a very good friend to him and had never let him down. On the other hand he rebelled against every prohibition. He was inwardly furious if forbidden to go out at night, he objected to his father's views on politics and music ; in short, he objected to everything the father said or did. He very seldom dared to show his feelings openly, and when he did he was usually forced into submission by his fear of the father's reactions, though he was more afraid of the father's stern attitude than of actual punishment. He had very similar feelings towards his headmaster. During the mother's pregnancy he was very worried because he had once been told that she was very ill after he had been born, and he was afraid she might die during her confinement. After his delinquent act had become known he was not afraid of the official proceedings and did not mind appearing in court ; the only thing which really worried him was his father's reaction. It puzzled him that the father had not punished him immediately and had not talked about the matter, which was kept secret from his sister. But he was expecting the storm to break at any moment.

It is certainly true that the most superficial motive for the boy's antisocial act was his wish to hide his dismissal from work and to have a good time with the help of the stolen money. That this cannot have been the only motive immediately becomes clear when we study his former history. Though he intensely disliked his school he never played truant. Never before in his life had he chosen an easy way out of a difficult situation. Four nights a week he had been engaged either with the Sea Cadets or in club work of some kind or another. He never missed an evening, although this made it impossible for him to go to the pictures or to play football with his friends, as he was not allowed to go out more often. These facts arose out of a careful study of the boy's history and show that there must have been additional reasons inducing him to adopt this course. He could have avoided his father's contempt at the loss of his job by at once finding himself another, which would not have been very difficult in wartime conditions. In fact his father had told him beforehand that if he did not like the work in his first job he could easily change.

This superficial motive for the delinquent act may also be described as the conscious motive. It is striking, however, that during these five weeks the boy never seriously considered what would happen when the money was finished—he had already taken more than half—or if it were discovered that he had no right to sign the book, for he made no attempt to imitate the owner's handwriting. He walked through the streets daydreaming, generally imagining that he was already grown-up and in the Navy.

THE UNCONSCIOUS CONFLICT.

A more deep-lying and unconscious motive for his delinquent act is to be found in his hostile attitude towards his father. He could not easily have found a better weapon for hurting his father and inflicting an injury on his pride than the commission of an anti-social act, especially as the father's hobby was club work with boys of his son's age, whom he wanted to keep from living an anti-social life. It was certainly very awkward for the father as a magistrate to see his own son in a police court.

For the last year or two Peter had been conscious of hostile and rebellious feelings towards his father. He very rarely expressed these feelings openly, and it became clear that he regarded the father as so strong that it would be completely hopeless to try to hold his own in his presence. These hostile feelings against the father were the unconscious motive force behind the antisocial act. We have seen that the rebellion against the older generation is a normal development in puberty, eventually helping the boy to grow up and to cut loose from the infantile dependence on the parents. We may therefore assume that the hostility which Peter felt was due to this phase of development. But this aggressiveness at puberty need not lead to the commission of a delinquent act. Peter, as we saw, did not express his feelings, even in the usual way by arguments about politics or other intellectual subjects. He did not dare to show his hostility openly and was very baffled about his own feelings. He could not understand their origin at all. Peter's experiences at home when he was between 13 and 14 years of age account for the fact that in his case the hostile feelings towards the father were particularly strong, and also that it was against his conscience to express them. We have seen that with the maturing of the sexual organs in puberty the remnants of the Oedipus conflict are reawakened, and the struggle to free oneself from the first objects of love expressed itself in the conscious desire to become independent of the parents.[1] When Peter had reached this stage the mother became pregnant. As we have seen, during the absence of the father at this period the boy took over the father's rôle towards the mother, and when the baby was born adopted it as his own. It is very likely that these occurrences just at this stage strengthened the

[1] Part I, Ch. X, p. 64.

boy's old feelings for his mother, which he now wished to keep repressed, and increased his hostility towards the father as the rival in his love for the mother. It was the more difficult for him to give up his old infantile feelings as the mother insisted on his demonstrating his affection and showed her displeasure when he wanted to stop her tucking him up at night. It will now become clear why it was so dangerous for him to show his hostility against the father. We have seen that at the end of the Oedipus phase the retaliation which is feared for this hostility towards the parent of the same sex actually leads to the renunciation of the Oedipus wishes.[1] The situation at home at the time when the remnants of the Oedipus conflict were reawakened caused a revival of the old wishes and increased hostility towards the father. This hostility had to be repressed as far as possible, as it was too closely related to the desire to possess the mother. On no account could the hostile feelings towards the father be openly expressed, as unconsciously this would have meant admitting the incestuous wishes. But, as we have seen, instinctive urges will find expression, if not directly, then in a more disguised form. So the hostility was first of all transferred to the people in authority at school. This apparently was not a sufficient outlet, and consequently a weakness in the boy's Ego and Super-Ego allowed him to express his desires through an antisocial act. Quite logically, therefore, he expected punishment not from the magistrate in court, of whom he was not in the least afraid, but from his father. And he expected the father to take away the activity which allowed him the best outlet for his wish to be a grown-up man. That was why he believed that his father would forbid him to be a member of the Sea Cadets ; the punishment for his misdeed (which in his unconscious was not the stealing but the aggression against the father) would be the loss of his manliness.

Needless to say, the boy was utterly unaware of these conflicts. He was aware only of an acute feeling of guilt when he realized that his father was not going to punish him at all.

DIAGNOSIS. In this case antisocial behaviour occurred under the pressure of unconscious mental conflicts. Unlike Mary's delinquent symptom, the antisocial behaviour in itself shows no neurotic structure. But the fact that this boy had never before reacted to frustrations by delinquent behaviour and moreover the connection between his changed behaviour and events at home, show the dependence of the antisocial acts on

[1] Part I, Ch. VI, p. 40 ff.

unconscious conflicts aroused by the mother's pregnancy. The effect of treatment [1] confirmed the assumption as to the causal nature of his conflicts, while the examination revealed signs of a slight antisocial character formation.

As will be shown later,[2] the importance of a correct diagnosis in such a case cannot be sufficiently emphasized. The treatment decided upon will depend entirely on whether the antisocial act is the expression of an antisocial character formation of long standing and severe degree, or whether, as in this case, an unconscious mental conflict has found its way into antisocial action. For our purpose this case has been given to illustrate the fact that an antisocial act may have a neurotic basis which is revealed only when a very full history is taken. Disturbances of a similar kind are often encountered during puberty, and explain the great number of cases where antisocial acts are then committed for the first and—given correct treatment and a relatively good environment—for the last time.

(3) " Psychopathic Personalities "

DEFINITION. The conception of the " psychopathic personality " is as vague and as open to misinterpretations as was the former conception of " moral insanity " (25). Occasionally it is maintained that criminal behaviour is in itself a sign of psychopathy, but, as Henderson (19*b*) points out, only certain psychopaths are also criminals. This vagueness in the conception is due to a lack of knowledge on our part. Henderson (19*a*) has made an attempt to bring some order into this chaos by describing three different types of psychopathic personality : (1) the predominantly aggressive, (2) the predominantly passive or inadequate, and (3) the predominantly creative. Recent encephalographic studies promises a clearer definition of the first group. Evidence so far available seems to show that among the aggressive psychopaths there is a group whose behaviour is caused by some organic aberration—the nature of which is not yet clearly defined—which may etiologically belong to the epileptic group and will therefore be discussed with the organic cases.[3] The " predominantly creative type " does not produce criminals. But various cases have been described by different authors and under different headings which belong to Henderson's group of the " predominantly passive and inadequate type ".

[1] Part III, Ch. IV (*c*), p. 223. [2] Part III, Ch. II.
[3] Part II, Ch. VIII, p. 180.

Aichhorn (2) describes a type of boy who presents special difficulties in institutions, and the Borstal authorities also mention these boys among their special difficulties (16*c*). Unlike the aggressive youth,[1] these boys fit very well into the routine and the training school, are always friendly and obliging, behave irreproachably while under supervision and go out into life entirely unchanged, committing once more the same offences for which they were sent to be reformed. Roland Leaf[2] in Hawkspur Camp (30) was an offender of similar type. These people steal, forge, embezzle in a minor rather than in a major way. They continue, however, with their petty antisocial behaviour regardless of how often it may land them in prison. Henderson's cases in his latest paper on the subject (19*b*) are of an identical character. Aichhorn (2) called this type the " Impostor ", and it is closely related to what are known as the " Pathological Liars—and Swindlers ". Healy (18) has given extensive histories of twenty-seven such cases, many of them women, whose prime motive seems to be the pretence of coming from a higher social class—swindling and stealing being necessary to keep up this pretence. Burt (8) described cases of this kind among juvenile offenders. Behaviour described by Alexander (3*b*) as characteristic of the " Neurotic Character " is due to a similar psychological make-up.

Most authors agree that with this type of offender no change in behaviour can be achieved by the usual methods of treatment. Henderson (19*b*) seems to believe that an indeterminate sentence, allowing of re-education over a very long period, might show some result, but he states that he is not aware that so far any cures have been achieved. The very fact that no appeal to their moral outlook or to their common sense makes the slightest impression on these people has led to the belief that there is some inherited instability of character which is the fundamental and unalterable basis of this antisocial behaviour.

On the other hand, Aichhorn (2) was able to re-educate a number of such boys whom he had under supervision when they were still young, and Abraham (1) describes in great detail a patient who, after a happy marriage, seemed to change his way of life entirely, and became a respected member of the community.

So far there is insufficient evidence to enable us to state with any degree of certainty whether offenders of these types are

[1] Part III, Ch. V (*a*). [2] Also Ibid., Ch. IV (*b*), p. 215.

curable, and if so by what method. Opportunities for creating the atmosphere necessary for treating such offenders are non-existent. This problem will be discussed more fully in a later chapter,[1] but as such offenders are by no means rare and cannot be dealt with successfully by ordinary methods of treatment it will perhaps be of interest to study one such case in greater detail with reference to its psychological foundation.

An "Impostor Type"

CASE 5. FIRST COURT APPEARANCE.

Ronald was 16 when I had him for a few weeks under psycho-analytical observation. His delinquent career had started at the age of 7, but he had only once come before the court, a few weeks before the beginning of the observation. At that time he had associated with a known crook many years older than himself, and had stolen two bicycles with him. Both were caught, and Ronald, who did not give his name and address, was put in a remand home. He absconded, wandered about for a few days, was caught and brought back, absconded again, and when found for the second time was sent to prison for his remand period. He was put on probation for two years on condition that he did not meet his friend again.

PREVIOUS HISTORY OF DELINQUENT ACTS.

As Ronald came from a very good middle-class home his parents had so far not asked for help from the police. When he was 7 he was found out for the first time at home, though he had been stealing for some time. On this first occasion he had within a few days taken money from his mother's purse amounting to £1 4*s*. He denied having taken the money, and only 4*s*. were found on him, hidden in his shoe. A long argument followed, and in the end the mother said that she knew he must have more money because his elder sister had been hiding in a cupboard and had watched him while he stole. He then admitted that he had another pound, but would not show them his hiding-place, which was a pocket in one of his father's suits. From that time onwards he stole money whenever he could lay hands on it. At first he stole mainly at home, and later on also at the boarding-house where he lived for a few days, but he also stole repeatedly at one of the various schools which he attended. One of his later exploits was the theft of

[1] See also Part III, Ch. IV (*b*).

£50, which belonged to an aunt of his who shared his parents' house during the wartime evacuation period. With this money he bought a motor-bicycle from a man living near by. He wanted to run away with it to London, but the theft was detected almost immediately, and his purchase became known the same day. On this first and on the numerous subsequent occasions he denied having taken the money, and was very indignant when he was accused of theft without his parents having the necessary proof. He admitted his misdeed when his father told him the improbable story that the pound notes had been traced by the Bank of England. The longest period without any known theft was a few weeks, and this had been going on since the boy was 7 years of age.

HOME ENVIRONMENT.

Ronald's parents were well-to-do middle-class people. The father was much older than the mother and a distant cousin of hers. There were two sisters who were four and two years Ronald's seniors. The eldest sister was already married ; the younger had been rather difficult during her childhood, but not delinquent. There was no history of any nervous disease or abnormal behaviour in the family. The father was a quiet man who had worked hard all his life. He was very fond of the boy, and did not take his behaviour very seriously. The mother, who looked and dressed like a young girl and seemed more like a sister than a mother to the boy, was neurotic and not very sincere. She did not care very much for her daughters, though she had tried to bring them up well, but she was devoted to the boy. She always emphasized that she was his best friend and that he told her everything—which of course was quite untrue. He had never been punished for any of his thefts, and the mother left her handbag lying about in order to show the boy that she trusted him. She was convinced that his delinquencies had a sexual origin, and therefore frequently discussed sexual questions with him. She was opposed to his taking part in any kind of manly sport such as football, being afraid that he might hurt himself, and he could only by much persuasion get permission to join the A.T.C. He did not go regularly, but it must be admitted that he always had difficulties at home when he wanted to go out at night. Even the mother could not deny that the boy told a great many lies (sometimes in order to cover up his thefts, at other times for no obvious reason), but she was always inclined to believe him at first.

EARLY HISTORY.

Ronald had been in the hands of many nurses during the first years of his life. His education during that time was rather patchy, as there were many opinions about the way in which he should be brought up, and he very soon found out that he could play one person off against another. He was defiant from the start and always determined to get his own way, and in this he succeeded more often than not. The mother entirely dominated the household, so that the father took no hand in the boy's education until a short time before I saw him. The boy grew up with his two sisters and two girl cousins. When he was about 8 the mother's two sisters joined the household. He saw very little of his father, who was working. From his seventh to his fourteenth year Ronald had attended about ten schools, at none of which he had stayed for more than a few months. Every kind of school had been tried, progressive as well as more conservative ones, the last being a well-known boarding-school from which he absconded after being there for two terms. When he was 10 his mother went with him to see a psychiatrist on account of his excessive masturbation. Psychological treatment was advised, but the mother did not send him. It did not become clear whether the mother ever mentioned his stealing to the doctor at that time.

CHARACTER FORMATION.

Ronald was a very good-looking boy with pleasing behaviour; he was very intelligent (I.Q. 121) and looked older than his age. Despite his polished and manly attitude he was not attractive because of a rather shifty look in his eyes. Before committing himself to treatment he enquired in an intelligent and polite manner exactly what he would have to do, and in what way the treatment could help him; he apparently fully understood the explanations given to him. His whole manner during this first interview was much more that of a grown-up man than that of a boy at the age of puberty. But this outward appearance was very deceptive, and his behaviour during the treatment was in many respects much more that of a small child than of a boy of 16. He would come irregularly and think out the most ridiculous excuses. A pain in the stomach or chilblains kept him away on some days; at other times the excuse was that the alarm clock did not go off. Quite often he would ask his mother to ring up and to lie for him, which she would very obligingly do. When he had been coming for a fortnight, he had the impression that he had been having treatment for months, and it was difficult to convince him that this was not the case. He simply could not imagine continuing with anything, this treatment or a job, for any length of time. He could not understand that it was possible to do something which did not give immediate pleasure. He asked me quite seriously what he could do if he did not want to come ; the idea of coming if he found it unpleasant was absolutely beyond him. He had started to work in his father's factory during the period of treatment, and gave it up after he had encountered the first difficulty. He wanted to work at a machine straight away, and the foreman would permit him to do so only after he had worked at other jobs. He could not bear waiting for a few weeks until his wish could be fulfilled, and so after three weeks he gave up. He then started to work with a tutor for his matriculation, but was not able to concentrate on his work for an hour together. He became restless, wanted to do something else—and did it ! We have seen that this inability to wait and to endure tension is characteristic of the emotional life of the small child before the reality principle is enforced. Ronald's behaviour in this respect was very typical of delinquents in general.

THE STEALING AND LYING AS SYMPTOM.

In one thing alone was Ronald consistent, his stealing. And it soon became clear why it was quite impossible for him to give this up for any length of time. The stealing and everything connected with it, the planning, the actual taking of the money, the suspense as to whether he would be found out, and the arguments with his mother as to whether she could really prove that he was the thief—right up to the confession—provided him with excitement of the most pleasurable kind. When not engaged in one of his delinquent acts he had phantasies about stealing. These phantasies were identical with the acts themselves, and the climax of his excitement was always the question whether a theft could be traced back to him. The most striking feature about the phantasies, as well as the actual delinquent acts, was the unimaginative way in which he covered up his traces. One day he came with a particularly clear story : he imagined that he had been asked by the warden of the A.R.P. post in his district to take £50 to the post office. His idea was that he would steal the money and run away to the Navy. They would never be able to prove his guilt because when found he would say that the money was taken from him on his way to the post office. The police could not, he said, hold his former record against him, as they were allowed to bring that up only if he were actually found guilty.

Whenever he told me these phantasies, the boy would try to persuade me that the life of " a crook ", as he used to call himself, was the most exciting of occupations, and he saw no reason why he should give up the one thing which gave him pleasure. Anything else, jobs, reading, even travelling were all boring compared with stealing, and he just could not see how he would be able to stand such an empty life. The thought of having to spend half his life in prison if he pursued this way of living had no deterrent effect on him, although he had already had some experience of it. It was "just part of the game ", as he used to express it. From these descriptions, as well as from his attitude towards me during the treatment, it became clear that being caught and being offered the proof that he had stolen aroused pleasurable sensations in him in the same way as the act of stealing itself. As a matter of fact, the two were inseparable : the stealing did not afford enough excitement if there was not also the danger of being caught. That is probably one of the reasons why he did most of his pilfering in a rather clumsy way and not in accordance with his intellectual standards. In a minor degree, he got the same kind of excitement out of lying and being found out. He had not had treatment for more than a week when he started to try this game with me. He told me lies about his being late and tried his utmost to get me to prove to him that he had not given me the true reason. He made remarks which showed quite plainly that he had again stolen at home, and he tried hard to make me accuse him of it so that he might start an argument as to whether I could prove his guilt. When his attempts to get me to play this game with him failed, he was very dissatisfied, and experienced the same feeling of emptiness as on the rare occasions when he had an opportunity of stealing and did not do so. One day he saw £9 lying on the mantelpiece at home. He wanted to take it, but then thought he had better not do so. He walked to and fro about four or five times in this struggle as to whether he should or should not take it. In the end he did not steal, and as a result he felt dissatisfied and disappointed until about an hour later. Next day, however, he was quite glad that he could tell me that for once he had not taken advantage of an opportunity to steal.

THE UNCONSCIOUS MOTIVATION.

This boy's stealing had nothing whatever to do with want. He had sufficient pocket money, and his mother in order to prevent him from stealing would give him money whenever he asked for it, and he knew this was so. He did not often ask for it, for he did not want money to be given to him: he wanted to steal it in order to get this special kind of pleasurable excitement. There was a certain adventurous quality about the exploits, but this certainly played a minor rôle as a motive for his offences. What can easily be gathered from the description of his emotions is the fact that stealing and everything connected with it expressed a very strong impulse which had to be satisfied, whenever it arose, in the identical way and in every detail. The struggle described on the occasion when he did not steal is rather illuminating. This kind of struggle is similar to that put up by young people against the impulse to masturbate; and the dissatisfaction when refraining from stealing can be understood on this analogy; the stealing taking the place of masturbation. The first emotion then experienced would be the unpleasant sensation of not being able to satisfy a sexual urge, the satisfaction of having conquered one's desires coming only later.

There was a long history of masturbation in this case. Ronald started to masturbate round about the age of 5; at least that is the time when he first remembered having masturbated, and the habit had persisted ever since. There was a time of excessive masturbation of an obsessional kind when he was about 10. Then he had to masturbate during the day when his mother or other people could observe him, but it was no longer pleasurable. He had not stopped masturbating from that time on but did it now less frequently and always without getting any real satisfaction. He just had to do it, but he was convinced that he had damaged his brain by this habit. That, as he explained to me, was already an old story; he knew that this was so and that he would never be able to be any good or to learn enough to obtain a better job. He knew that his scholastic knowledge was inferior to that of a boy of 12, and he thought that this was due to the fact that he had damaged his capacity for learning. As he could not be of any use at ordinary work he intended, he said, at least to be a marvellous crook and so stop feeling inferior to other boys. But it was not this conscious and more or less intellectual idea which had driven him to steal. The excitement and pleasure which were originally connected with masturbation had become dissociated from sexual activity and had found an outlet in an antisocial activity. That is why he could not stop doing it. His ideal of being a crook was a secondary formation and provided a rationalization of his instinctive desires. The strange attitude of wishing to be found out now becomes clearer. His constant claim, " But you cannot prove it ! " belonged to the original fear of being found out when masturbating. It contained the wish that the other person should not be able to prove it, and that in turn would mean that he had not really damaged his brain—or perhaps his sexual organs in the original version. The easy confession every time after he had been told that he had been seen in the act of stealing is due to the fact that it was a relief to him to be found stealing and not masturbating.

This attachment of sexual excitement to an antisocial act was certainly not due solely to the prohibition of masturbation. Most children are forbidden to masturbate at one time or another, yet very few of them develop symptoms of that kind. The root of this maladjustment is to be found earlier, namely, in the boy's relationship with his mother and in the absolute lack of a consistent attitude towards his primary instinctive urges at a very early age. There was no sign of sublimation, there was no interest in any social activity, the whole of the instinctive energy having become attached to an antisocial urge. And as in early childhood, the mother still " played the game " with him. She tempted him by letting money lie about the house, though she already had years of experience by which to judge that this did not help to alter his behaviour. However, this was only a superficial item in her entirely wrong attitude towards him. She showered affection on him and wanted affection in return—at an age when the boy should have spent his time with friends of his own age. She had spoiled him from his earliest years, always covering up his misdeeds, and she prevented him from taking part in any kind of boyish or manly activity. Worst of all, she did not suspect that the boy was using her for his own ends when he made her discover a theft and argue for hours about his possible guilt. It was not to be expected that the mother should have had the psychological knowledge to understand why the boy behaved in this way ; but she must have seen the uselessness of her attitude, and if she had not had some pleasure in arguing herself she would very soon have tired of it. She shielded the boy, who in appearance was already a man, from every unpleasantness in the outside world, and lied to the father about his actions. The boy, of course, knew all this and used his mother for his own ends. In his home environment he could live out his instinctive pleasures, which consistently took the same form.

The relationship between mother and son was by no means the ideal one described by the mother. Though there was never any attempt from the mother's side to deal seriously with the boy's misbehaviour she was constantly behind him to find out whether he had stolen anything. She was always nagging at him, and quarrelling and arguing with him, never leaving him a minute's peace. But when he was attacked by anyone else, for instance his father, she took sides with him.

This relationship, which is rather similar to that between Billy and his mother, together with the whole family background, was the cause of Ronald's antisocial character formation.

In the chapter on treatment more will be said about the attitude which the persons of the environment would have to adopt to give a boy of this kind a chance to change.[1] The case has been described here in order to illustrate characteristic features of the so-called psychopathic personality.

DIAGNOSIS. Ronald displayed all the usual traits of an antisocial character. There was his inability to wait for satisfaction, his entire disregard for reality where his instinctive urges were concerned, his self-centredness and his lack of interest in social activities of any kind. He had no friends except the one with whom he had stolen, and the wish to gratify his desires was much stronger than any relationship with another human being. His conscience-formation was defective, and an ethical code seemed to exist only in so far as it did not interfere with his pleasures. In all these attitudes he is in no way different from the multitude of young offenders. What is peculiar to him is the driving force behind his antisocial actions. In Peter's case we saw that an unconscious conflict drove him to an action which expressed his aggression against the father and, at the same time, solved a real difficulty for him. The psychological mechanism at the basis of Ronald's behaviour is of a different kind. Here the sexual urge is not repressed, but has become displaced and attached to an antisocial activity which is no longer sexual in nature, although the excitement and satisfaction derived from stealing is still very similar to sexual excitement.

[1] Part III, Ch. IV (*b*).

The significance of the instinctive, or in other words sexual, basis of the urge to steal was of course entirely unrealized by the boy.

It could not be ascertained which factors were responsible for this kind of instinctive development. It was probably the combination of a very strong fear connected with masturbation on the one hand, and the inability to forgo direct instinctive satisfaction on the other. If this satisfaction could no longer be gained by masturbating it had to be forthcoming from another equally forbidden activity. But stealing was forbidden only by the outside world and merely led to being found out, which in itself in time had become pleasurable, while deriving pleasure from masturbation was infinitely more dangerous, as it might lead to the loss of manliness.

It is the combination of the antisocial character with the diversion of sexual urges to antisocial activities which causes this variety of stealing.

SUMMARY. In the majority of offenders grouped together under the heading of the " predominantly passive or inadequate " type of psychopathic personality, and especially in the types known as " pathological liars and swindlers " and " impostors ", a very similar mechanism is at work. Their antisocial actions are sexualized in the way described. In many cases the phantasy lived out in the antisocial action is the " family romance ".[1] These people are not satisfied with day-dreaming about their descent from a higher social class ; they actually want to live out their day-dream. That leads them to lie and to steal, to forge and to swindle in order to support these lies. The transformation of instinctive urges into action in daily life may not always be so direct as it was in Ronald's case, but we have seen that the family romance takes its origin from the Oedipus phantasies which in their turn were once masturbation phantasies. This development of the instinctive life is not confined to delinquents. It is found in people who have never committed an antisocial act, but who destroy their own happiness because they are forced to repeat the same irrational actions over and over again. It is only when this instinctive development accompanies an antisocial character that this type of delinquent behaviour results. The fact that the antisocial action is so closely related to sexual gratification explains on the one hand the constant repetition of the offence, and on the other the uselessness of ordinary methods of social treatment.

[1] Part I, Ch. IX, p. 61 ff.

(4) The "Criminal from a Sense of Guilt"

DESCRIPTION.

Freud (12*b*) was the first to describe a specific psychological mechanism which may lead to criminal behaviour. He showed that there are offenders who are driven by feelings of guilt to commit a crime and who, after committing it—and especially after punishment—regain their mental balance. He was able to show that the feeling of guilt experienced could always be traced back to the Oedipus conflict; that the antisocial act was committed in order to earn punishment; and that the relief was due to the fact that the crime committed was not the one which the offender unconsciously intended to commit: namely to kill the father in order to get rid of his rival for the mother's love. There are some offenders in whom this mechanism—again on the basis of an antisocial character development—accounts for every single delinquent act they commit. Alexander (3*a*) describes one such case in detail. More often it is found that this psychological mechanism is merely a contributory factor in delinquent behaviour. Again, it is of extreme importance in the choice of treatment to know in any given case whether this mechanism plays any decisive part in causing delinquent behaviour. In these cases punishment relieves the feeling of guilt and has therefore neither a curative nor a deterrent effect.

Mary's last act of stealing is a good example of this mechanism. There we saw how a child was driven by her feelings of guilt to steal again in order to be punished. We saw also that her stealing had a symbolic significance and that by it she could to a certain extent satisfy her aggressions against her mother, while on the other hand the fact that she chose a mother-substitute instead of her real mother convinced her that she had not really expressed her inner hostility and therefore need not really be afraid that her mother would leave her alone. The reason why Mary's conscience developed because her mother never punished her for stealing and so made her feel responsible for her actions will be discussed in a later chapter.[1]

DIFFERENTIAL DIAGNOSIS.

Where this neurotic mechanism predominates in any particular case it gives rise to what Freud has described as "The criminal from a sense of guilt". We must distinguish this attitude from those which have their origin in a regression to the anal-sadistic level of

[1] Part III, Ch. V (*a*), p. 244.

development. Both in Billy's case and in that of the "Aggressive Youth" punishment also satisfied an instinctive urge. It was the anticipated response to the offender's own aggressive attitude and satisfied his sado-masochistic object relationship. But these antisocial actions are not caused by a feeling of guilt, and the offenders do not wish to be punished in order to be relieved of guilt. Quite the contrary: if in these cases punishment is withheld for any length of time, they will begin to feel guilty about their actions. We saw this happen after Mary's stealing with the gang, and it is usually the first sign that the conscience, which formerly was entirely dependent on the persons of the outside world, is becoming independent, and that the delinquent is beginning to take responsibility for his actions.

CHAPTER VI

THE SEXUAL PERVERSIONS

RELATIONSHIP BETWEEN SEXUAL OFFENCES AND PERVERSIONS.

A thorough knowledge of the genesis of sexual perversions is necessary in order to understand what are legally called "sexual offences". Sexual offences and perversions are not identical. Many perversions are not punishable by law, for instance homosexuality in women, or fetishism if not related to assault of any kind. There are also sexual offences which do not necessarily involve a perverted sexual instinct, as, for instance, intercourse between a young boy and a girl under 16. On the other hand, many sexual offences are committed by persons who suffer from a perverted sexual instinct, while again there are many people who satisfy their illegal perverse sexual activities without ever coming into conflict with the law. The problem is an intricate one, and the first step towards a fuller understanding will be a scientific knowledge of the aberrations of the sexual instinct. This is the more necessary as the attitude of the public towards sexual offences is still largely based on irrational motives.

PERVERSIONS IN THEIR RELATION TO THE NORMAL SEX INSTINCT.

The maturation of the instincts, with special emphasis on the sexual instinct, has been discussed previously.[1] It has been shown that the sexual instinct makes its appearance soon after birth, runs through certain stages of development during the first five years of life, and emerges in puberty as the genital impulse. Only in this last stage of development at puberty do we find the genital impulses with all the characteristics which constitute the sexual life of the adult. Freud's theory of the development of the sexual instinct from birth onwards, as opposed to earlier conceptions which placed the origin of the sexual impulse at puberty, has been amply confirmed during recent decades by direct observation of children. But even without this confirmation, merely from the study of adult sex life, the facts can be explained by Freud's theory while they remain inexplicable on the assumption of a ready-made sexual instinct. There are occasions when a person who was formerly normal in his sexual behaviour may find sexual satisfaction in what has hitherto been

[1] Part I, Ch. III.

regarded as an abnormal way. This happens often in camps, in prisons, or on expeditions, in other words, in situations where men are thrown together for any length of time without the possibility of sexual relationships with a woman ; they may then resort to homosexual practices and be nevertheless able to revert to a normal sexual life when the environment changes. Shortly after puberty, a homosexual phase in girls and boys is so common that it has to be regarded as a normal phase of development. These facts, which have always been well known, show that homosexual tendencies are part of the mental make-up of every individual, but that under normal conditions they do not lead to homosexual practices. If persons who have been able to lead a normal sex life are capable, under certain environmental conditions, of resorting to homosexual practices, then surely those individuals who can find satisfaction only in intercourse with a person of the same sex are not entirely different from the normal person, but can for certain reasons express their sex life only in the abnormal and not in the normal way. The original assumption that homosexuals are degenerates does not explain why a large number of these people show no other sign of inferiority and are often useful members of the community.

But, it has been argued, other sexual aberrations, such as sadism or fetishism, are so far removed from the normal sexual life that persons who exhibit them cannot possibly be classed with those who lead a normal sex life. But once again we find that, unnatural as such practices may seem, they still have some connection with the normal. Objects belonging to the beloved person are cherished by a lover ; sadistic tendencies are always present in the man ; looking and being looked at are part of the preliminaries of lovemaking. That is to say, we find ingredients of sexual intercourse, increasing the desire or heightening the pleasure, which if they lead to intercourse with a person of the opposite sex are considered as normal. If any of these tendencies of itself leads to sexual satisfaction we receive the impression of very abnormal sexual behaviour, and we call these aberrations of the sexual instinct " perversions ". Again we see that the primary tendency towards perverted sexual activity is present in every individual, but to a much slighter extent and for a different purpose than in the true pervert.

We already know the origin of these ingredients in intercourse. They are the remnants of the early component instincts of the sexual urge. Normally some of the energy behind these instinctive tendencies has become sublimated ; the repressed tendencies are changed by reaction-formation, while the rest have been submerged in the genital impulse, under whose primacy they will remain, to increase the desire and pleasure in intercourse. If we now find that in a number of people one or the other component instinct has more importance than the genital instinct, or that the connection between the genital instinct with its normal object and aim has not been achieved, we shall suspect either that this one component instinct has been abnormally strongly developed for constitutional reasons, to the detriment of the genital instinct, or that for some as yet unknown reason the normal development has been in some way arrested or disturbed.

FREUD'S CLASSIFICATION OF PERVERSIONS.

We have shown [1] that the sexual instinct has a source, an object and an aim, and that, contrary to popular opinion, a firm relationship between the sexual instinct, its object and its aim occurs only after puberty, when the genital instinct emerges as the last phase of a long development. According to Freud (12*f*), sexual perversions can therefore be classified as

(1) aberrations in relation to the sex object :
- (*a*) inversion,
- (*b*) intercourse with children and animals,
- (*c*) fetishism ;

(2) aberrations in relation to the sexual aim :
- (*a*) looking and being looked at (exhibitionism, viewing),
- (*b*) sadism and masochism.

CLINICAL CONSIDERATIONS.

There is no sharp dividing line between normal and perverted sexual activities. Some individuals are able to derive satisfaction from both normal and perverted practices, though in all these cases the trained observer will find that the genital instinct is not very strong, and that more satisfaction is derived from the perverted than from the normal sexual activity. Very often it is found that the sexual activity as practised is normal to all appearances, but that sexual satisfaction can only be gained by masturbating with perverse sexual phantasies. This is not a perversion in the true sense of the word, but leads to the manifold neurotic disturbances of the sexual life of the adult. In these disturbances, strong perverse wishes are repressed and interfere unconsciously with a satisfactory sex life, either leading to complete inhibition, as in impotence in the man or frigidity in the woman, or else interfering in various

[1] Part I, Ch. II and III.

ways with the achievement of complete sexual satisfaction. The sexual disturbances of the adult, in men as well as in women, are manifold and varied, and it has been found that in all the neurotic disturbances encountered in adult life there is always a disturbance of the sex life as well. It has been shown that the sexual instinct has to go a long way before it emerges in its final form, and some of the factors influencing this development have been discussed above. It is only natural that a development which is not only dependent on maturation but is to a large extent influenced by the environment, especially by the emotional relationship of the child towards its parents, should be very liable to disturbances. We have to conclude that the occurrence of a perversion is one way in which a disturbance of the development of the sexual instinct may manifest itself.

GENERAL PRINCIPLE OF CAUSATION.

It was for some time an open question whether in some perversions, such as exhibitionism or homosexuality, the later perverse tendency was constitutionally so strongly developed that it overshadowed the other component instincts and especially the genital instinct. This idea was strengthened by the fact that perverts in their conscious recollections did not remember ever to have been sexually attracted by another object or to have had any sexual aim other than that of their perversion. But when psychiatrists became able to bring repressed conflicts to light by the psycho-analytical method, it was seen that in all cases so studied there were at least traces of manifestations of the genital instinct, though possibly only for a short time. This leads to the assumption, which has been confirmed by each case undergoing psycho-analytical treatment, that in perverts the development of the sexual instinct also follows the lines described ; that in all these cases the Oedipus conflict has been experienced, and that there is usually a short time after puberty when normal desires are present, if often only in phantasy. These case histories which include hitherto unconscious recollections also show that the component instinct which later becomes the focus of the whole of the sexual energy was strongly developed from the very start and was too freely satisfied during the early stages of development. Here we again meet with the simultaneous action of two series of factors—the constitutional and the environmental—in producing a disturbance of development. For several reasons, one of which is always an excessive fear at the phallic stage, a regression of the sexual energy takes place to the component instinct which has given satisfaction previously, and this component instinct now becomes charged with the whole of the sexual energy. The normal genital impulses have to be kept in repression. Though it may seem that the adult pervert is " oversexed ", this is actually not the case. He is unable to have normal sexual relationships on account of his fear of having intercourse with a woman, and if he wants to get sexual satisfaction at all, and that is a normal desire, he can get it only in the perverted form. His sexual instinct is certainly not stronger, in fact in the majority of cases it is weaker, than that of the normal individual.

Very often not only one but several perverse tendencies are manifest in the same individual. Psychologically the development is the same as that just described, with the difference that regression takes place to an earlier phase of instinctive development and that not only one but several component instincts are reinforced by the reversion of the libido.

EVALUATION OF ENDOCRINE DISTURBANCES.

In recent years, much valuable research work has been devoted to the influence of the endocrine glands and their secretions, known as hormones, on sexual tendencies. As has been stressed, Freud's theory of the instincts presupposes the organic origin of the primary instinctive urges, and Freud himself at a time when hormones were still rather unknown quantities had assumed that the difference in instincts might be due to some chemical agency. Further research will show whether what we call the constitutional factor in the strength of an instinctive urge is due to a lack of balance in the hormonic make-up. Cases have already been described where, owing to a growth in one of the glands with internal secretion (usually the cortex of the suprarenal gland) manifest homosexuality may appear for the duration of the illness. But such cases are very rare, and in the majority of cases of homosexuality, for instance, no gross disturbance of the hormonic balance can be detected with the means of research at present at the disposal of scientists. It would of course be very valuable if eventually methods of research could be refined to such a degree that in cases where the disturbance is mainly due to a lack of endocrine balance the long and tedious process of psycho-analysis could be replaced by organic treatment. Up till now, attempts at therapy on the basis of endocrinological findings have been very disappointing.

Owing to the fact that the development of a perverse sexual activity is influenced by environmental circumstances, no two cases are psychologically identical. But certain factors are common to the outcome of this development. In homosexuals we find as a rule a very strong fixation to the mother, an intimate early relationship with her, and an identification with the mother instead of with the father at the end of the Oedipus period. In exhibitionists, a strong fear of castration has caused a regression, and the exhibition of the male sexual organ, together with the shock this evokes in the female onlooker, serve as a reassurance that the genitals are intact. In fetishists this same fear leads to a fixation on an object, the fetish, which is always a phallic symbol. Both these perversions are unknown in the female. The significance of the perverse sexual activity is entirely unconscious, and an intellectual knowledge of these facts would not help perverts to find their sexual satisfaction in a more normal way.

PSYCHOLOGICAL GENERALIZATIONS.

A Homosexual Phantasy

We shall attempt to illustrate some of the psychological factors involved in the development of a perverse sexual phantasy, though in this case only those which play a part in the sexual development can be discussed, and not the psychological development as a whole. It must be emphasized that this case illustrates only one possible development of homosexuality in a man.

CASE 6.

The material here presented is taken from the analysis of a man of 35 years of age, Mr. A., who was suffering from an obsessional neurosis. He had never actually had a sexual relationship with a man, in fact he had never had any sexual relationship at all, but he masturbated with homosexual phantasies. He was attracted by men only and sexually repulsed by women, though in his social contacts he preferred the company of women to that of men. In his behaviour, though in no way effeminate, he was extremely passive and unaggressive. After a happy early childhood, during which he was said to have been a very lively and active little boy, he contracted hip disease at the age of 5 and had to remain on his back until he was 11 years of age. When he started to walk again he was at first lively and communicative; but then he was once more laid up for a few months, and after recovering from this second illness he became silent, shy and awkward, and had remained so ever since. At the age of 14 he was about to be sent to a boarding school. This prospect put him into such a panic that this shy and easily frightened boy ran

EARLY HISTORY.

away from home and stayed away for a few days until he was picked up by the police. The analysis revealed that shortly before his father had told him that he was to be sent to boarding school, his eldest brother had written home about the expulsion of a boy from school for homosexual practices. His panic at going to school was connected with the vision of a dormitory full of boys and the possibility of coming in physical contact with them. It became clear that at this time he was afraid of his own impulses, which made him think that the close proximity of many boys would be attractive, and so he fought very hard against these impulses. After puberty, at the age of about 16, he had phantasies about women, but only for a very short time : soon his sexual phantasies centred around the figures of men and more especially of boys between the ages of 14 and 16, and these phantasies, though greatly elaborated, had since remained sexually attractive to him.

The analysis showed that this man, whose father was very often abroad for long periods during his early childhood, had, when small, an especially strong attachment to his mother. Owing to his delicate health his mother devoted much more attention to him than to his older brother.

These few items of the case history have been selected because they throw some light on the development of the sexual instinct in this man. There was no gross endocrine disturbance in this case, and the family history gave no indication of inherited tendencies of a homosexual kind. In his early childhood there was this strong fixation to the mother, which was certainly enhanced by the frequent absence of the father ; especially between his fourth and fifth years, when he was alone with his mother and imagined that she belonged to him and not to the father. The absence of the father during the Oedipus phase is an environmental factor quite often met with in the history of homosexuals. The father's absence during this important period of the child's development allows too strong a development of the sexual wishes which are centred round the mother and does not give the boy the opportunity of identifying himself with the father : this, as we have seen, is an important factor in the renunciation of the Oedipus wishes. At the important age of 5 the patient contracted the illness which robbed him for years of the use of his limbs. This illness was unconsciously perceived by him as punishment for his sexual wishes towards the mother, and it impressed him as a very

SEXUAL DEVELOPMENT.

severe and incapacitating revenge. Shortly afterwards his father came back, and the boy, who before had been very friendly with him, was now terrified of him. Unconsciously he connected his father with his illness and was afraid of further punishment, especially as he masturbated at that time with very aggressive phantasies. As the boy had no motor outlet whatsoever his whole aggressiveness became centred in his phantasy life. With the return of the father it became imperative that he should give up his desires for the mother, so as to avoid further punishment. In order to gain some instinctive gratification in an object relationship, he now identified himself with the mother instead of with the father, and his wish to be loved began to centre round the father : he wished to be loved by the father in the same way as the father loved the mother. We saw that in puberty he was fighting to suppress his homosexual tendencies which had re-awakened with the maturing of the sexual instinct. His phantasies began to centre round women, but they were not very pleasurable : unconsciously he was afraid of sexual thoughts about women, as he was fixated to the mother and yet was forbidden to desire her. He then returned to men as sexual objects for his phantasies : but not to older men, as they would represent his father, and such an open phantasy would also arouse fear. His love objects were young boys of the age at which his male object choice was definitely established. He was always tender towards these young boys in his phantasies, he protected them, and in short, treated them in the way in which he himself once wished to be treated by his mother. It was soon very clear that the young boys represented himself, and the patient expressed the position very well when he said one day that he seemed to be in love with himself all the time.

CAUSATION OF PERVERSION.

Various factors were combined in this case to bring about the inversion, ranging from external and accidental ones to purely psychic mechanisms. There was a more or less normal libidinal development, with a slight emphasis on sadistic impulses. The absence of the father, the devotion of the mother and the illness which necessitated his being handled by a woman, either the mother or a nurse, all effected an undue stimulation of his Oedipus desires. The illness, with its unconscious significance of punishment for his Oedipus wishes, caused an exaggerated fear of castration and, as an escape from this, he identified himself with the mother instead of with the father in order to avoid further rivalry with him and also to gain instinctive gratification. But at the same time, owing to this strong fear, the Oedipus desires had to be quickly and completely repressed, and consequently a partial regression took place to the anal-sadistic phase. With the repression of the Oedipus conflict, the figure of the father had to disappear from the phantasies, as these were still too close to the original desires. In the patient's everyday life this was also shown by the fact that he did not dare to be alone with his father or to have any kind of friendly relationship with him. But the objects of his sexual desires were still represented by men, or rather boys. We have seen that the further we go back in instinctive development the greater the importance attached to the self as compared with the persons of the environment. We say that the small child is narcissistic. Owing to this regression which had taken place in the libidinal development of this man, his object choice became narcissistic : in the end, the love of his own body and person was predominant in the final shaping of the perverse phantasies. He loved young men in the way in which he wished that his mother could have loved him.

The psychological mechanism here described is the basis of what has been called active homosexuality : men who desire to have intercourse with young boys and who to a certain extent at least assume the male rôle. In the type which has been called the passive homosexual, the passive attitude towards the father is not so deeply repressed and can therefore be satisfied : these are the men who want to be loved by another man and who then assume the female rôle.

It would be impossible here to give an adult case history in such detail that the material in itself would be convincing. The material chosen has been given in order to show what kind of mechanisms are at work in producing a perverted sexual phantasy, which in this case never led to manifest perverse behaviour because this man had a severe neurosis as well. The material, however, may be sufficiently lucid to demonstrate why it is that the kind of treatment usually given to sexual offenders does not meet the case.

CHAPTER VII

SEXUAL OFFENCES

INTRODUCTION. Young people do not often commit sexual offences; they are more often objects or victims of sexual assaults. Those sexual offences which do occur in young offenders, as for instance exhibitionism, are committed in the same way and for the same psychological reason as in the adult. Special emphasis will therefore be laid on those sexual offences which already occur in the young person, and those adult sexual offences which implicate a child or young person.

In the *Report on Sexual Offences against Young Persons* (27) emphasis is laid on the very varied type of offenders who commit the same kind of offence. Loafers and vagrants as well as business or professional men of great respectability have been found guilty of a single type of sexual offence. The same publication states that though the mental expert classifies sexual offenders into certain well-defined types, such classifications are technical, and it has not been found practicable to base methods of treatment on them. This Report dates back to the year 1926, and since then the idea of directing treatment to the cause of the trouble and not to the actual behaviour itself has penetrated to the public to a certain extent. The necessity of understanding the causes holds good not only for antisocial behaviour in general but more especially in cases of sexual abnormality. These conditions have been studied much more thoroughly by experts than has antisocial behaviour. The layman on the other hand is very liable to be unconsciously influenced by emotional factors and to act on feelings such as disgust and horror instead of going to the root of the trouble. J. Watson (29) has recognized this danger, and advises prison visitors not to discuss sexual questions with their wards but to refer them to the prison doctor. C. Mullins (23) also emphasizes that in cases of sexual offences he always tries to get a psychiatric report.

An understanding of the variety of sexual offences may be reached by classifying them according to whether they originate in perverse sexual behaviour, are on the borderline between normal and abnormal behaviour, or are a manifestation of a developmental phase which normally is kept in repression.

(a) Perversions

THE PERVERT AND THE AUTHORITIES.

We have seen in the preceding chapter that perversions are disturbances in the development of the sexual instinct. It has been explained [1] that a certain amount of direct sexual satisfaction is necessary if mental balance is to be preserved. Therefore, it would seem that whenever a pervert wants to obtain sexual satisfaction, a desire in itself normal, he will necessarily come into conflict with the law. Alexander (3*a*) has stressed this point in demonstrating the irrationality of punishment for offenders of this kind. This is very important, and will be more fully discussed in the section on treatment. But it leaves out of account the fact that the majority of perverts do satisfy their sexual desires without being brought before a court. The probability that the attention of the outside world will be aroused is naturally greater with some perversions than with others. With exhibitionism, where the perverted sexual activity consists in repeated exhibition in front of a woman in a public place, there is more danger of being noticed than with homosexuality.

PERVERSION WITH NEUROSIS.

There are two cases in which the pervert may become a public nuisance. One is when he himself is not happy in his sexual behaviour and can allow himself gratification only if punishment is expected to follow. The other is when there are strong aggressive tendencies against society, which are expressed in the perverted action in the same way as hatred against authority is expressed in other delinquent acts. Those perverts, therefore, who come before a court are in most cases either persons with at least a tendency towards antisocial character formation or who suffer from a neurotic disturbance in addition to their perversion. We have seen that perverse sexual behaviour, antisocial character formation, and neurotic disturbances all have their root in factors which disturb early instinctive and emotional development. We shall therefore not be surprised to find in some people not merely one alone of these disturbances, but several in combination.

PERVERSION WITH ANTISOCIAL CHARACTER.

CASE 7. HOMOSEXUALITY.

A typical case is that of Mr. B., a man of 44 years of age, in a good job and thoroughly respectable, who had come before the courts twice, once at

[1] Part I, Ch. V, p. 33.

the age of 30, and the second time shortly before I saw him. He had on each occasion tried to seduce another man in a public lavatory, on both occasions attracting the notice of a police officer. For as long as he could remember he had been attracted only by men. He would have liked to have a homosexual relationship, but felt that it would be extremely wrong to do so. On the other hand he did not want to be treated, as he did not desire to be attracted by women. He admired women ; his mother, with whom he still lives, he loved dearly, but he did not care sexually for girls. When he was brought before the court at the age of 30, he had for the first time tried to find a man friend, and was found out before his attempt succeeded. He was then sentenced to a short term of imprisonment, and he felt that the punishment was absolutely justified. In the intervening years he was in love with a friend without having a manifest homosexual relationship with him, and was perfectly satisfied. He loved this man with an adoration typical of boys at puberty. His friend having to join the Army, he felt very lonely, and after a time became restless and sexually dissatisfied. He disapproved of having a homosexual relationship for himself, but was able to justify such behaviour in other people. The pressure of his unsatisfied desires increased until he found himself once again accosting a man in a lavatory, whereupon a police officer intervened.

WISH FOR PUNISHMENT.

It was quite clear from his story that he could not allow himself to seek for sexual satisfaction in a more inconspicuous way, and that he therefore chose a situation in which the danger of being caught, prevented and punished was very great. The conflicts of this man were very complicated, as in addition he was suffering from an obsessional neurosis. This example has been given to illustrate the fact that it was not so much his homosexual tendencies as his feelings of guilt that drove him to display his perversion in such a way that the public became aware of it.

SEDUCTION OF YOUNG BOYS.

In the preceding chapter a case of active homosexual phantasies has been described. It is in people with a disturbance of this kind that the danger of seducing young boys exists. Again, such persons will become dangerous to the community only if they combine anti-social tendencies of an aggressive nature with their perversion. The danger for young boys in undergoing such experiences should not be minimized, especially as the first experience may lead the boy towards male prostitution as a profession. But it should be borne in mind that it is very rare for boys who do not already display homosexual tendencies to be exploited in this way. We have described how Billy used to talk to men in the street and take money from them, and it has been shown that this tendency was due to his passive attitude towards his father, which we have seen, in the case described in the last chapter, led to homosexual behaviour. More often than not, young boys will offer themselves, if not in words then by gestures, to older men. This is not meant to excuse the behaviour of the adult in introducing a young boy to homosexual practices. It is rather meant to draw attention to the fact that such boys should be examined with regard to their own mental condition and, if they are still young enough, should be helped to develop in a healthier way.

EXHIBITIONISM.

Exhibitionists are, on the whole, more likely to come to the notice of the police than are homosexuals. In cases which have been studied by the psycho-analytical method the perverse act usually includes hostility towards women, which forces the man to choose situations in which he can shock and frighten a woman. Sometimes this hostility towards women is very much to the fore.

CASE 8.
THE OFFENCE.

Mr. C. was a man of 23 who had already been before the courts twice on a charge of indecent behaviour. Two years before the last charge he had exhibited himself in front of the same girl whom he knew by sight, and in the same place, repeatedly for about a fortnight before he was caught. He was given the choice of three months' imprisonment or psychological treatment. He naturally chose the latter, but very willingly went to prison when he found himself in a mental hospital amongst defectives. Two years later he masturbated in an open field and was observed by a girl whom he alleged he had not seen.

HISTORY OF SEXUAL DISTURBANCE.

In this case there was a long history of sexual difficulties. Between the ages of 4 and 8 he lived with an older male cousin, with whom he played some kind of sexual games. At that time he began to masturbate with sadistic phantasies. At the age of 14 he was brought before the juvenile court because he had accosted a slightly older boy in the street for the purpose of having a sexual relationship with him. He was put on probation, and psychological treatment was recommended. On coming home from the court his father birched him so thoroughly that the court's wise recommendation did not bear fruit. The boy transferred his fear of the father to the psychotherapist and saw him only twice. Between his fourteenth and eighteenth year he had various homosexual relationships without getting into trouble. Then he fell in love with a girl who did not want to marry him, although she allowed him to make sexual advances to her. He was furious with her and began to hate all women. He then joined the Merchant Navy. After a few months of close proximity with men he feared that he might want to have a homosexual relationship. He consulted a doctor, who recommended his being discharged from the Navy. Since then he has married, out of spite, a girl whom he does not love and has settled down in a good job. Although he has learned to like his wife as a personality he cannot get sexual satisfaction from intercourse with her. This again causes him to hate women, whom he apparently holds responsible for this lack of sexual gratification. His real sexual satisfaction he derives from masturbation with sadistic phantasies, in which he imagines beating and torturing women, and also from his exhibitionistic acts, which he desires to avoid at all costs, and which have occurred only since his marriage.

After his prison sentence he went to an out-patient department in order to get treatment. Here they promised that they would give him an appointment in the near future, but the next thing he heard was that an official had visited his father and asked him to sign a request for his certification. As this man has an I.Q. of 113, such a procedure seemed an inadequate way of dealing with his disturbance. It roused him to greater hatred of society in general, and, as he was fighting very hard all the time to suppress his perverse desires he naturally felt that he had been very unjustly treated. A short time later he committed his last offence after a quarrel on the same day with some men in the factory where he was working.

NEUROTIC TENDENCIES.

Although this man had sadistic phantasies he was unable to express his aggressions in a normal way. If provoked to a fight he would always get out of it for fear of killing the other man. At home for long spells he would not remark on anything he did not like, but later he would suddenly burst out with great aggressiveness quite unwarranted by the usually negligible nature of what he found disagreeable. His exhibitionistic actions were another outlet for his hostile tendencies ; yet another disturbing conflict was his fear of being inferior to other men, which led to an exaggerated ambition and to his finding it impossible to go on trying to do anything he had failed in at the first attempt. This feeling of inferiority was closely related to the idea of having harmed himself by masturbation.

We find again in this case a mixture of perverse phantasies and actions together with neurotic conflicts and an inability to deal with hostile impulses too strong to be safely expressed. This case is typical of those of a large number of exhibitionists, and though it is not given in any great detail, will allow of an analysis in a later chapter,[1] showing why penal methods of treatment, far from diminishing, only enhance the urges which lead to the perverse actions.

Exhibitionism and allied perversions occasionally occur very early, at the age of 13 to 14. It is then of extreme importance to recognize the perverse behaviour at this early stage for what it is, as the treatment employed will probably decide the boy's future.

CASE 9. HISTORY OF SEXUAL OFFENCE.

Richard was 13 when he was brought before the juvenile court for the first time. He had tried to take down a little girl's knickers, and he did it so conveniently in front of the girl's home that her mother rushed out and prevented him. He was put on probation, and when he repeated the same offence six months later with another girl he was sent to an approved school. There he stayed for three years, in great favour with his headmaster, as his behaviour was excellent and he was very good at school subjects. Nevertheless, once when he was out for a walk alone the same trouble occurred again ; he was sent back to school and psychological treatment was advised. He had started to masturbate at that time and was very worried about it. He asked the psychiatrist very earnestly to help him to suppress this habit, and apparently succeeded while he was undergoing treatment. When released from the approved school he was given manual work in a factory, an occupation which was entirely uncongenial to him. But having had his school life interrupted in this unfortunate way, even his superior intelligence (I.Q. 140) could not compensate for his lack of training. At the age of 18, after working for two years, he exposed himself in front of two girls in a wood. The girls screamed, and he rushed off on his bike, but stopped very soon to ask the way at

[1] Part III, Ch. IV (*c*), p. 234.

a place from which he could still hear the girls shouting. He must have behaved in a highly suspicious manner, for the person who was talking to him took him back to the girls, and he readily gave his name and address. During his remand, before the trial at Quarter Sessions, he had some psychological treatment, which, although much too brief, helped him to a certain extent. Owing to the report of the doctor he was not sentenced but put on probation. Treatment was advised, but no steps were taken to obtain it.

During the following year he committed no new offence, but began to have a craving for the cinema. He had a strong urge to see certain historical films, but felt impelled to go as often as possible to different picture houses, even if that meant his seeing the same film twice. The probation officer noticed that the boy had grown very restless and had stayed away from work for a day now and again to go to the pictures. He tried to get treatment for him. This was about a year after he had committed the last offence. But, unfortunately, he was too late. The boy suddenly disappeared altogether, and stayed away for a week until he was found by his father at the recruiting office nearest to his home. What had happened during this week was revealed only during psycho-analytical treatment. He had felt sexually excited and restless and wanted to go with a prostitute. So he stayed away from work and went to Piccadilly. He had £1, which he supposed to be the sum he needed. But while walking about Piccadilly not quite knowing what to do he got into a conversation with another youth who succeeded in getting 10*s*. from him by promising to show him one of these girls. After taking the money the boy disappeared and Richard was stranded. He went home, took his bicycle, and rode to Liverpool in order to join the Merchant Navy. There he was told that he would have to join in his home town, and it was then that to his great relief his father found him.

At this stage the boy was examined, and treatment was recommended; which, together with certain alterations in the environment, proved very successful.

HOME ENVIRONMENT AND EARLY HISTORY.

Richard, though very tall, looked much younger than his age. He came from an excellent home, the father being a professional man. He had one sister, four years younger than himself, whom he adored. He was not a difficult child, apart from showing deep jealousy after the birth of his sister. All he consciously knew of his attempts to see the genitals of girls was his wish to see what they looked like, as he alleged that he had never had any opportunity of knowing what a girl looked like. During the treatment recollections came back of very often seeing his sister naked, as the two children had had their bath together. When he was 9 years of age, the ceiling of the bathroom came down on one such occasion. He was slightly hurt and his sister was terrified. He succeeded in calming her. A doctor was called, whom the boy heard tell his mother that it was bad for the children to have their bath together. Unconsciously he perceived this as a warning directed against his sexual games with his sister in their bath, and he obediently altogether forgot what a girl looked like. Shortly after this incident he was emotionally disturbed, and did not succeed at the age of 11 in winning a scholarship.

THE NEUROTIC CONFLICT.

Before he had committed his first offence he heard the boys in his class describe how they succeeded in taking down little girls' knickers and how the girls apparently liked it. This gave him the idea of trying it himself, but he did it in such a way that he had to be caught. He already felt very guilty about his sexual wishes at this time, partly on account of the incident in the bathroom. His guilt feelings increased with the increasing strength of his desires, and in the ensuing years he succeeded in being caught every time he attempted to satisfy his desire to look at a girl's genitals. In committing his last offence he showed the other side of the picture: he exposed himself. The incident in the bathroom proved to be what is called a " cover memory ". It increased his castration anxiety—he was hurt—but it was not the first incident in which he had experienced such a fear. This incident covered the fears connected with his Oedipus desires, which were particularly strong at the time when his little sister was born. When at puberty he started to masturbate he was convinced that he had damaged himself, and as we have seen, he asked the doctor to help him to stop masturbating. It would probably have helped him more if his guilty feelings could have been relieved at that time. In his talks with the prison doctor before he was brought up at the Assizes he understood that his sexual behaviour was not morally wrong. And though the time was much too short for more than an intellectual understanding, this helped him at least to stop exposing himself. He succeeded in partially sublimating one of his sexual desires, namely the wish to look. He began to crave for the cinema. The obsessional character of this activity shows its origin in an instinctive source. But he was not yet normally balanced. One of the reasons for his difficulties certainly was that in his occupation he had no opportunity for sublimating his instinctive energy. He was unskilful with his hands, but was clearly gifted intellectually.

DIAGNOSIS.

This case offers some features, especially in regard to sublimation, which will be discussed further in the section on treatment. Here it is meant to illustrate the combination of neurotic symptoms, particularly guilt feelings and obsessional tendencies, with perverse sexual activities which made their appearance as early as the age of 13. I think that this case shows how necessary it is to examine such a boy very thoroughly at the earliest possible moment. It is quite true that his first sexual act might be interpreted simply as boyish naughtiness, but in fact it was the first sign of a perverse sexual activity, and the recognition of this fact would have prevented the damage to the boy's entire future. A boy with an I.Q. of 140 and an excellent home should never be sent to an approved school where he cannot possibly obtain a secondary education ; this is especially important if it is realized that his perverse sexual behaviour cannot be cured in this way.

FETISHISM.

In fetishism sexual satisfaction is gained from the possession of an object usually belonging to the body or person of a woman. If possession of this object has to be gained by force, or if it is a condition of the individual perversion to damage the object, the fetishist may come into conflict with the law.

CASE 10.
THE EXTERNAL SITUATION.

George was a very amiable and friendly young man of 21. He came from a good home, with devoted parents and one younger brother. He was not only a good son but had an excellent record at work as well. His intelligence was average (I.Q. 107). From his sixteenth year he had occasionally had short-lived affairs with easy-going girls until he got engaged at the age of 19 to an intelligent and pretty young woman of the same age, whom he had known practically all his life and who worked in the same factory. Both families were delighted with the match, and marriage was contemplated as soon as housing facilities were available. Then all at once a series of disturbing factors entered George's life. He was transferred from his factory to another three miles away and put on a slightly different job.

He hated being separated, at least during the daytime, from his girl, and he was even more worried lest, owing to the different type of work he was doing, his apprenticeship of four years' standing should be jeopardized by the transfer. At the same time his girl wanted to have an operation for the removal of her tonsils, and that bothered him considerably. Since he was engaged he had occasionally had intimate sexual relationships with his fiancée, and their opportunities for meetings were also endangered by the separation. As his girl was very pretty he got madly jealous and thought that all the men in his old workshop would be pursuing her. George had up till then had a very easy life, and everything he intended to do had worked out according to plan. These difficulties, slight though they were, apparently put him off his balance.

SEXUAL DISTURBANCE.

In the next six months he had experiences which seemed to him very odd, though he had not the power or probably the wish to stop them. He often found himself, especially when he had not seen his girl for a day or two, suddenly attracted by a woman in the street or on a bus in which he was travelling. All these women wore mackintoshes. His sexual excitement at the sight of these women, whose faces did not interest him at all, would rise, and strangely enough would increase with the inevitable realization that he could not sleep with them. He never made any attempt to make sure that this was really the case. Then while still sexually excited he would become very angry, and if opportunity allowed, in the blackout for instance, or when queueing for a bus, would damage the woman's mackintosh, either cutting it with a knife or soiling it with ink or paint which he sometimes happened to have on him. With this act his sexual excitement rose to a climax, and then died down. After he had had this experience about a dozen times he was at last caught in the act and came before the court. During the period of about six months when he was undergoing these experiences, he had become depressed, moody and irritable. His girl friend knew that something must be troubling him, but did not want to bother him with too many questions. Before he had to go to court he told her the whole story and left it to her whether she wanted to break off their engagement. She stuck to him, and they were married.

THE EXAMINATION.

When George came for his psychiatric examination the court procedure was over; he had been put on probation, and had then already been married for four months. His sexual relations with his wife were normal and satisfactory to both parties. The impulse to damage a woman's mackintosh had never reappeared, and he felt happy and satisfied except that he was still troubled because he did not understand at all what had caused him to behave in so strange a way. However, it appeared that since the age of 14 he had masturbated with a phantasy that he would touch a woman's mackintosh. He had ceased masturbating on beginning to have sexual relationships with his girl, and had not begun to do so again when he was separated from her so that they could meet only much more rarely. Instead he had put his sexual phantasies into action.

DIAGNOSIS. The unconscious significance of the mackintosh as fetish could not be ascertained in this case, as there was no need for psycho-analytical treatment. But it is not an unusual fetish. George's ability to have satisfying sexual relations with a woman showed that he was not yet fixated to the fetishistic sexual activity and that, given a satisfactory external situation, which so far he had created for himself, he would probably not have to resort to it again. Apart from this perverse sexual activity he showed a very strong attachment to his mother and did not appear to be a very strong personality altogether. This accounts for the fact that he reacted to the difficulties described with the outbreak of a perverse sexual activity. The outstanding difficulty in this period was the separation from his girl friend, and the impossibility of getting sexual satisfaction in the normal way. The deeper reasons why he chose this particular method of dealing with his difficulties could have been ascertained only by a thorough analysis, which, as has been mentioned, was not here necessary. But this case also illustrates how narrow the borderline between the normal and the abnormal can be. This young man was not abnormal in any other way, and would probably never have indulged in his perverse activity had he not met with external difficulties with which he could not cope. There are, however, other cases of fetishism where the fixation to the particular activity concerned has occurred very early in life, and where the possibilities for a normal sexual life are non-existent. These true perverts may be able to perform the sexual act, but without gaining the sexual satisfaction which is open to them in the perverse act. Then no change in external circumstances can alter the way in which they obtain sexual gratification.

(*b*) Borderline Cases

There are certain types of sexual offences which on superficial investigation cannot really be classed amongst the perversions; only an examination which would take account of unconscious motives could decide whether the behaviour is due to external circumstances or solely to a perverse urge.

SEXUAL ASSAULT. In all cases of sexual assault, from rape to the molestation of women, the behaviour may be caused by external circumstances, that is, by the impossibility of obtaining sexual satisfaction in the ordinary way so that increased aggression is necessary to satisfy a normal sexual urge, or it may be due to a sadistic perversion, that is, the assault may be a necessary original condition for gaining sexual satisfaction. Sexual crimes of violence have become rarer during recent decades. The repression of sexual activities imposed on the individual by the community has become much less strict since the First World War, and this would explain the decrease. It is very probable that in the majority of cases of assault there are external circumstances which tend to make sexual satisfaction difficult for the offender, and that in addition there is a rather stronger mixture of aggressive tendencies with the sexual urge than is usual.

ASSAULT ON CHILDREN. The same two factors are very often at work in cases of indecent assault by men on small girls. In all cases of this kind which have come under my observation the man involved was usually not very young and his sexual capacities were weak. There were opportunities for being with young children; this type of sexual offence is occasionally committed by teachers in girls' schools, but in all cases there was also a strange curiosity to see the genitals of a small girl, a desire which is a remnant of the normal infantile curiosity. This was very clear in the case of a man who had never committed a sexual offence but who was under psycho-analytical treatment because he was suffering from an obsessional neurosis. He had never had any sexual relationship at all. During a period of his treatment just before recollections of early sexual games with a little girl came back to consciousness he used to go into a park with the intention of seeing the genitals of little girls. He would sit for hours near a children's play-ground waiting for an opportunity of obtaining satisfaction for his impulse, and always came away with the fear that the park attendant had guessed what he was after. This desire could be shown to be directly connected with his infantile sexual games, the knowledge of which was fully repressed as belonging to the forbidden sexual urges of the Oedipus period.

CASE II. THE SEXUAL OFFENCE.

A similar conflict may have been at work in causing Mr. D. to come before the court on the charge of indecent assault. Mr. D. was a man of 43 years of age, married and with two small boys. His conduct up to the time when he was charged had been irreproachable, at home as well as at work. He was accused of having on two occasions touched the genitals of a little girl who used to play with his boys. When charged with the offence he at once admitted his guilt, and furnished the further information that he had on the same occasion handled a second girl also. He could give no other explanation for his action than that he was suddenly seized with an intense curiosity to see what a girl was like, as he had never before had occasion to do so. To the probation officer this explanation seemed rather weak, coming from a married man.

THE EXTERNAL SITUATION.

Mr. D. was a healthy man, physically as well as mentally. On closer investigation it appeared that though his marriage was perfectly happy his sexual desires were rather weak. At the time when he committed his offence his wife was again pregnant, and he wanted a girl very badly. He had always wished for this, every time his wife was going to have a baby, and he was disappointed that twice the child had been a boy. He had always been interested in playing with little girls, and the two children whom he had assaulted had both been frequent visitors to his house for at least a year. He had not been aware of his curiosity over the girl's genitals until two occasions when the children were playing with his boys and in doing so exposed themselves. On both these occasions he had managed to be alone with them for a short while and to touch them.

PROBABLE CAUSE.

Mr. D. had a sister two years younger than himself, and it is very likely that as a child he had had ample opportunity of observing her. He had no recollection of any sexual game with his sister or of any curiosity towards her. But it was only to be expected that if the curiosity which he displayed in the sexual act with the small girls was derived from an infantile curiosity directed towards his sister, his desire should have remained in the unconscious until the moment when it reappeared in action. Between his offence and the time when he was charged with it—three weeks elapsed between the two dates—he had nearly "forgotten" the whole incident, but when reminded he felt very guilty and readily admitted his misdemeanour, furnishing facts which were not known to the police. After he had been sentenced to a heavy fine he again intended to forget the matter as quickly as possible, and he succeeded very well. This attitude shows the tendency towards repression which was at work on the original desire when he was a small child. There was no possibility in this case of verifying this assumption, for this could be done only by psycho-analytical treatment, but all the circumstances and especially the high ethical code which Mr. D. otherwise maintained would go to prove that his offence was caused by an old infantile repressed desire.

In all such cases the effect upon the little girl of an assault of this kind is of even greater importance for the field worker than the understanding of the psychology of the offender. As such an offence is usually committed by older men, the problem of the effect on the girl is very similar to that caused by an incestuous assault, and will be dealt with under that heading.

(*c*) Incest

Incestuous relationships between father and daughter or brother and sister are much more common than would appear from court statistics, for obvious reasons. Such cases are difficult to prove, as there is very rarely corroborative evidence, and, what is not so often realized, the girl in question, whether daughter or sister, herself feels much too guilty and too fond of the aggressor to furnish sufficient proof.

GENERAL PSYCHOLOGICAL CONSIDERATIONS.

The complications met with in court cases of this kind will be more easily grasped if all the psychological factors involved are taken into account. It has been seen that during an early period of the girl's life the desire for a sexual relationship to the father is part of her normal emotional development; during this time children very often indulge in sexual games with one another, driven by their own instinctive urges and the desire to imitate adults. The elder brother therefore very often represents for the girl a substitute for the father. Incest is one of the taboos of civilized society. The factors which lead to the repression and resolution of the Oedipus desires have been described in detail,[1] and it has also been shown that very often the Oedipus desires are simply repressed and remain untouched by further modification in the unconscious. There is, therefore, an unconscious preparedness for incestuous relationships in every human being, and it depends on the further emotional development and on environmental factors whether there is any likelihood of their being put into action. It is important to keep this factor in mind since it explains why girls give in easily to their father's or brother's desires, and why they are likely to keep it as secret as the male partner. For the man the desire is very often prompted by opportunity. Incest is in the majority of cases a problem of overcrowding. The psychological motive arises in the man also from the Oedipus conflict ; very often in these cases it will be found that the age difference between father and daughter is not insuperably great ; that the mother is of the father's age or older, and occasionally that the daughter has been away from home during her early years, so that the father is suddenly confronted with a young girl whom he has not seen grow up.

PSYCHOLOGICAL EFFECT ON THE GIRL.

(1) IN LATENCY PERIOD.

The effect on the girl of a relationship of this kind will vary according to her character formation and instinctive development. The psychological significance for the girl consists in the fact that a desire which has to be repressed before the age of 6 suddenly finds satisfaction. We have stated above [2] that one of the most potent reasons for the suppression of the Oedipus desire is the fear of punishment from the parent of the same sex. The fear of the mother's retaliation together with her love for her mother help the girl to renounce the wish for the father. It will therefore be significant at what stage of the emotional development the incestuous desires find fulfilment. If the father not only shows admiration for the girl, but actually handles her sexually at a very early age, it will be unlikely that she will be able to solve her Oedipus conflict in a satisfactory way, and this may be reflected later on in her character development. It is very likely that she will remain fixated to her Oedipus desires, and all kinds of disturbance will be encountered, from antisocial character to the formation of a neurotic illness after puberty. But, and this is an important point when considering treatment in such cases, there need not necessarily be any disturbance in later life. The fulfilment of

[1] Part I, Ch. VI.

[2] Ibid., p. 41.

Oedipus desires need not necessarily have a greater after-effect than the fulfilment of aggressive wishes or any other instinctive urge which eventually has to disappear.

The situation will of course become much more complicated if a child should have to give evidence against the father, a necessary condition if the father is to be charged with the offence. Then her feelings of loyalty towards the father and her own guilty feelings connected with the Oedipus desires will make it extremely difficult for her to accuse the father. Very often such accusations are made not at the beginning of an incestuous relationship but rather when the girl for one reason or another believes that her father's attention has been withdrawn from her. The motive for her accusation is then jealousy and revenge rather than the knowledge that the relationship is forbidden.

(2) IN PUBERTY.

All these conflicts are enhanced if, as is usually the case, the girl is at or nearing puberty when the relationship begins. It is then very often the girl's first sexual relationship, and it occurs at a time when normally she should be able to free herself from infantile love objects and to transfer her feelings to boys of her own age.

There is again no hard-and-fast rule as to the further development of a girl who has had an incestuous relationship at the age of puberty. There need not be any severe disturbance at all, and on the other hand it may cause an upheaval from which she will never properly recover.

THE PSYCHOLOGICAL EFFECT OF COURT PROCEEDINGS.

There are difficult problems connected with cases of incest. If such a relationship is discovered means should be found to break it off. But in every such case court proceedings with the unavoidable statements and the necessity of accusing the father will make the psychological situation much worse than it was before. However tactfully the investigations may be conducted the girl will always be the cause of the father's imprisonment, and as she has at least some faint knowledge of her own wishes, even when they are consciously repudiated she is bound to feel very guilty. Many cases are known where the girl made the first accusations and then withdrew the charge. This does not necessarily mean that the first statement was untrue. It may be an indication that she is not strong enough emotionally to stand the strain of having her father punished for an offence of which she herself also feels guilty. The situation is very often complicated by the mother's attitude towards the girl, an attitude which is very rarely rational because her deepest emotions are involved as well. A solution should be found which would make it possible to remove the girl from home, if this course seems best, without the need for court proceedings. In cases of incest, for the reasons detailed above, not only tact, but a profound knowledge of the psychological factors involved is necessary in order to avoid damaging the girl's later character and emotional development.

A short case may illustrate some of the points mentioned.

CASE 12.
EARLY HISTORY.

Milly was brought up by an aunt until she was 12 years of age. The reason why Milly, an only child, had been removed from home at the early age of 2 has never been satisfactorily explained. The mother, herself a very good-looking and still young woman, stated that the child's health was rather delicate and the relatives lived in the country. When Milly was 12, the aunt with whom she stayed died, and she was sent to other relations. School holidays were usually spent at home. During her year's stay in this new home she began to be difficult ; she romanced and invented phantasies and showed a marked preference for boys. She spent another holiday with her parents and complained that her other relations were cruel to her. This accusation had never been substantiated, but it induced the parents to take the child home. She lived at home for three years, going to a convent school. Her school record was mediocre, and she decided that she wanted to become a hairdresser, while the parents wanted her to take up a profession. During the war the home broke up, and Milly was sent into the country, where she got a good job in a hairdresser's saloon. She fell in love with her employer, a man aged 34, who wanted to marry her, and she took him home to see her parents. When it became known that she had already had an intimate relationship with this man, her father strongly objected to the marriage and forced her to give up her job. Milly, though very much in love, obeyed. When she started her new job she was very depressed and disturbed, and her new employer asked her what was wrong. She then told him that during the three years she lived at home she had had an

THE INCESTUOUS RELATIONSHIP.

intimate relationship with her father. She was glad when she fell in love, because she did not want to go on living with her father. She felt sure that the father objected to her marriage only because that would mean separation. Her employer, with the girl's consent, informed the police, and the father was summoned. As there was sufficient evidence, the nature of which cannot be described here, the matter came before the court, but the case was dismissed mainly on account of the fact that the mother accused the girl of having always been too interested in men and drew attention to her romancing. The girl herself was not very firm in her accusations and stated that she had not known that her father would be punished. She was very glad when the case was dismissed.

DIAGNOSIS. It had been ascertained without doubt that the girl's statement was true, and there could also be no doubt about the fact that she had been quite willing to comply with her father's wishes so long as she stayed at home. This made it difficult for her to appear as the accuser in court, though it could be proved that the mother's allegations about the girl's conduct were untrue. Interestingly enough, once away from home the girl was able to form a good relationship with her employer, who represented a father figure to her, and the fact that her sexual relations with him were very satisfactory proves that her emotional development was not unduly disturbed by the incestuous relationship. This may be due to the fact that she had not grown up in the presence of the father, and that when she returned home at the age of 13, the father was a stranger to her. The girl's relationship to the mother was complicated. There could be no doubt about the mother's hostility towards her, promptly expressed in her wish to have the child brought up away from home, and later in her accusations. It may be that the mother's open unfriendliness and hostility made it easier for the girl not to feel too guilty about her relationship with the father.

In this case, the girl's difficulties were due not so much to her original relationship to the father as to the parents' attitude when she had succeeded in cutting herself loose from home. Under this difficulty her resolve to keep away from the father broke down. She was not able to rebel against his wish that she should not marry, which showed his affection for her, but she gave in to him. In her further development she was helped by some psychological treatment, and she succeeded in the end in taking work in another town and so at least avoiding contact with her parents. But two years after the court proceedings she had not yet formed another satisfactory relationship with a man.

CHAPTER VIII

ORGANIC AND PSYCHOTIC EGO-DISTURBANCES

It has been shown that antisocial behaviour may be due to a faulty character development: under such conditions the Ego is unable to control or to keep in repression the innate primitive instinctive urges.

Criminal actions may also occur if the Ego is paralysed by an organic illness of the brain. The psychological conception of the Ego cannot be expressed directly in terms of brain physiology. But it is possible to say that a disturbance of the higher functions of the brain has its correlate in a disturbed Ego-function.

Criminal actions caused by a disturbed function of the brain are fully discussed in textbooks on psychiatry (10*a*, 20) and will only be shortly enumerated here, especially in their relationship to juvenile delinquency.

(1) Mental Defectiveness

Statistics as to the number of mental defectives among offenders vary to an astonishing degree, from about 4 per cent. up to 80 per cent. in some American investigations. It has of course to be borne in mind that only statistics compiled during the last few decades, since intelligence testing has become an objective science, can be considered as correct. Healy (17*a*) and Burt (8) as well as Rhodes (9) come to the conclusion that though only a low percentage of defectives can be found among their cases, the percentage is in each case slightly higher than that found among the population as a whole.

INTELLIGENCE AND CHARACTER DEVELOPMENT.

The importance of the innate intelligence in the development of the Ego and also in the modification of instinctive urges has been stressed. In lower-grade mental defectiveness the development from the pleasure-principle to the reality-principle, which as we have seen plays a paramount part in social adaptation, is disturbed by the lack of the necessary intellectual knowledge required for adjusting actions to past experiences and future considerations. Lack of ability will prevent a satisfactory sublimation of instinctive energy into socially acceptable channels.

As a result the Ego will remain weak and unable to control the instinctive urges. Very careful training under good environmental conditions will make it possible to achieve a certain standard of attainment, but the environment has to be such that it is adapted to the defective.

In the cases of mental defectiveness it is the organic functional disturbance of the brain which endangers normal development, and not emotional factors. On moving upwards in the scale to higher-grade mental defectiveness and especially on considering dull and backward children, the conditions become slightly different. Only a very careful diagnostic examination will help to decide whether antisocial behaviour is due to lack of intelligence or whether attainments are influenced by an antisocial character formation. We have seen that the lack of modification of instinctive urges leads to a lack of interest in school subjects and thus often causes backwardness without innate intellectual defects. In such cases, the treatment of the character disturbance will result in an apparent increase in intellectual abilities. Educational psychologists, accustomed to testing delinquents, will be able to decide whether the disturbance is more on the intellectual or more on the emotional plane.

(2) Organic Illnesses of the Brain

In certain organic illnesses of the brain, such as General Paralysis of the Insane, brain tumour, and brain injury, the moral conduct of the patient may change. This is due to the non-functioning of the higher brain centres. Expressed in psychological terms, this again causes the Ego to lose control so that instinctive urges, hitherto inhibited, can come to the fore.

ENCEPHALITIS. An organic disturbance due to encephalitis lethargica is of interest in juvenile delinquency (if the acute illness has been contracted before puberty). These cases may have the appearance of the usual antisocial behaviour with emphasis on sudden cruelties towards other children and animals. Such cases do not, of course, respond to ordinary methods of treatment, and special institutions have been set apart for their segregation. The illness has become rare in recent years. Hill (21) develops an interesting theory based on the similarity of behaviour between encephalitic children and aggressive psychopaths.

EPILEPSY. Much severer diagnostic and therapeutic problems are involved when antisocial behaviour occurs in an epileptic personality. States of fugue equivalent to an epileptic fit, during which criminal actions are committed without the conscious knowledge of the offender, are comparatively rare, and are not known to occur before puberty. Much more common are cases in which there is antisocial behaviour, in no way differing from the behaviour we have seen to be caused by emotional factors, together with a history of epileptic illness. Usually such cases do not respond to methods of treatment, social or psychotherapeutic; encephalography makes it possible to detect the epileptic nature of an antisocial disturbance even if there is no history of fits, and allows us to distinguish in our diagnosis between a purely emotional and an epileptic disturbance.

In recent years encephalographic studies have enriched our knowledge of functional disturbances in certain cases of antisocial behaviour. Hill (21) has examined the Electroencephalogram (E.E.G.) of cases belonging to the "predominantly aggressive group" of psychopathic personalities (19*a*). He records that in this group the E.E.G. is abnormal in 65 per cent. of cases. Moreover, he states that "electroencephalographic examination shows strong grounds for thinking that there is a kinship between the D.A.B. (dysrhythmic aggressive behaviour) patient and the epileptic". In his paper, Hill develops a very interesting theory of the physio-chemical abnormalities of constitution which may form the background of cerebral function in disturbances of this kind. No attempt has been or can yet be made to correlate these physiological findings with psychological findings. The causes of antisocial behaviour in this group are probably organic.

ALCOHOL AND DRUG ADDICTION.

The psychological basis of an addiction to alcohol or to drugs does not concern us here; but under the influence of alcohol crimes of violence may occasionally be committed. Alcohol, though apparently stimulating in small quantities, in slightly larger quantities removes inhibitions arising from the higher nervous centres. Expressed in psychological language, alcohol impairs the function of the Ego and thereby allows antisocial instincts to find expression in action. The same mechanism is at work when antisocial actions are committed under the influence of drugs.

(3) Psychotic Ego Disturbances

In insanity, for reasons so far unknown, the patient loses contact with reality. Instinctive urges and conflicts formerly repressed become conscious and are for the patient much more real than anything going on in the outside world. His Ego breaks down, and his actions and thoughts are directed only by the unconscious. Sometimes, therefore, crimes are committed during a state of insanity (20, 10*a*).

Insanity is very rare in children and in young people until after puberty. Occasionally difficult diagnostic problems arise in certain cases of antisocial behaviour beginning after puberty, when there are as yet only very slight indications that the disturbance may be due to incipient insanity, usually belonging to the schizophrenic reaction type. The sudden onset of antisocial behaviour, the severity of the criminal action, the lack of emotion displayed by the offender, the impossibility of finding an adequate motive, and other disturbances of the emotional life of the young person may draw attention to the fact that the criminal act is linked to an incipient psychotic disturbance. Very often only a period of observation can clarify the diagnosis. Psychotic illness should be suspected in all cases where a young person suddenly commits a severe crime such as murder or assault, but there are many cases in which the antisocial behaviour in itself is not very different from that displayed by offenders with an antisocial character formation.

CASE 13.

BEHAVIOUR DIFFICULTIES.

Dorothy was 20 when her relations thought that her behaviour perhaps called for medical help rather than for educational methods. The girl had been perfectly all right until about two years before she came for examination. She had passed matriculation, and had never been difficult in school except that she was rather solitary and did not get on too well with her schoolfellows. At the age of 17 she worked in the domestic department of a school where she fell in love with the headmaster, an old man, and talked about her wish to marry him. She had to be removed from the school and took a job as governess to two small children. By the kindness of her mistress she was able to stay there for half a year, but was found to be very difficult from the start. She had no sense of responsibility. She could not be left alone with the children because she was apt to abandon them and stroll dreamily round the countryside. When it was explained to her that she would have to change her attitude if she wanted to stay she would be very friendly, but her mistress had the feeling she was talking to a wall instead of a girl. She had also begun to steal food from the larder. After she had been dismissed from her job as governess she spent some time in a camp with other people of her own age where she still pilfered food and was unable to form any kind of friendship. She then wanted to become a nurse, and it was at this stage that she was sent for examination.

PSYCHIATRIC EXAMINATION.

Dorothy could give very little explanation of her behaviour. As regards her attitude towards food she explained that it was impossible for her to see other people eating because it was disgusting, and suddenly she would be seized with the desire to have great quantities of eatables, especially sweets, which she then had to obtain at all costs. She also complained that her difficulties were due to the fact that she had no lover, but that she had never been attracted by anybody she had met. She was afraid that she was changing : when she looked in the glass her chin seemed out of place and different in shape from what it had been before. During the interview she smiled occasionally but without reference to what she was saying. Otherwise she did not display any emotion, and was neither sorry nor disturbed about her difficulties. The only emotion which could be inferred was anxiety about this feeling of being changed.

DIAGNOSIS.

The suddenness of the onset of the disturbance with this phantasy about a love relationship with a man who had never looked at her, her delusion that she was physically changed and her inadequate emotional responses led to the diagnosis of an incipient schizophrenic disturbance, though the evidence was slight at the time of examination. A period of observation produced no definite result, but a year later the girl had to be admitted to a mental hospital.

CHAPTER IX

A CLASSIFICATION OF JUVENILE DELINQUENCY

During the last century delinquent behaviour was classified according to the distinction, either mental or physical, between the delinquent and the law-abiding citizen.[1] No attempt was made at that time to classify the "normal delinquent" into different groups. Healy (16*a*) and Burt (8) made some progress by giving up all attempts to classify the delinquent, classifying the causative factors in delinquent behaviour instead. This, as has been shown,[2] led to a great advance in the study of the individual offender.

FORMER CLASSIFICATIONS.

Since then, and with the knowledge gained by these extensive investigations into causative factors, attempts at classification from various angles have been made, and the "normal delinquent" has been included in these schemes.

HAMBLIN SMITH.

Hamblin Smith (28), who was the first author in this country to recognize the importance of psycho-analytical knowledge in the understanding of delinquent behaviour, in his chapter on "Various Classes of Offenders", discussed groups of offenders without claiming to attempt a classification based on causation. His first four groups include the various types of mental defectives and the epileptics. In his group of "psychopaths" he includes all the known neurotic disturbances as well as sexual offences. His group of "constitutional inferiors" would nowadays by most authors be classified amongst the psychopaths. He then assigns a special group to "offences at puberty and adolescence"; he criticizes the conception of "moral insanity" and doubts the occurrence of such disturbance, and lastly classes together alcoholism and other toxic conditions. In this classification Smith intended to discuss groups already known and the value of keeping the various headings or discarding them rather than to create a new classification.

ALEXANDER.

Alexander (3*a*) attempts a classification on more causal lines and from the point of view of the criminologist. The basis of his classification is the degree of Ego-participation in the criminal act; the punishment or treatment should depend on whether or not the offender's Ego parti-

[1] Introduction, Ch. II. [2] Ibid., Ch. IV.

cipated in the antisocial act. He distinguishes two main groups: "chronic" and "accidental" criminality. The first group is subdivided into those criminals whose Ego is put out of action by a toxic or organic disturbance, those whose criminal behaviour is conditioned by a neurosis, those whose Super-Ego is criminal as a result of upbringing, and those who are "genuine" criminals. Alexander is doubtful whether this last type really exists. The "accidental" criminal group is subdivided into crimes resulting from "mistakes" like manslaughter and "situational" crimes, where the Ego is put out of action by a sudden overflow of emotion.

I.S.T.D. The diagnostic groups used at the I.S.T.D. (15) have been set out for the practical purposes of the clinical work undertaken at the Institute. They include: mentally defective, borderline mentally defective, psychotic, borderline psychotic, psychoneurotic, character cases (including psychopathic personalities and sex perverts apart from neurosis), behaviour problems, cases of organic origin, non-delinquent, normal, and alcoholic cases. Though this classification serves a very good practical purpose it does not give enough scope for etiological grouping.

In the preceding chapters some cases, representing different types of delinquent behaviour, have been discussed in greater or less detail. The examples have been chosen to illustrate certain points, but they do not by any means give a full picture of the variety of behaviour found among young offenders. Probably in time, when fuller psychiatric material is available, a typology of delinquent behaviour, based on causative factors, will be created. But it is already possible on the basis of the available literature and long years of experience in diagnosis and treatment of delinquents to attempt a classification which may facilitate further research.

This classification will be valid only on very broad lines. Just as normal imperceptibly merges into delinquent behaviour, so one type of delinquent behaviour gradually merges into another. Although therefore this classification will not allow every case to be placed in one or another category, the relative strength of the characteristics revealed on careful examination will facilitate the choice of treatment.

AUTHOR'S CLASSIFICATION. The classification put forward here has some resemblance to Alexander's in so far as the disturbance in Ego control is its basis. It differs in the assumption set out in the preceding chapters,[1] that at the basis of delinquent behaviour—whether complicated by neurosis or not —is the antisocial character formation on the one hand or an organic disturbance of the Ego on the other.

Generally speaking, delinquent behaviour is the result of a disturbance in the relative strength of the three domains of the mind, the Id, the Ego and the Super-Ego. The only exception to this statement would be a criminal who has become such merely because he had adopted the ethical code of his environment. Alexander (3*a*) seems to believe in the existence of such a type. As the Super-Ego is primarily formed in identification with the parents,[2] it is assumed that children growing up in a criminal environment have adopted this code of behaviour without any disturbance in their character development. It would then have to be assumed that the child, up to puberty, had not had any contact with the community outside the home, which is unlikely. It is even more unlikely that criminal parents should be able to bring up children in such a way that their character development is normal. The criminal environment of course exerts an important influence on the mind of the growing child, but by creating the conditions for an antisocial character development rather than merely by submitting the child to an ethical code different from that of the rest of the community. The effect of the criminal environment on the child is well described in *Branch Street* (24). Such children show the antisocial character formation to a high degree, and they are unable to conform to a normal ethical code later on, because their first environment has produced a disturbance in their mental structure which cannot be deleted by a change in environment.

If, therefore, criminal environments produce more criminals than normal communities, this is not simply due to the absorption of the criminal code, but to the disturbance which such an environment causes to character formation.

It is possible to classify the disturbance of the three domains of the mind into three groups which are susceptible of further subdivision. Thus it may be due to an antisocial character development, to organic illness, or to psychosis.

[1] Part II, Ch. I.

[2] Part I, Ch. VII, p. 47.

Group I

The Antisocial Character Formation

Into this group fall the majority of juvenile offenders. Constitutional and environmental factors are responsible for the development of the antisocial character, which may be present in various degrees, and the delinquent behaviour may be caused—

(1) by the antisocial character formation alone; delinquent behaviour will be manifest from the latency period onwards without long interruptions and without serious provocation other than the environmental factors which have caused the disturbance in the first place.

In the latency period, children of this type are often "beyond the control" of their parents (Case 1).

During and after puberty the criminal career becomes habitual unless adequate treatment is undertaken. Special types at puberty are Aichhorn's "aggressive Youth" (2) and the "wayward" girl (Case 2).

(2) by a lesser degree of antisocial character formation with the addition of severe environmental or emotional stress, the latter being usually due to an unconscious mental conflict.

Many offenders who commit their first antisocial acts at puberty belong to this group (Case 4).

(3) by a slight degree of antisocial character formation together with neurotic conflicts, on the basis of which symptom formation may occur. The resulting symptom will be a delinquent instead of a neurotic one (Case 3).

Kleptomania, incendiarism, occasional crimes and certain sexual offences belong to this group.

(4) by a certain degree of antisocial character development together with the neurotic disturbance of "acting out" a phantasy in daily life (Case 5).

Reich's "Triebhafter Charakter" (26) (impulsive character), Alexander's "Neurotic Character" (3*b*), Aichhorn's "Impostor Type" (2) belong to this group, which, as has been said, is classified by Henderson (19*a*) as the "predominantly inadequate group" of psychopathic personalities.

Group II

Organic Disturbances

In this group of cases the Ego is put out of action by toxic or organic disturbances or a malfunctioning of the nervous centres.

(1) Toxic disturbances:
 Crimes committed while under the influence of alcohol or drugs.

(2) Organic disturbances:
 (*a*) mental defectiveness and backwardness, if the lack of intellectual capacity has been found at the basis of the delinquent behaviour.
 (*b*) Tumours of the brain, General Paralysis of the Insane, Cerebral Trauma, etc.
 (*c*) Encephalitis, if acquired before puberty.

(3) Malfunction of the Nervous Centres.
 (*a*) Epilepsy.
 (*b*) Hill's (21) dysrhythmic aggressive behaviour.

Group III

Psychotic Ego-disturbance

The Ego is unable to control instinctive urges on account of its inability to distinguish between reality and phantasy. A diagnosis of psychotic illness cannot be made unless other pathological symptoms are present apart from an inexplicable delinquent act.

This classification, especially in so far as Group I is concerned, is, I believe, an etiological classification so far as our present state of knowledge goes. Future research will allow us to amplify it and will probably necessitate various changes. At present, this classification, provided a careful diagnosis has been made, may form the basis for the choice of treatment.

BIBLIOGRAPHY. PART II

1. Abraham, K.: "Die Geschichte eines Hochstaplers im Licht psychoanalytischer Erkenntnis." *Imago*, Bd. XI, Heft 4. 1925.
2. Aichhorn, A.: *Wayward Youth.* London, 1936.
3. Alexander, F., and Staub, H:
   (*a*) *The Criminal, the Judge and the Public.* London, 1931.
   (*b*) "The Neurotic Character." *Intern. Journal of Psycho-Analysis.* 1930.
4. Alexander, F., and Healy, W.: *Roots of Crime.* New York, 1935.
5. Bagot, H.: *Juvenile Delinquency.* London, 1941.
6. Burlingham, D.: "Die Einfühlung des Kleinkindes in die Mutter." *Imago*, Bd. XXI. 1935.
7. Burlingham, D., and Freud, A.:
   (*a*) *Young Children in War Time in a Residential War Nursery.* London, 1942.
   (*b*) *Infants Without Families.* London, 1943.
8. Burt, C.: *The Young Delinquent.* London (4th edition), 1944.
9. Carr-Saunders, A. M., Mannheim, H., Rhodes, E. C.: *Young Offenders. An Enquiry into Juvenile Delinquency.* Cambridge, 1942.
10. East, Norwood:
    (*a*) *Introduction to Forensic Psychiatry in the Criminal Courts.* London, 1927.
    (*b*) *The Adolescent Criminal.* London, 1942.
11. East, Norwood, and Hubert, W. H. de B.: *Home Office Report on the Psychological Treatment of Crime.* H.M.S.O., 1939.
12. Freud, S.:
    (*a*) "Analysis of a Phobia in a 5-year-old Boy." *Coll. Pap.*, III, 1925 (1909).
    (*b*) "Einige Charactertypen aus der psychoanalytischen Arbeit." III: Die Verbrecher aus Schuldbewusstsein." *Ges. Schriften*, Bd. X.
    (*c*) *Introductory Lectures on Psycho-Analysis.* London, 1922 (1918).
    (*d*) *The Interpretation of Dreams.* London, 1913 (1900).
    (*e*) "Selected Papers on Hysteria." *Coll. Pap.* I, 1921.
    (*f*) *Three Contributions to the Theory of Sexuality.* New York, 1910 (1905).
13. Friedlander, K.:
    (*a*) "The Antisocial Character Formation." In: *A Psychoanalytical Study of the Child.* New York, 1945.
    (*b*) "Delinquency Research." *New Era*, May, 1943.
14. Gillespie, R. D.: "Neurotic Illness and Crime." In: *Mental Abnormality and Crime.* English Studies in Criminal Science. London, 1944.
15. Glover, E.: *The Diagnosis and Treatment of Delinquency, being a Clinical Report of the work of the Institute during the Five Years 1937 to 1941.* I.S.T.D. Pamphlet, No. 1. London, 1944.
16. Healy, W.:
    (*a*) *The Individual Offender.* London, 1915.
    (*b*) *Mental Conflict and Misconduct.* London, 1919.
    (*c*) and Alper, B. S.: *Criminal Youth and the Borstal System.* New York, 1941.
17. Healy, W. and Bronner, A.:
    (*a*) *Delinquents and Criminals. Their Making and Unmaking.* New York, 1926.
    (*b*) *New Light on Delinquency and its Treatment.* New Haven, 1938.

18. HEALY, W. and HEALY, M. T. : *Pathological Lying, Accusation and Swindling.* Criminal Science Monographs, No. 1. 1915.

19. HENDERSON, K. D. :
  (*a*) *Psychopathic States.* London, 1939.
  (*b*) "Psychopathic Constitution and Criminal Behaviour." In : *Mental Abnormality and Crime.* London, 1944.

20. HENDERSON, K. D. and GILLESPIE, R. D. : *Textbook of Psychiatry.* London (5th edition), 1943.

21. HILL, D. : "Cerebral Dysrhythmia : Its Significance in Aggressive Behaviour." *Proceedings of the Royal Society of Medicine.* May, 1944.

22. LOMBROSO, CESARE : *L'Uomo Delinquente.* 1906–7.

23. MULLINS, C. : *Crime and Psychology.* London, 1943.

24. PANETH, M. : *Branch Street.* London, 1944.

25. PRICHARD, J. C. : *Treatise on Insanity.* London, 1835.

26. REICH, W. : *Der triebhafte Charakter.* Vienna, 1925.

27. *Report of the Departmental Committee on Sexual Offences against Young Persons.* Home Office, 1926.

28. SMITH, HAMBLIN M. : *The Psychology of the Criminal.* London, 1922.

29. WATSON, JOHN A. F. : *Meet the Prisoner.* London, 1939.

30. WILLS, D. W. : *The Hawkspur Experiment.* London, 1941.

PART III

TREATMENT

CHAPTER I

THE ATTITUDE OF THE PUBLIC

The boy Billy complained one day that he was constantly being smacked, He was very indignant and made it clear that that kind of treatment would cut no ice with him. A little later we were talking about a naughty boy, and I asked Billy how he would deal with him. Billy looked at me with wide, astonished eyes: "What he wants is a jolly good hiding, that would make him see reason."

DESIRE FOR PUNISHMENT.

There, in a nutshell, is the emotional reaction of the public,[1] which holds back all progress towards a rational treatment of crime. The *lex talionis* principle has been alive in the minds of human beings from the beginning of time. As civilization has progressed, the establishment of guilt and the punishment of the guilty has been taken out of the hands of the individual and has become the task of a special authority. So long as that authority fulfils its function in conformity with the unconscious tendencies of the majority of the members of a given community, all is well.

The wish to see the criminal punished is rooted in the history of mankind as well as in the individual history of every human being. The painful process of social adaptation during the first years of life has been fully described, and we have shown that the very impulses which are modified in the normal human being find an outlet in action in the delinquent. Attention has been drawn to the fact that even in the healthy individual some of the antisocial impulses escape modification and are repressed. We have shown [2] that experiences which strengthen the repressed impulses are apt to arouse anxiety; they undermine the power of the repressing forces, the Ego and the Super-Ego. If, therefore, the ordinary human being tends to be harsh towards the lawbreaker, there are several reasons for this. Consciously, this attitude is rationalized in the belief that attempts to undermine the law are a danger to the community and must therefore be repressed by

UNCONSCIOUS MOTIVATION.

[1] Introduction, Ch. I, p. 1.

[2] Part II, Ch. V, (*b*).

punishment. Unconsciously, the fear is due not to concern for community life, but to the danger which threatens our own equilibrium. If antisocial actions are not punished by the outside world the power of the Super-Ego is weakened, and the danger arises that our own antisocial impulses may break out in action. This fear is strong, not because the punishment of antisocial action is severe, but because it arouses the old childish idea of retaliation. The danger at that time was not loss of liberty, but damage to one's own body, and the fear is therefore much stronger than reality warrants.

In insisting, therefore, on punishment for the criminal, the public not only obeys the age-old retaliation principle, but also satisfies an inner need, namely that of safeguarding itself against a loss of mental equilibrium. If progress is to be made in the treatment of offenders it is important to recognize the strength of the unconscious trends which hinder any loosening of the connection between crime and punishment. It is also important to realize that " common sense " alone is not an adequate weapon against these unconscious tendencies. Common sense is very valuable in all those instances where intellectual judgment is unhampered by unconscious emotions. But it is helpless against influences arising out of our own unconscious. History, not in the field of criminal research alone, is full of examples showing that only expert knowledge can remove prejudices based on unconscious motives. The treatment of the insane before the emergence of psychiatric knowledge is but one example of the crass error of judgment committed by " common sense ".

The unconscious, and therefore purely emotional, motives for the maintenance of punishment as a treatment for antisocial reactions can at once be recognized in the reaction of the public when the efficacy of penal methods is challenged. It is interesting to note that invariably, when attention is drawn to the fact that punishment has proved to be ineffective, the alternative seems to the layman to lie in pampering the criminal or letting him run wild and thus further endanger the community. But neither psychologists nor criminologists nor sociologists have ever suggested this. Scientists fully agree with the public that the community has a right to safeguard itself against its criminals ; the question is how best to achieve this : by punishment, which, as has been shown over and over again, does not reform and must therefore constantly be repeated, or by other methods which make re-education and rehabilitation possible.

NEED FOR SCIENTIFIC EVALUATION OF FACTS.

Owing to the unconscious trend which arouses the wish to see the criminal punished, it will be doubly necessary to base all conceptions of treating delinquents on scientific facts and not on "common sense". The scientific facts set out in the preceding chapters go to show that the offender, through no fault of his own, has been unable to build up a character which of itself would enable him to respect the claims of the community and, in certain situations, to regard them as more important than the satisfaction of his own desires. We have also seen, at least by implication, that if we are law-abiding citizens, it is merely because we have had the opportunity to become socially adjusted. Treatment of the offender must therefore aim at rectifying his maladjustments. This, as will be shown in greater detail later on, will involve a repetition of the processes which tend to bring about social adaptation in childhood, under better conditions than those which the offender had met with in his early family setting.

The question of punishment, therefore, does not arise at all when deciding how any given offender may be enabled to develop a different character structure.

PUNISHMENT VERSUS TREATMENT.

There will be many cases in which this re-education will be impossible, especially when the criminal is too old or his innate endowments are too poor. The question will then arise how best to protect society against such an individual, and segregation may be the only possible method. This does not mean that such segregation is intended as punishment, although our motives may make little difference to the prisoner. But our motives will decisively influence the fate of other offenders who need not be imprisoned in order to become law-abiding citizens. Punishment, or better, frustration of certain impulses, may play a part in re-educating the offender as it does in education generally. But the verdict on any individual offender should be based on facts and not on our own emotions which, as we have seen, are opposed to scientific methods of treatment for the offender.

The only rational way to avoid basing our decision on unconscious emotions instead of on facts will be careful investigation into the causes of delinquent behaviour in any given case and the application of treatment which will counteract these factors. Constant revision of the treatment and re-estimation of its result at intervals will gradually increase our knowledge.

CHAPTER II

PROBLEMS OF DIAGNOSIS

The diagnosis of delinquent behaviour is one of the most difficult tasks in psychiatry. As long as diagnosis distinguished merely between organic and psychotic disturbances, and mental deficiency, as opposed to " normal criminality ", that is to say, as long as the task of psychiatry consisted mainly in establishing the fact of irresponsibility, it was difficult, but it proceeded, so to speak, on strictly orthodox lines. When, as is now the case, emphasis is laid on the understanding of " normal " delinquent behaviour, a new body of knowledge has to be built up. No classification of delinquent behaviour of general validity yet exists. Healy and Burt, the pioneers in the research into normal delinquent behaviour, made a great step forward when they discarded all former classifications and considered behaviour under the headings of its various causative factors. The classifications used by the courts are confined to the various types of delinquent actions and are useless from the psychiatric point of view.

But this lack of classification is only one difficulty. A correct diagnosis of a young offender cannot be reached by the psychiatrist alone. We have discussed the many factors which contribute to the development of the antisocial character formation, and we have seen that delinquent acts, in themselves indistinguishable from one another, may be caused by disturbances other than this character formation. We have seen that even if antisocial character development has been diagnosed, the behaviour may be complicated by a neurotic illness. In all these different cases treatment will be different. Experts in the various branches of science will be needed for the necessary examinations.

The diagnosis of organic illness is the task of the physician. The offender's innate intelligence must be tested by a psychologist. Not only his immediate environment but also his past history from birth onwards, and his emotional relationship to parents and brothers and sisters will have to be carefully studied by the psychiatric social worker. It is for the psychiatrist to examine the offender's mental condition and to ascertain which of the factors elucidated by all the other examinations play a decisive part in causing his delinquent behaviour.

NECESSITY FOR DIAGNOSTIC CLINICS.

Not only the psychiatrist but also the psychologist and the psychiatric social worker should have special experience with delinquent children and young persons whose behaviour, as we have seen, is different from that of neurotic or other disturbed individuals. For this reason, and because of the number of investigations required—and these can only gradually be integrated into a single picture—the diagnosis of delinquents can be satisfactorily undertaken only in clinics specially adapted for this purpose. Healy (20*a*) was the first to put this idea into practice when he created the Judge Baker Foundation in Chicago. In England, the I.S.T.D. (Institute for the Scientific Treatment of Delinquency) was established in 1932 for the same purpose (18). Child Guidance Clinics have the necessary staff to undertake investigations of this kind in the case of children under 14, though not all of them take a special interest in the delinquent.

Even with the facilities afforded by this type of centre, the diagnosis of delinquent behaviour is not an easy task. The presence or absence of organic illness can usually be established by one examination, and the innate intelligence can nowadays be ascertained with a reasonable degree of certainty at one interview. But some factors in the child's home life and in its other surroundings may in one single interview or in one single visit to the home entirely escape the notice of even the experienced social worker. Attention has been drawn [1] to the wrong impression which Billy's home might have given on a single visit, and to the fact that it took weeks before Billy's mother made any truthful statements about her relationship to her husband. To give another example : A boy of 12 was brought for examination because he soiled himself day and night and was cruel to smaller children and animals. The condition of the child when seen for the first time was such that it was assumed that he was in a pre-psychotic state. Enquiries into his environment showed that although the boarding school where he had been living for the past three years was perhaps not ideal for him, the headmistress was so devoted to him, having helped him in many ways, and the boy was so fond of her, that no better environment could be found. The school being too far away from London, no visit could be made, and it was only by chance that the boy was brought to the clinic for one of the interviews by another

SOCIAL HISTORY.

[1] Part II, Ch. I, p. 81.

teacher who proved to be the main cause of his abnormal behaviour. Removal from the school and from the grip of this teacher, who himself was an abnormal and dangerous personality, resulted in an immediate change of behaviour. It is even doubtful whether one visit to the school would have brought this most important environmental factor to light. It cannot be sufficiently emphasized that in assessing environmental factors we have to consider, not only the actual environment, the cleanliness of the house, and the number of rooms—though these factors are significant—but even more carefully the influence which the environment exerts on the child. In the same way, not only must the overt attitude of the parents be studied, but means must be found to penetrate deeper and to assess their emotional attitude towards the child, which may be in contrast with their overt behaviour. This emotional attitude cannot often be ascertained in a single interview.

PSYCHIATRIC INVESTIGATION.

The same difficulties confront the psychiatrist. The younger the child, the less likely he is to put his emotions into words. Even with young people it is only in a second or third interview, when a relationship to the psychiatrist has already been established, that the really important aspect of their emotional conflicts may come to light. And although, with experience, it is not too difficult to decide into which group of offender one or another case will fall, the particular details, of equal importance of course, will come to light much later. There are some cases in which psychiatric diagnosis will be possible only after a period of observation, and there are other cases, especially if a psychotic disturbance is suspected, where diagnosis would be infinitely easier if observation centres were available.

PRESENT SITUATION.

Having regard to these difficulties it is astonishing that the majority of young offenders are never sent for such an examination and are treated without a diagnosis. The majority of delinquents are dealt with only in the court. It is true that before a decision as to the disposal of the delinquent is arrived at, the probation officer makes enquiries into his home life, and school reports are sent in. And it is very often due to the efforts of the probation officer that a case is referred for psychiatric diagnosis. Some juvenile courts, notably that of J. Watson (32), have made a special study of juvenile delinquency so that they are much better equipped to deal with the offender than others. But if we really want to be able gradually to develop a scientific scheme for the treatment of young offenders, and to assess the merits of the various types of treatment, each single offender would have to be examined on the lines discussed above. If such a procedure were adopted some children would have to be examined whose delinquent acts are not the outcome of an antisocial character formation or of any other disturbance. But even in these cases an examination would not be wasted. If the parents could be advised how to deal more satisfactorily with their children, this might prevent a further disturbance in development.

PROPOSALS BY OTHER AUTHORS.

This is not the first time that the adoption of such a procedure has been advocated. Healy (20*a*) and Burt (10) have repeatedly emphasized the importance of a thorough examination in every case. Recently Mannheim (26) has suggested from the point of view of the criminologist how to put such a procedure into practice, namely by creating " Treatment Tribunals ". Another of Mannheim's proposals, to raise to 12 years the age at which criminal responsibility is assumed, and to have cases below this age dealt with by Chancery Courts, would help considerably in removing certain difficulties. Very often an offence is committed by a gang of children. Some of these children may be healthy, others may be " in need of care and protection ", others again may already be severely antisocial. All these different types have to have different treatment, so that one is dismissed under the Probation of Offenders Act, while others may have to be put on probation and others again perhaps sent to an approved school. Such discrimination appears unjust to the public, and will continue to do so, so long as probation and other methods of treatment are looked upon as forms of punishment and not, as they really are, helps towards a more normal development. It is not for the psychiatrist to find the means by which such difficulties can be overcome. But even though the psychiatrist may be aware of their existence, his suggestions for treatment should be concerned solely with helping the children to become socially adapted. This calls for close collaboration between psychiatrists and criminologists in order to achieve their common aim : not only to keep children out of the Courts, but also to help them to become good citizens.

Whenever it is proposed to examine every individual offender it is argued that this procedure would be too expensive. This, of course, is a fallacy. The method of trial and error, largely adopted at present, proves much more expensive. Many cases are sent to approved schools which, if they had been examined in the beginning, could be dealt with at home. There are other young offenders who, because they are not being treated in accordance with their disturbance, develop into habitual criminals later on. The only difference in expenditure would be that in the one case the money would be spent in the beginning with the idea of preventing criminal careers, while in the other it would be spread over the whole of the offender's lifetime.

A physician who prescribed treatment without first examining the patient would be accused of gross negligence. The same applies in principle to treatment for young offenders, and it is to be hoped that in fifty years' time the attitude of the public towards the diagnosis of delinquency will be the same as it now is to the diagnosis of organic illness.

CHAPTER III

TRANSFERENCE

Before we discuss the various forms of treatment appropriate to the different types of delinquent behaviour, the theoretical basis for curing delinquent behaviour has to be considered. So long as it was thought that the delinquent was antisocial of his own free will the situation was easy : it was assumed that he could choose to be socially adapted, and that punishment would induce him to do so. To-day we know that neither delinquents nor we ourselves are able at will to alter fundamentally our attitude towards the community. We know more : we have seen that the disturbance which under certain environmental and psychological conditions leads to antisocial behaviour, is a very deep-rooted one. It is not an illness, inflicted upon a healthy personality, but a character-disturbance rooted in experiences during the first years of life. How is it possible to clear up such a disturbance? Is it likely that attitudes which have been formed so early can be fundamentally changed? Have we not seen that the delinquent does not as a rule suffer from his disturbance, but finds as much satisfaction in his way of life as we do in ours?

CAN CHARACTER BE CHANGED?

Unless we are able to rectify the faulty character development all our efforts may remain patchwork. They may lead to a temporary change in behaviour, but each new environmental difficulty and each new emotional upheaval—situations to which nobody is immune—may arouse the old antisocial reaction once more. Looking at the enormous figures of recidivism one would be inclined to believe that this really happens. Sheldon Glueck's (19) analysis of 500 criminals also points towards the difficulty of modifying delinquent behaviour fundamentally. On the other hand, experiments like the "Little Commonwealth" (7), Aichhorn's Institution (2*a*), the "Hawkspur Camp" (34), and the successes of Approved Schools and Borstal Institutions, and from the point of view of psychological treatment, the Report of the I.S.T.D. (18), as well as various publications on the treatment of individual offenders, go to show that under certain conditions even hardened young offenders can develop into useful citizens.[1]

[1] See also W. Healy and A. F. Bronner, *Treatment and what Happened Afterwards*, Studies of the Judge Baker Foundation Centre, 1945.

The fact that a small number of young offenders have fundamentally changed their attitude towards society shows that the possibility of change exists. Perhaps it does not occur more often because the correct methods of treatment are not always adopted. Though at first the treatment of offenders had to be proceeded with by the trial and error method, to-day we are already able to discuss theoretically under what conditions such fundamental changes can occur. Only by doing so shall we be able to increase the number of successes and to decrease failures.

What scientific factors allow us to assume that character traits formed in early childhood may under certain conditions undergo a change?

PSYCHO-ANALYTICAL FINDINGS.

The psycho-analytical treatment of patients suffering from neurotic illness or character disturbances of various kinds showed that through the release of repressions and the bringing of unconscious conflicts into consciousness, the adult personality may undergo a profound change; neurotic symptoms will disappear by the resolution of fixation points and by progress in the formerly arrested libidinal development; undesirable character traits, built up as a defence mechanism against morbid anxiety, will disappear also.

The knowledge of the structure of the mind gained by the psycho-analytical method has enabled us to understand the causes of delinquent behaviour. The effect of psycho-analytical treatment shows that character traits, even if acquired in early life, can be modified.

The mental disturbance which results in antisocial behaviour is different from the disturbance which causes neurotic illness [1]: it is a failure of early education in its widest sense. If, therefore, the delinquent could be brought back to the dependence of the small child on an adult person, a process of re-education could perhaps undo the faulty character development.

Freud (16*b*) has been able to investigate a characteristic of the human mind which allows the re-establishment of former emotional relationships—of which the mother-child relationship is the most important and most intimate. This factor, which is of vital importance in the treatment of delinquency, can be readily observed as a phenomenon of our daily life.

Let us imagine that we are invited to listen to a lecture on

[1] Part II, Ch. V (*a*), p. 117.

an interesting subject by a well-known authority. According to our mental make-up we shall have differing attitudes towards the lecturer. We may be disposed to be friendly or critical, we may be inclined to agree or to disagree, and we shall feel these inclinations before the lecture has taken place. If we examine our own attitude more closely we shall find that we have similar expectations in similar situations. We shall find that our attitude towards people in authority is in the first place dictated by something in us and not in the other person.

THE TRANSFERENCE IN DAILY LIFE.

If we now imagine that we are magistrates and that the same lecturer is brought before us on the charge of exceeding the speed limit, our attitude might still be friendly, but it would be entirely different from that which we would adopt if we expected to meet the same man in a position of authority. It would now be the attitude which we usually adopt if we ourselves are in authority.

In trying to analyse our own behaviour towards the persons in our environment we shall therefore find that according to the situation in which we meet a given person for the first time we adopt an attitude which at first is based not on his personality, but rather on our own mental make-up. Moreover, we shall find that our attitude towards persons in authority may be similar to our attitude towards our teachers when we were young. We transfer to the persons in our environment certain emotional expectations which arise out of our own personal experiences, often going back to our childhood. If we are mentally healthy we quickly adjust our feelings to the real persons ; our relationships with various people in our environment may eventually be quite different from our first anticipations, and these first anticipations may pass almost unnoticed.

This transference of former emotional attitudes is more evident in neurotic people. A young scientist, for instance, had a number of unpleasant experiences. He went to work in a large concern and was at first very pleased with his new position. After a few weeks he began to have difficulties with his immediate superior. At first they were only slight, but after a short time he believed that this man was trying to wrest his scientific discoveries from him. The young man had no real grounds for his suspicions, but he felt them strongly enough to withhold important information from his superior. In the end he changed his job because the

TRANSFERENCE IN NEUROTICS.

situation had become too involved. We do not yet know whether the young man's suspicions were justified. But his previous history shows that he had had the same difficulty in three former jobs and that the story had constantly repeated itself. His suspicions always arose after a few weeks, with nothing concrete to substantiate them, and in the end the young man put himself in the wrong and conspired against his superiors behind their back. It would seem as if these situations had been created by the young man himself, and this is confirmed by the fact that his attitude towards his own father was very similar to that which he adopted towards all persons in authority, irrespective of their personality. It seems very unlikely that all these superiors should have behaved in exactly the same way towards the young man who, by the way, had not yet made the discovery of which he was afraid he might be robbed. We shall assume—and in this case the assumption was proved correct during psycho-analytical ,treatment—that this man transfers his old infantile conflicts with his father to persons in authority, irrespective of their appearance or their personality.

This example, which is by no means unusual, shows that in certain cases the transference of old emotional attitudes over-shadows the real relationship which may arise between two people. Needless to say this young man was entirely unaware that his relationship to his superiors was due to his own unconscious conflicts. The difference between this transference and that of mentally healthy people lies in the fact that no adjustment to the real personality has taken place, but that quite on the contrary, in the course of time, the real person of the superior has become in the young man's phantasy more and more like the person of his father.

TRANSFERENCE IN THE DELINQUENT.

The firmer the fixation of an individual to the objects of his early childhood, the more uniform will be his reaction to the people of his environment. We have seen that the delinquent never really becomes independent of his early family circle. We have explained in detail how Billy transferred his sado-masochistic relationship with his mother to his teachers, to the psychiatrist, in short, to all persons who represented authority for him, and to all his friends who were older than himself, while towards younger children he behaved as he felt his mother had behaved to him : he bullied them. It is therefore to be expected that delinquents, taken away from their home and put into an entirely different environment, will not be able to react immediately to the differences in personalities and will behave in the old manner to any person they meet. This is the invariable experience of foster-parents and institutions, and it explains many of the failures of social treatment. The author of *Branch Street* (29) describes very well the reaction of antisocial children towards adults who are in every way different from the people with whom they otherwise mixed : though these children had had many instances of the sincere friendliness of their wardens, they continued to regard them with suspicion, to hate them and to do their utmost to thwart their efforts. Aichhorn (2*b*) analyses in great detail the transference reactions of his aggressive group, which were rather unpleasant, and Wills (34) draws attention to the emotional outbursts of delinquent youths in a free environment.

So far the transference does not seem to be very helpful in the modification of antisocial behaviour. Quite the contrary : the fact that these offenders transfer their thwarted emotions to every other person in their environment seems to make the task of curing them even more complicated. In a way this is certainly true. The educator's good intentions towards these children, or the psychiatrist's wish to help them, will not impress them in the slightest degree, for more reasons than one. It is not only that their former disappointments have made them suspicious of every adult. We have seen that Billy's sado-masochistic relationship to his mother, the constant interchange of hostility from his side and punishment from hers, provided him with instinctive gratification. This kind of relationship was more gratifying to him than any other. To react in a friendly way to the friendly behaviour of adults is not attractive to the majority of delinquents.

DISADVANTAGE OF TRANSFERENCE.

ADVANTAGE OF TRANSFERENCE.

Yet this transference of infantile emotional attitudes, though it renders the first contact with the delinquent more complicated, in the long run makes treatment possible. We have shown [1] that the modification of the primary instinctive urges does not come about by imitation, but is made possible by the emotional relationship of the child towards the mother and later on the father. In every human being there is the urge to establish an object relationship, at first with the person who provides his physical care. We have seen how the wish to be loved by the mother

[1] Part I, Ch. V, p. 36.

and the fear of being left alone drive the child to give up instinctive gratification; and in the delinquent this aim has not been satisfactorily achieved. Though this primary urge towards an object relationship was present in the delinquent just as in the normal person, it was not employed by the mother so as to bring about a modification of instinctive urges. The person of the mother and her substitutes are therefore still necessary in order to give instinctive satisfaction on a low level of development. It is this distorted object relationship which the delinquent transfers to the persons of his environment. The wish to be loved and not to be left alone is still present, but is entirely overshadowed by the constant clamour for gratification, and if satisfaction is not forthcoming, open hatred is expressed.

As the transference reaction is based on the former mother relationship, it gives us the weapon with which we can attack and, by various methods, readjust the faulty character development. Without the establishment of this strong emotional relationship we should be utterly helpless. We have shown that the delinquent's Super-Ego, or his own moral code, is non-existent. Appeal to his better feelings can therefore have no effect; there is nothing to appeal to. His values are entirely different from ours. But his need for love and attention is present, though it is overshadowed by the distorted object-relationship.

Different forms of treatment can make different uses of the delinquent's emotional relationship to the persons of his environment, and the different methods, which have partly been tested by experience and can partly be reconstructed on a theoretical basis, will be discussed in detail later.

SUMMARY.

The factor, therefore, which explains the successful treatment of delinquents and which, if handled in a rational way, can increase the successes and diminish the failures, is to be seen in the automatic establishment of an emotional relationship to the persons of the environment. This emotional relationship is of an infantile character, and gives the educator the weapons which were once, during the early years of life, in the hand of the mother. This power has now to be used to bring about a modification of instinctive urges, an aim which was not achieved, this failure permitting the faulty character development.

CHAPTER IV

PSYCHOLOGICAL METHODS OF TREATMENT

(*a*) Introduction

Only in a minority of cases is psychological treatment without environmental adjustment the best method. The reason for our discussing it before the more widely-used method of environmental treatment is a purely technical one. When we have considered the factors which help to produce a cure by psychological treatment, the conditions necessary for a modification of behaviour in environmental treatment will emerge more clearly.

Psychological methods of treatment have been applied in some form or other since the days of Hippocrates. But their scientific application is an achievement of the last fifty years, and new methods are still being elaborated. The use of the various psychotherapeutic methods for the treatment of offenders is of still more recent date, and it will take many years of research to assess its full value. The results so far obtained justify neither the optimism which hopes to use these methods exclusively, nor the opposition to their application which is frequently expressed. Their full development is dependent on the provision of facilities which do not as yet exist to any great extent ; they will be provided only if the public is made aware of the problems involved. It therefore seems justifiable to discuss the various methods of psychotherapy in some detail and to show under what conditions they can be applied to the young offender.

The original application of psychological treatment was to the cure of neurotic illnesses in adult patients. There are two fundamentally different methods of approach.

(*b*) The Psycho-analytical Method

CATHARSIS.

Freud (8) began his investigations into the nature of hysteria by using the " cathartic method ". The patient was hypnotized, and in this condition of impaired consciousness, while *en rapport* with the doctor, was given the opportunity of abreacting some of his repressed emotional conflicts. In recent years this method has been revived as narco-analysis, helpful in cases of acute states of anxiety caused by traumatic experiences ; but the impairment of consciousness is no longer induced by hypnosis, but by the use of drugs, especially penthatol. Useful though this method is in combating acute mental distress caused by external experiences, Freud found its application rather limited in cases of chronic neurotic illness. It permitted the psychiatrist an insight into the patient's unconscious conflicts, but in a situation in which the patient himself was unaware of his revelations. In the state of normal consciousness the patient, when confronted with the conflicts which he had revealed under hypnosis, could not recognize them as his own, and though he may have achieved temporary relief from tension, there was no guarantee that new conflicts would not develop in the future.

Freud (16*a*) then found that it is possible for the trained observer to understand the unconscious processes underlying neurotic symptoms from the narratives of the patient, if certain conditions are observed. The patient is asked to express every thought which comes into his mind during the hour of analysis, including those ideas which in ordinary conversation he would suppress by reason of their unpleasantness or seeming irrelevancy. To permit greater concentration on the processes going on inside the mind, certain conditions were taken over from the hypnotic treatment. The patient lies on a couch and is asked to relax. To prevent his being guided in his associations by the expression on the face of the psycho-analyst, the doctor sits behind the patient. The theoretical background which allows us to use the patient's associations as material for building up the structure of the unconscious is to be seen in the theory of determinism. It is assumed that thoughts which follow each other are connected, and that the first thought has given rise to the second. Using this method of free association Freud made the further discovery that certain thoughts met with strong disapproval on the part of the patient and a resistance against their utterance. It proved necessary to remove this resistance by a slow process of interpretation before unconscious drives could be brought into consciousness. The analyst is aided in this process of making the unconscious conscious, or in removing the resistance against these instinctive drives—emanating from the Ego—by the state of increased suggestibility into which the patient is brought almost instantly when he begins treatment of this kind. In the psycho-analytic technique, suggestion is used only to help the patient to

FREE ASSOCIATION.

RÔLE OF SUGGESTION.

overcome his resistance against disclosing his thoughts, and to a certain degree in inducing him to consider an interpretation of such thoughts. It is not used to induce a belief in the analyst's interpretations ; even if a patient, especially at the beginning of treatment, takes every remark of the analyst's for gospel truth, this does not influence the unconscious to produce phenomena suggested by the analyst.

The fundamental process in psycho-analytical technique, therefore, is to bring into consciousness those unconscious drives or conflicts which have caused the neurotic illness, thus making possible a further process of modification of hitherto repressed instinctive drives. It has been explained how, under certain conditions, the infantile conflicts are repressed, and how in this way the economy of the psychological forces may be severely disturbed. The repressed instinctive urges strive for satisfaction and find it—in a disguised form—in neurotic symptoms.[1] The analytical process aims at a resolution of these repressions and allows therefore of a better disposal of psychic energy. By decreasing the severity of the Super-Ego some of the instinctive drives will find an outlet in direct gratification, while others will be modified by reaction formations and sublimations.

ANALYSIS VERSUS SYNTHESIS.

It has often been said that by the removal of repressions, antisocial instinctive urges would be allowed to come to the fore to the detriment of the personality and the patient's activities, and that therefore analysis should be followed by a process of synthesis. This process is envisaged as active help from the side of the analyst in building up a new pattern in the patient's life. Knowing the dynamic processes at work in analysis, it is clear that this second stage in the treatment is unnecessary. The danger of satisfying antisocial instincts is, as all experience goes to show, non-existent in the neurotic, whose Super-Ego is much more severe than that of the normal person. Owing to the inherent tendency of instinctive drives to strive for further development, the freeing of repressed urges leads by itself to further modification, that is to say to an increase in socially accepted activities. By the release of instinctive forces formerly repressed in the unconscious, the horizon of consciousness is enlarged and energy is freed for further sublimations. The intervention of the analyst at this stage would substantially interfere with the individual's freedom. The patient has to

[1] Part II, Ch. V (*b*).

build up his own life or to correct his former pattern of life in the way he thinks fit, and not in the way the analyst would wish. The analyst's task is finished when he has given the patient free access to his available psychic energy.

TRANSFERENCE.

The reluctance of the analyst to advise his patients is still further justified by the phenomenon of transference which plays an important part in psycho-analytical treatment. From the beginning of the treatment onwards the patient develops a relationship to the analyst—who purposely remains a shadowy figure in the background—which is coloured much more by the patient's former emotional relationships than by the analyst's actual personality. Under the special conditions of the psycho-analytical technique, this relationship develops more and more on the lines of the infantile pattern. The patient, for instance, expects his analyst to react in the same way as his father once did, and his attitude towards the analyst is more and more influenced by irrational motives. Within this emotional relationship old conflicts are revived and acted out during the hour of analysis. The analyst, by remaining aloof from any emotional entanglement, is able to demonstrate the character of this relationship to the patient and thus to show him his irrational attitudes in action. The patient's experience in the process of analysis is therefore first and foremost an emotional one. In contradistinction to other methods of psychological treatment, the transference is constantly made an object of investigation and should, towards the end of the treatment, be completely dissolved : the analyst should become once more an ordinary human being and not a father figure invested with magical powers, as he occasionally seems to the patient during the treatment. The fact that the analyst is envisaged during the various stages of treatment in entirely different lights makes it imperative that he should undertake no actual intervention in the patient's life.

CONDITIONS FOR TREATMENT.

This very brief summary of the forces at work in an analysis will enable us to draw some conclusions as to the necessary preconditions for successful treatment. The treatment is long and tedious. The patient has to come four to five times a week for a period of an hour. Longer intervals between the sessions would make the work of reducing the resistances almost impossible. The average length of an analytical treatment is two years, during which time a gradual process of readjustment takes place. Only a person suffering severely from neurotic symptoms will be willing and able to undergo such treatment ; only if the patient is at least of normal intelligence, of good ability and fairly young (preferably between 20 and 30 years of age) will it be worth while to undertake a treatment of this kind for the purpose of a cure. As psycho-analysis gives an increased insight not only into one's own mind but also into the working of the minds of other people, it is very often undertaken for the purpose of training for various professions. In such cases the decision will rest rather on the patient's intelligence and ability than on his age or symptoms.

SUITABLE CASES.

As already stated, psycho-analysis was originally devised for neurotics, for persons suffering from hysteria and obsessional neurosis. Soon other disturbances, such as inhibitions in one's profession, character difficulties, and so on were made the subject of analytical treatment with very good results. The attempt has occasionally been made to analyse psychotic patients, but although in chronic psychotic conditions the patient may in this way be helped to live outside an asylum, no cure has been achieved. The results of analysing so-called psychopathic personalities are inconclusive ; more often than not the condition remains unchanged. The results of psycho-analytical treatment in cases of sexual disturbances of all kinds will be discussed later.

PSYCHO-ANALYSIS OF DELINQUENTS.

Psycho-analysts soon noticed that the repressed desires and impulses of the neurotic were identical with the actions of criminals.[1] Similarities and dissimilarities between neurotic and delinquent reactions could only be ascertained by treatment. For many years selected offenders have been undergoing psycho-analytical treatment, although the number of cases still remains very small. The treatment is long, and the necessary external conditions rarely exist for the criminal. Reik (30), Staub and Alexander (5), and Alexander and Healy (4) have made valuable contributions by the psycho-analytical treatment of the adult offender ; Zulliger (35*a*, *b*) Schmiedeberg (31), and, mainly, Aichhorn (2) by treating young offenders. The scientific value of these contributions has not merely lain in ascertaining the possibility of psycho-analytical treatment and cure for the offender. By analysing an offender, the structure of his mind and the unconscious motivation of his antisocial behaviour could be understood even if a given case

[1] Introduction, Ch. III, p. 7.

could not be cured. This understanding of the unconscious forces which cause criminal behaviour is necessary if it is desired to create social conditions in which crime is less likely to occur, and to devise environmental methods of treatment by which the bulk of offenders can benefit. Even if it had been proved that psycho-analysis can cure all offenders, which is by no means the case, it would always be impossible in practice to analyse more than a very small percentage of them. As a method of research, therefore, the analytical treatment of offenders is invaluable as it is the only method which will reveal the conscious and unconscious factors of an individual's antisocial development.

ALEXANDER'S AND HEALY'S RESEARCH.

Alexander and Healy (4) in their work attempted to ascertain the therapeutic value of psycho-analysis for offenders. The experiment lasted only for ten months, a period too short to allow any patient to derive full benefit from the treatment. The majority of patients were treated during detention, with all the disadvantages inherent in prison atmosphere and the interference of the untrained and partly hostile prison personnel. The cases chosen were desperate ones, although young; recidivists who had already spent years unsuccessfully in reformatories and prisons. According to the classification put forward in this book, they belonged to the type described in Group I, (4) : individuals who in their daily life have to dramatize unconscious conflicts, and because of their antisocial character formation find relief in antisocial actions.

The results of this therapeutic experiment are encouraging if allowance is made for the fact that in no case could the treatment be finished, and that some of the patients left prison in a time of severe depression and unemployment. It is impossible to summarize the results, but in some cases which had been treated for some length of time distinct changes in character formation could be observed. As the book appeared two years after the treatment ended, no conclusions could be drawn as to their further career. It is, however, of great practical value that the authors were able to show that in the seven cases fully investigated, readjustments in their early life—undertaken by psycho-analytically trained social workers—could most probably have prevented the criminal career.

Generally speaking, amongst adult offenders those cases in which neurotic symptoms are most pronounced will not respond to environmental treatment but should be considered for psycho-analytical treatment. These are the cases classified under Group I (3) and (4) in our system[1]; a cure can be achieved only if the underlying unconscious conflicts are brought into consciousness and at the same time resolved. In cases of this kind, the Super-Ego is severe, though it may not control all instinctive urges. The patient, therefore, is suffering as a result of his abnormal behaviour and will be able to co-operate in the difficult process of psycho-analysis.

CASES SUITABLE FOR PSYCHO-ANALYTICAL TREATMENT.

Cases of this kind form a minority of the total number of offenders. For practical reasons it is at present impossible to treat even the comparatively small number of cases found suitable for psycho-analytical treatment, and untreatable by any other method. The number of trained psycho-analysts is small, and each of them is able to deal only with a very limited number of cases over a long period of time. The majority of offenders suitable for psycho-analytical treatment are unable to pay a fee, and so far no funds are available from official sources for this purpose. Psycho-analysts, therefore, are seldom in a position to take on more than one such case at a time, and treatment lasts for about two years. An even greater obstacle than the financial one is that of time. The offender's place of work is usually not very near to a specialist's consulting room, and working hours are long. It is imperative that a treatment which lasts over so long a period should not affect his working capacity, and often such cases, though otherwise suitable, cannot be advised to undergo treatment.

A further difficulty arises in the legal aspect of the case. The best chances for psycho-analytical treatment are met with in those cases where the offender is either dismissed or put on probation, and voluntarily comes for treatment, so that it is not a condition of probation. If the offender is sentenced to imprisonment, the chances of success after the sentence has been served are slender, especially in those cases where the underlying motive was an unconscious sense of guilt. Once this guilt feeling has been relieved by punishment the urge for treatment disappears —until the next offence is committed. For various reasons psycho-analytical treatment inside an institution is impossible under present prison conditions. Alexander and Healy (4) describe the difficulties presented by prison personnel and the

PSYCHO-ANALYSIS IN PRISON.

[1] Part II, Ch. IX, p. 186.

exceptional status of the prisoner under treatment, even though their investigation was undertaken as a research with the full co-operation of all the authorities. A patient undergoing psycho-analytical treatment should pursue his normal life and not be restricted in his activities. During detention in prison the patient is robbed of his activities and, what is more important, of his responsibilities. This situation in itself causes psychological changes. Usually regression takes place to the early phase of absolute dependence on the mother, and oral traits—such as increased emphasis on food and increased envy—and passive feminine traits in men appear and overshadow the original picture. Treatment will have to cease when the offender leaves prison and faces the most difficult problem of his readjustment to the outside world. Moreover, the discrepancy in values between ideas explained to the patient during a psycho-analytical treatment and the prison environment, with its emphasis on punishment, will make it impossible for the ordinary offender to solve his conflicts during detention.

For these reasons only a small number of those adult offenders for whom psycho-analytical treatment would be advisable can be treated. Whenever such an attempt has been made, notably that of Alexander and Healy, valuable results—of greater importance than the cure of a single offender—have been achieved.

Alexander and Healy (4) propose that more facilities should be given for the psycho-analytical treatment of a larger number of suitable cases under suitable conditions, and they stress the point that the expenditure involved would be amply justified, as criminal careers could be prevented. This suggestion seems a reasonable one, especially in the case of young offenders where the financial burden of a long criminal career is certainly much greater than the initial expense of psycho-analytical treatment.

Extension of facilities for psycho-analytical treatment would be particularly valuable if applied to young offenders classified under Group I, (4).[1] The majority of Alexander's and Healy's cases belonged to this group. As mentioned above,[2] such cases have been psychiatrically classified as the "predominantly inadequate" group of psychopathic personalities, and have been found unsuitable for environmental treatment. Most authors are inclined to emphasize constitutional factors as the basis of the disturbance. Our psycho-analytical experience, though not yet extensive, seems to show that the psychological basis of the

[1] Part II, Ch. IX, p. 186. [2] Ibid., Ch. V (c), (3), p. 139.

disturbance is of much greater importance than has hitherto been acknowledged.

A case of this kind has been described, though not analysed, by Abraham (1).

ABRAHAM'S CASE.

Abraham saw this man first at the age of 22 in a military hospital; he was accused of desertion, of wearing an officer's uniform, and of several fraudulent actions. During the examination it became apparent that X had started to lie at the age of 6, pretending to be of higher social standing than he actually was, and supporting his stories by frequent thefts which enabled him to pose as a rich boy. He had been to an approved school, where his conduct was excellent, and he was well liked owing to his superior intelligence and his charming manners. When released he continued his life of lies and frauds without interruption until he was examined. The prognosis was considered to be very bad, and X was sentenced to three years' imprisonment. When released in 1918, he continued his old life and committed several offences, for which he was brought before a civil court five years later. Then X himself asked for a psychiatric examination, contending that for the last four years he had led an entirely blameless life, and that the offences for which he was now to be punished were committed by him while still under his old compulsion.

Abraham saw him again and found to his astonishment that his allegations were perfectly correct. Not only had he discontinued his antisocial activities, but in the meantime he had managed to obtain and keep a responsible post with an important business firm, and his employers, who knew his former history, testified to his absolute honesty in money matters. Abraham describes in detail in his paper how this change in behaviour was brought about by a happy marriage, which for certain reasons connected with his early childhood history was able to effect a change in character formation. This case was the first instance of a lasting change in attitude in an "impostor type"

The description of this case represents a very important contribution to our psychological knowledge, since it was the first proof that behaviour of this kind can be altered and yields to treatment.

RONALD'S TREATMENT.

Ronald (Case 5)[1] was a similar type, and the psychological investigation—undertaken for a period of three months—gave an opportunity of

[1] Part II, Ch. V (*c*), 3, p. 140 ff.

studying the conditions under which treatment might be successful. While Ronald came for treatment he was still living at home, in the same environment which, as has been shown, was largely responsible for his abnormal development. The relationship to his mother remained the same as before, and she was incapable of co-operation. We have seen how the stealing and the subsequent " trial " provided Ronald with excitement and pleasure—the only instinctive pleasure he could gain. We have also described how Ronald was unable to come for treatment regularly as he could not bring himself to do anything which did not give immediate satisfaction. In such a case, psycho-analytical treatment could be successful only if satisfaction of the morbid desire—to steal and to be found out—were not forthcoming. Under the existing conditions this could be prevented only during the analytical session, and Ronald was most disappointed when I did not try to find him out or to argue with him. But the treatment lasted for one hour each day, and during the other 23 hours, except when he was asleep, he could get as much abnormal satisfaction as he chose. There was not one person in his environment whom he could not provoke into arguing ; first and foremost his mother. It was apparent that Ronald could not be cured under the existing environmental conditions. He was not unhappy ; he had rationalized his desire to steal by building up an ideal figure of a " crook " whom he wished to resemble. There was no means of inducing him to come for treatment regularly, as he could not be brought against his will, and his mother was very willing to lie for him if he stayed away. On the other hand, no environmental change alone would have had the slightest effect on him. He had been to four different types of boarding-school, from the most progressive to the more conservative, without the slightest effect—he did not stay anywhere for more than about two terms. If he had been sent to Borstal his conduct there would probably have been excellent—and his behaviour when leaving quite unchanged. Wills (34) quotes a case very similar to Ronald's whom he could not keep in Hawkspur Camp and who, he believes, was acting under a compulsion.

PROPOSED CONDITIONS OF TREATMENT.

Such cases should be sent to a place like Q camp, where the general atmosphere is one of freedom and understanding. In such an environment it would be possible to frustrate Ronald's morbid desires : nobody would be inclined to find him out and argue with him. This would put a boy of that kind into a very disagreeable psychological position : he would no longer get the accustomed instinctive gratification. In such an environment psycho-analytical treatment might be successful. Under the pressure of instinctive frustration and the resulting dissatisfaction and tension, the urge to satisfy his desires in more socially adapted ways would become stronger, and so create the wish to understand and to modify his old behaviour. Unfortunately facilities are not yet available for the combination of environmental with psycho-analytical treatment. Experimental institutions are usually some distance away from large towns, and never have the funds to provide even the daily fares. Although some boys living in Hawkspur Camp could come for psychotherapeutic treatment to London once a week or once a fortnight, this would not have helped in a case like Ronald's or Roland Leaf's (34). Only continuous, daily treatment could cope with the tensions and dissatisfactions arising every minute of the day and trace them back to their original source. A week's interval would seriously interfere with the continuity of treatment. Such boys are constantly compelled to act out and to dramatize their unconscious conflicts. Every item of these dramatizations must be known to the analyst, so as to enable him to understand it and to transmit this understanding to the patient. The development and analysis of the transference would also be quite impossible in weekly interviews. It will be difficult to create a situation in which this combination of treatment is possible, but " difficult " does not mean " impossible ".

To have a psycho-analyst attached to an institution of this kind would not be a good plan. Wills (34) describes the difficulty of transference in a free environment, and he too believes that treatment inside the institution would considerably complicate matters. The solution would be an institution or hostel close to a town to which individual offenders could be sent daily for treatment, and close co-operation maintained between the analyst and the staff. Aichhorn (24) came to the conclusion after many years of experience that for young offenders whose neurotic conflicts did not allow them to readjust their lives by means of re-education alone, a treatment in two stages would be advisable. The first stage should be a process of re-education which would include a strengthening of the Super-Ego. At first, absence of suffering, their inability to endure delay and their utter unreliability would

AICHHORN'S PROPOSALS.

make psycho-analytic treatment of these youths impossible. If re-education succeeds the picture changes. The antisocial youth becomes more and more neurotic, begins to suffer from his symptoms and to gain some insight into his own disturbances. At this stage psycho-analytic treatment could begin and should result in a solution of the conflicts.

DIFFERENCES IN TECHNIQUE.

In discussing psycho-analytical treatment of the young offender, a slight difference in technique from that used for the neurotic adult has already been indicated. We have said that in Ronald's case the analyst would have to keep close contact with the staff of the institution, to learn details of the boy's behaviour there and to advise the staff step by step as to the form their educational efforts should take. In the analysis of adult neurotics, the analyst is in contact with the patient alone and strictly avoids getting any outside information or advising the patient or his relatives about their actions. This difference of technique, which is taken over from the technique of child analysis as described by Anna Freud (15), is necessary on account of the incomplete development of the Super-Ego and the disturbance in Ego-development; the young offender is psychologically more like a child than an adult. These characteristics make psycho-analytical treatment very difficult and often impossible unless the environment is changed.

PSYCHO-ANALYSIS OF DELINQUENT CHILDREN.

With offenders between the ages of 7 and 10, psycho-analytical treatment promises to be successful, and it is necessary in cases where other methods are ineffective on account of the depth of the disturbance. In children of that age the structure of the personality is not completed, and analysis proceeds with a different technique from that of the adult patient, making use of the active co-operation of the mother in bringing the child for treatment and often in adapting her educational efforts to the stage of the analysis. There are of course differences in the psychological make-up of the neurotic and of the antisocial child, which also necessitates slight changes in technique.

BILLY'S TREATMENT.

Billy (Case 1) was analysed for a period of two years. The psychological foundation of his disturbance has been described.[1]

The first step towards a change of behaviour occurred when Billy understood that his aggressive behaviour was a defence against his fear of being weak and feminine. The analysis of

[1] Part II, Ch. I, p. 84 ff.

Billy's fighting phantasy led in time to a relief of anxiety and opened the way for progress in libidinal development from the anal-sadistic to the phallic level. Hand in hand with the analysis of the instinctive urges went the analysis of his character disturbance. We have described how Billy could not stand any unpleasantness and how this failure of his Ego to adopt the reality-principle led to his antisocial behaviour. After 18 months of treatment, Billy one day remarked that he should not have stayed out late the night before, as then he would not have had to stay in to-day. This forethought, which we expect to find in children of 5, was the first sign in Billy's case that the urge of the moment had begun to give way to consideration for the future. This was possible only because the strength of instinctive urges had declined and Billy was now able to bear some tension. From that time onward his attitude in school fundamentally altered. He did not play truant any more, he could now learn, being able to admit failure and to stand disappointment, and his interest in school subjects increased in proportion as instinctive energy became free for sublimation. Shortly afterwards he developed a very positive relationship to the mother's friend, the father having left the home about half a year previously. He wanted to become an engineer like this man, and therefore became rather keen on learning to read and write, mastering this in a short time. He began to save money and ceased extracting it as a bribe from the members of the household. He made friends in school, a sure sign that his relationship to other boys no longer consisted in bullying and being bullied. He was still not a model boy when treatment ended, but he had succeeded in adapting himself to the reality principle and in developing an independent Super-Ego. This was first indicated by his identification with the mother's friend, who represented for him a better father figure than his real father. With this difference in character structure, normal methods of education will succeed in shaping his further development.

PSYCHO-ANALYSIS VERSUS ENVIRONMENTAL METHODS.

Although the psycho-analytical treatment succeeded in clearing up the faulty character development in this case, it might be asked whether the same result could not have been achieved by different methods. This is of course very difficult to assess, as it is impossible to let the same boy undergo two different kinds of treatment. No outside influence such as supervision by a probation officer could possibly have had the slightest effect on Billy's development. The mother was entirely uncoöperative and quite unable to modify her attitude towards the boy. This presented a severe obstacle during the analytical treatment, and could only be counteracted by seeing the boy regularly every day and by keeping the mother at least superficially friendly during the whole period of treatment. The mother's tendency to use the analyst as a bogy could not upset the treatment, as the boy's experience during the analytical session was such that it lessened his anxiety. The probation officer, by seeing the boy once a fortnight, would never have been able to gain his confidence. But it is likely that if the boy had been removed from home to a suitable foster-home or boarding-school specially adapted to difficult children, where he would have had the possibility of attaching himself to some person or other on the staff, he might have been able in the course of some years to achieve a similar change in character development, though his neurotic conflicts, as for instance his passive feminine attitude, would have remained unchanged. Such a measure would have made a separation from his mother necessary, and would have been a severe shock. On the other hand, it was this relationship which made it so impossible for Billy to adjust himself to the needs of school life and to the outside world in general.

Looking back on Ronald's childhood history, it seems probable that an analysis at the age of 7, at the time when he had just started his antisocial activities, might have been successful and thus have prevented the practical certainty of a criminal career.

Psycho-analytical treatment is no exception to the rule that the earlier antisocial behaviour can be checked, the more certainty there is of success. For many reasons only a small number of cases can be analysed. Wherever there is a possibility of this extensive treatment for children between the ages of 7 and 10, cases should be selected in which antisocial behaviour has a compulsory character and where the environment is not such that it would fully explain the aberrant behaviour, at any rate at first sight. Intelligence must be good and abilities satisfactory, even if school attainments are very poor.

Summary

Psycho-analytical treatment of offenders of all ages offers a unique opportunity of studying in detail the psychological foundation of antisocial behaviour and the interaction of environmental and constitutional factors in bringing about the typical character formation. In order to use this method, not only as a means of research but for the purpose of cure, cases have to be carefully selected. The best prospects of success are probably with children between the ages of 7 and 10, to whom the method of child analysis can be applied. Environmental conditions have to be such that the regular attendance of the child over a long period of time is guaranteed. Only very selected cases of young offenders, notably those of the "impostor" type, should be chosen for an attempt at psycho-analysis at puberty; the environment has to be such that the acting out in daily life can remain under the control of the analyst. Otherwise puberty is not a suitable age for psycho-analytical treatment. Among adult offenders, those in whom the neurotic basis of antisocial behaviour is more pronounced than the antisocial character, especially cases of true kleptomania and cases with an unconscious sense of guilt which acts as a driving force, should be selected. At the present stage of our knowledge, such cases could be diagnosed and selected for treatment at the time of the first investigation. Psycho-analytical treatment should then be advised in the first place and before any other methods have been tried and failed. Otherwise the chances of treatment are considerably lessened.

In all cases selected for psycho-analytical treatment intelligence and abilities should be average, not only because this facilitates treatment, but also because such people can later become valuable citizens. The justification for undertaking such a long and tedious treatment with one offender lies in its value for research; moreover, these selected cases do not usually respond to any other method of treatment. The choice, therefore, is not between a longer or shorter method of treatment, but between a criminal career and a possible cure.

(*c*) Psychotherapeutic Methods

FUNDAMENTAL DIFFERENCE BETWEEN PSYCHO-ANALYSIS AND PSYCHO-THERAPY.

The aim of psychotherapy is to bring about the disappearance of symptoms by pushing the conflict back into the unconscious, in contrast to that of psycho-analysis, which is to bring the unconscious conflict to light. If we take as an example a patient who suffers from a hysterical symptom, for instance a functional paralysis of a limb, psycho-analysis would aim at a complete disclosure of the nature of the repressed instinctive urge which has made its appearance in this symbolic form, and a disclosure of the forces emanating from the Ego which have kept this instinct in repression. In this way psycho-analysis not only achieves relief from the one symptom, but also prevents the development of new hysterical symptoms at a later date. Psychotherapy, in contrast, would aim at driving the instinctive urge beginning to find a way to action in the hysterical symptom, back into unconsciousness. The means by which this can be achieved are manifold. Abreaction in hypnosis or under the influence of drugs would lead to a withdrawal of emotion from the conflict and thus allow it to disappear again into the unconscious. Suggestion under hypnosis or suggestion and persuasion with the waking patient aims at a strengthening of the Ego and with it of the repressing forces, and may thereby lead to a disappearance of the symptom. The advantage of this method as compared with analytical treatment, is its brevity, its disadvantage that it is not successful in chronic neurotic cases, as for instance obsessional neurosis, and that it does not prevent the development of new symptoms. On the other hand, it is a very valuable method in cases of minor disturbances, and in an out-patient department, for instance, these by far outnumber the major neuroses. Shortly before and especially during the Second World War a new method of psychotherapy has been developed, or rather a very old method of influencing people has been put to scientific use. In hospitals, especially in rehabilitation centres, group psychotherapy has proved valuable in influencing not one, but a number of patients at the same time. This is made possible by effecting changes in the Super-Ego, under the condition of group formation.[1] The evaluation of this method, which may be even more potent in its effects than individual psychotherapy, is still in flux.

GROUP-THERAPY

TRANSFERENCE.

As psychotherapy and psycho-analysis have different aims, they handle the transference situation in different ways. Its development at the beginning of treatment is in no way different. But in psychotherapy the patient is not made aware of the nature of his relationship to the psychiatrist. The state of increased suggestibility is used for inducing the patient to believe the psychiatrist's theories about the nature of his disturbance and for making him consent to change his behaviour. The transference, therefore, is not analysed, but it is the most potent weapon in the fight against the

[1] Part I, Ch. IX, p. 58.

patient's morbid beliefs. During the later stages of the treatment it does not come into the open as in psycho-analysis, either in its positive or its negative form—if the psychotherapist is skilful in handling the patient.

It is not intended in this book to give more details about the employment of psychotherapeutic methods with the neurotic patient. The brief and over-schematic description we have given is meant only as an introduction to the use of psychotherapy in treating delinquents.

PSYCHOTHERAPY WITH ADULT OFFENDERS.

The results of psychotherapy with adult offenders are very difficult to assess. The treatment is undertaken in very varying situations and the type of case to which it is applied is not always clearly defined. East and Hubert (14) give a report of their four-year investigation on the psychological treatment of crime in prisons. So far as their adult group is concerned, probable successes have been achieved with offenders who co-operated well, who were intelligent and who, so far as can be judged, belonged to Group I (2) in our classification : offenders whose antisocial character formation becomes manifest under the stress of unconscious conflicts or adverse environmental circumstances. The investigation was not undertaken with the purpose of defining certain types, and it is difficult to be certain of its conclusions ; the case-histories of the offenders treated are given in fuller detail and the psychological foundation of the antisocial behaviour is clearer than in those cases which were seen only once. Co-operation on the part of the offender is of course essential if psychotherapy is to succeed ; but it is open to doubt whether the same type of offender would not show a higher degree of co-operation if treated while under probation. Although East and Hubert are justified in warning us against excessive optimism, certain types among the early recidivists, the group to which all the offenders treated belonged, responded well to psychotherapy while in prison. As Mullins (27) states in his criticism of the Report, the result is biased because cases of psychotic or organic disturbances are cited among the unsuitable cases. The authors' object probably was to counteract the belief that every offender can be cured by psychotherapy. But no psychiatrist has ever suggested this ; it has always been maintained that cases selected for psychotherapy must first be diagnosed and investigated to ensure their suitability. It is for this reason that other statistics,

[1] Quoted by Mullins (27).

such as those of the Tavistock Clinic [1] and the I.S.T.D. (18) show a much larger percentage of cures; it has to be borne in mind that results achieved in prison and out of prison can in no way be compared. In the report of the Tavistock Clinic, 58 per cent. of adult cases were reported as "relieved" three years after conclusion of treatment. Statistics are very difficult to interpret unless full details are available as to the types of cases treated, the length of treatment and the technique adopted. Applying all necessary precautions, Glover (interpreting the results at the I.S.T.D.) gives the figure of cures as 32 per cent., allowing for a 20 per cent. margin of spontaneous recoveries. These figures are sufficient proof that psychotherapy can achieve good results with selected cases of offenders.

DIFFERENCE IN TREATMENT WITH NEUROTICS AND DELINQUENTS.

There is one fundamental difference between psychotherapeutic treatment of offenders and that of neurotic patients. In the former case psychotherapy is almost invariably applied in conjunction with environmental methods. The exceptional situation created by imprisonment has already been mentioned.[1] Cases treated in freedom are usually on probation, and the influence of the probation officer will make itself felt in various ways. Quite apart from these penal methods, however, in clinics specially adapted to the treatment of delinquents, as in the I.S.T.D. or in Healy's Clinic in America, very few cases are dealt with solely by the psychiatrist. The psychiatric social worker has usually direct contact with the patient and tries to effect such environmental changes as are thought desirable. As Glover (18) states:

> Moreover, it has been proved up to the hilt, that the problem of delinquency is a highly specialized problem, calling for special organizations (Institutes, Clinics, etc.) special forms of training and special techniques of treatment. In a word, delinquency work constitutes a new medico-psychological "speciality".

This is true for the adult offender, but it is even more important in assessing the results of psychotherapy in the young offender and child. The only cases which can be excepted from this contention are those of sexual offenders, which will be discussed in a later chapter.

It is very important to realize this difference in technique. Psychiatrists who happen to see delinquent cases in their practice or in an out-patient department remark on the impossibility of

[1] Part III, Ch. IV (*b*), p. 212.

treating them on account of their unreliability and unresponsiveness. The same remarks are often made by psychiatrists and social workers at child guidance clinics not specially adapted to the treatment of delinquents. The difference in character formation has been amply described in previous chapters. The technique of treatment must take account of this difference, otherwise it will be unsuccessful. So far as their unconscious conflicts are concerned there is no difference between the two groups of cases : but the means of expressing these difficulties are entirely different. The unreliability which springs from the dominance of the pleasure-principle and the faulty development of the Super-Ego must be counteracted either by environmental changes—which are apt to bring about a modification of character—or by a long preparation for treatment. The delinquent usually does not suffer, and it will take some time to make him realize that his conduct is damaging himself and not society, and that this conduct is not under his conscious control. In the neurotic the conflict is internalized ; the tension between the instinctive desires and the severe Super-Ego has to be lessened. The environment which may originally have caused the development of a neurotic illness is no longer the paramount factor, and a change in this environment will very rarely have a beneficial effect on the neurotic illness. In the delinquent, the conflict is still between the desires and the outside world. Certain changes in the environment are therefore bound to bring about a modification of behaviour by influencing the character formation. In so far as unconscious conflicts are concerned the same holds good for the delinquent as for the neurotic. In treating the delinquent as if he were a neurotic he is given a responsibility for his reactions which he is unable to bear. In the delinquent with neurotic conflicts, both the antisocial character formation and the neurotic conflicts have to be treated, and the treatment for these disturbances is not the same. Even in those cases in which the neurotic conflicts have to be treated, slight variations from the usual technique employed with neurotics are indicated.

PETER'S TREATMENT.

In Peter's case (Case 4) only very few interviews were possible, for various external reasons, though these were influenced by the uncoöperative attitude of the father. The problem had become clear during the investigation : puberty conflicts were increased by the situation at home, and an antisocial character formation led to their expression in a delinquent act. Treatment had to succeed in making Peter realize his hostility towards the father and decreasing his feelings of guilt. The true reason for his aggression could of course not be explained during a few interviews, therefore an indirect method had to be used. By taking Peter's side in his complaints against the father and by emphasizing his right to have his own opinions we gave the boy emotional relief. Added to this were occasional remarks about the normality of rebellion against the father in a boy of his age which were apt to increase insight into his emotional condition.

But in Peter's case these few interviews were not sufficient. The home environment had to be modified as well, as otherwise the tension would not have been sufficiently relieved. Two interviews with the father succeeded in undermining his sternness towards the boy to a certain degree and making him realize that his anger with the boy was really a reaction to Peter's hidden aggression. This realization and the further explanation of the normality of this reaction at puberty helped the father slightly to modify his attitude. In the meantime the psychiatric social worker had interviewed the mother and explained to her the necessity for the boy's becoming more independent of her physical care and attention. No great change in attitude can be expected from a few interviews of that kind but they often help to ease a tense atmosphere at home. This is what occurred in Peter's case, and after a few weeks it was reported that his moodiness had entirely disappeared, that he seemed much more settled and that he enjoyed the work he was doing, had not been late and never stayed away. No further delinquent act was committed during the next six months, which of course is much too short a time for assessing the result. The change of mood, however, indicates that the conflicts had at least receded into the background. If Peter had been neurotic no interference with the home environment would have been necessary ; the given explanation might or might not have helped him, but changes in the environment would not at all have affected the internalized conflict.

COMBINATION OF PSYCHOTHERAPY AND CHANGES IN ENVIRONMENT.

This combination of psychotherapeutic treatment of the offender with environmental treatment, either by modifying the parents' behaviour or by finding a new environment altogether, has been extensively employed by Healy (20*b*). It is the method used at the I.S.T.D., though the relationship between the extent of psychotherapy and environmental measures varies from case to case. Details about environmental treatment will be discussed later. It might be argued that the results would perhaps be equally good if environmental treatment only were to be adopted and that positive results may be due to the environmental change and not to psychotherapy. But without the psychotherapeutic effort it would have been impossible to bring about the environmental change : the knowledge of the home influences very often emerges only during the course of treatment.

To sum up : cases especially suitable for psychotherapeutic treatment are those classified in Group I (2). The conflict which has caused the delinquent reaction is usually not very difficult to unearth. It has then to be considered which aspect of the conflict is nearest to consciousness and in what way one can succeed in strengthening the offender's resistance to his instinctive urges. Very often the understanding and impartial attitude of the psychiatrist helps to relieve feelings of guilt. The severity of the faulty character development has to be assessed and environmental treatment has to be instituted accordingly. Some cases belonging to Group I (3) can also be dealt with in this way, if the disturbance is not of too long standing and not too severe. The chances of success are of course much greater if the offender is young and his delinquent behaviour has only just begun.

In clinics adapted to delinquency work, a combination of environmental and psychotherapeutic method is used. This method, which is only in its infancy and still awaits further elaboration, promises much better results than could be achieved by either method alone.

(*d*) The Treatment of Sexual Offenders

RICHARD'S TREATMENT.

Richard (Case 9) [1] was first seen at the age of 18, a year after he had committed his last offence. The difficulty which induced the probation officer to seek our help was not another sexual offence, but his absence from work and running away from home. Since the age of 13, at which Richard committed his first offence, he had had various forms of treatment with varying results. First he was put on probation ; this did not prevent him from attacking a girl once more after half a year. The three years of approved school life also did not influence his sexual inclinations, nor did the brief psychotherapeutic treatment for which he was sent from

[1] Part II, Ch. VII (*a*), p. 165 ff.

the approved school after he had again committed a sexual offence. During this treatment Richard's only concern was to provoke the doctor to prohibit his masturbation. It may be assumed that the psychiatrist did not do so, but he apparently failed to relieve the boy's feelings of guilt, for otherwise Richard could not have succeeded in ceasing to masturbate during the period of treatment. It is not a sign of success if psychotherapeutic treatment leads to the giving up of masturbation at the age of 15. We have already said [1] that for a boy of that age masturbation is the most normal sexual outlet. Richard's sexual offences, as we saw during the psycho-analytical treatment, were a sign of his fight against masturbation ; this perverse sexual activity seemed to him less forbidden than the auto-erotic one, and the constant suppression of his sexual urges led to the sudden outbreaks of the desire to look at a girl's genitals. This wish was intimately connected with his fears about masturbation. He thought that his genitals had been damaged by this activity and, as a small boy, was confirmed in this idea by observing his little sister. He succeeded in completely repressing this unpleasant memory, and what remained was a doubt : what do girls look like ? He unconsciously wished to deny the anatomical difference in sex in order to mitigate his fear of castration.

THE UNCONSCIOUS SEXUAL CONFLICT.

As in the case of Billy, the boy's strong fear of castration had led to an identification with his mother and a passive attitude towards his father. Out of this wish to gain the love of the father arose the desire to be like a girl ; this wish was strengthened by the father's devotion to the little sister, so that the loss of the penis was in phantasy pleasurable as well as frightening. Both attitudes, the fear of losing the penis and the desire to do so, existed together in the unconscious. What emerged into consciousness was a strong sexual desire to see a girl's genitals, and this wish broke out in action on the various occasions mentioned. If, at the age of 15, for practical reasons only psychotherapeutic and not psycho-analytical treatment was possible, the line to be taken by the psychiatrist would have been clear if the underlying motives had been taken into account. The fear of masturbating was conscious, and the dangers which he feared had to be minimized. Intellectual explanations cannot do away with unconscious conflicts. But they might have achieved a certain relief from anxiety, especially if the boy had a good transference to the

[1] Part I, Ch. X, p. 64.

psychiatrist. It will emotionally impress a boy of that age if a man in authority, a father figure, gives him permission to do something which he believes the father had once forbidden under the threat of castration. If psychotherapy at that age had succeeded in this aim the boy would have continued to masturbate with fewer feelings of guilt. This would have led to a decrease of tension and dissatisfaction and might have resulted in a cure : at puberty the masculine tendencies are strengthened by the maturation of the sexual organs, and at this stage the passive tendencies may spontaneously recede into the background—if the fear of being a man is not too strong. In Richard's case psychotherapy did not succeed in lessening his fear of being a man, perhaps because it was too strong and too deeply repressed. He committed two more sexual offences, the latter of which took a different form, namely that of exposing himself. In the intervening years the faulty development led to the formation of a perversion. If a girl is shocked by seeing his genitals he can convince himself that he is a man. We have described [1] how the component instincts of looking and being looked at are present in the pregenital stages of development of the sexual instinct, and owing to Richard's strong fear of castration the libido had regressed to that earlier stage.

THE FIRST PSYCHOTHERAPEUTIC ATTEMPT.

THE SECOND PSYCHOTHERAPEUTIC ATTEMPT.

At this stage he had a further course of psychotherapy which did succeed in lessening his fears. He had a very good transference to the psychiatrist who saw him while he was under detention awaiting trial. It relieved him when the psychiatrist understood his wish to see a girl's genitals and when he learned that masturbation at his age was normal. His desire to see and to exhibit himself lost its strength ; but the energy behind it did not at once flow into the right channels, namely those strengthening his masculine desires. He made some attempts at contact with girls, but he was not successful. He believed that he was uninterested in girls, but on closer examination it was clear that he was afraid of them. He now became very fond of his sister and wanted her to go out with him all the time. He could not yet turn his desires away from his first love objects, but the nature of the desire had changed ; it was centred on the possession of the love object and no longer on looking and being looked at—which indicates that his libidinal development

[1] Part I, Ch. III.

had progressed. At the same time he developed an obsession : he had to go to the pictures nearly every day, sometimes twice a day. He wrote down in a diary all the films he wanted to see and the picture houses he had to inspect, and he could not bear to be thwarted in this desire. Therefore he had to stay away from work occasionally. This preoccupation with films was the first step towards sublimating his desire to look : not a very successful sublimation, as his craving for films overshadowed all his other activities and in the end got him into trouble once more. The obsessional character of this otherwise normal desire is explained by the fact that the instinctive drive behind it was much too strong and was still too closely related to the former sexual aim. Richard's work at that time was so uncongenial to him that he could not sublimate his instinctive drives by increasing his interest in it : on leaving the approved school he was given manual work in a factory. He was specially unskilful with his hands and hated occupations of this kind. Nevertheless he stayed in this job for nearly three years. After he had played truant he had a row with his foreman—the first difficulty he had ever had with any man in authority. He then stayed away altogether and had the experiences already described.[1] His desire to have intercourse with a woman became conscious to him, but he was too fearful to carry it out. So he wanted to go into the Navy, and thus testify to himself and to the outside world that he really was a man.

THE FIRST INDICATION OF SUBLIMATION.

It was at this stage that the case was investigated and the decision made that he should be analysed. The treatment could not start at once, as it was necessary to make arrangements which would give a guarantee of at least some months' treatment without interruption. The psychiatric social worker got in touch with the probation officer so as to arrange for more suitable work. The probation officer was very much in favour of Richard's idea of joining the Army, as he thought that strict discipline would do him good. This idea of the beneficial effect of discipline dies hard. In Richard's case it was easy to see that there had been much too much discipline all along, and that army life, far from making him more manly, would probably have increased his passive tendencies and fostered homosexual trends. After all, the Army is not intended as a place of treatment for sexual disturbances.

THE PSYCHO-ANALYTICAL TREATMENT.

[1] Part II, Ch. VII (*a*), p. 166.

So the co-operation of the probation officer had to be won over to make possible a plan which had suggested itself during the psychiatric investigation and which was based on Richard's attempts to sublimate his desire to look. The boy was very clever, and interested in intellectual subjects, and by training him to be a librarian his wish to see could be satisfied in a social activity of higher value than that of going to the pictures. At the same time the psychiatric social worker made contact with Richard's parents. The home was an exceptionally good one. It was significant that the father, though clever, was rather quiet and passive, while the mother was much more active and was the leading personality in the house. Both parents had a good relationship with the boy, and had been wholeheartedly opposed to his being sent to an approved school at the age of 14. They thought at the time that the boy needed treatment and were very glad that he was now given the opportunity to receive it. The treatment began when Richard had been working in a library for about a fortnight. The sexual disturbance as it came to light step by step during the treatment has been described above.

The most striking fact in Richard's attitude at the beginning of treatment was his entire lack of hostility towards the authorities who, as Richard now knew, had wrongly decided to send him to an approved school and had thereby taken away his chance of a secondary-school education. He felt no anger at his having been given a job which he detested and for which he was unsuited.

UNCONSCIOUS SENSE OF GUILT.

Moreover, it became clear that all his offences had been committed in so clumsy a way that he could not but be caught. Again Richard tried to gain help in ceasing to masturbate. The realization of his feelings of guilt led to the uncovering of his sexual games with his sister between 8 and 10 years, and then to the time of his sister's birth ; some of his Oedipal desires could be analysed. After this phase of analysis he felt the wish to have some contact with girls, and he became aware of his fear of having any sexual desires towards them. Formerly, he had rationalized this fear by a very severe ethical code. This boy, who for his precocious sexual behaviour had been three times before a court, and had been sent to an approved school, thought that it was wrong to kiss a girl before marriage and that to have such "improper" thoughts was immoral. The analysis of his mother-relationship gave him more freedom in his attitude towards girls, and he made friends with a number of girls belonging to his church club, girls whom he could take home and who could share his intellectual interests. Richard in the meantime had settled down very well in his work and was given more responsible jobs. He was extremely interested in books, and his greatest pleasure was to look over them, and to read a great deal so that he could advise the public. After three months of treatment his compulsion to go to the pictures had entirely disappeared. He was still fond of going to the cinema, but was quite satisfied if he could do so about once a week, and he did not mind giving it up altogether in order to go to evening classes.

After six months the treatment came to an end. It became increasingly difficult for Richard to attend, on account of an extension of his working hours. Though his passive tendencies could not be fully analysed, he had made sufficient progress to give ground for the hope that his sexual abnormality had been cured. His phantasies and desires towards girls were entirely normal, and it was due to his social environment that he did not dare to have a sexual relationship with a girl of his own social class. The successful sublimation of his desire to look in his work as librarian guaranteed the cessation of his abnormal sexual desires. His father stated that the boy was entirely different at home: his irritability and moods had given way to a cheerful attitude towards life, he was ambitious, and seemed to the parents very normal for a boy of his age. Two years after treatment ceased Richard still held his post in the library and was on the way to taking his matriculation examination. He had built up a social life of his own around his church club of which he was an active member. He had become a member of the Youth Hostels Association and had organized cycling parties amongst his boy and girl friends. He had never since had the impulse to exhibit himself or to look at little girls. Richard may be considered as cured of his perverse sexual activity. Whether he will be able to have a satisfactory sex life is not so certain. But he will be given the opportunity of continuing his treatment if he should later on discover a disturbance of his potency.

EFFECT OF TREATMENT.

The treatment of Richard has been described in such detail in order to demonstrate that environmental methods of treatment cannot modify a sexual disturbance. Even the fact that Richard at the age of 18 had the opportunity of being treated cannot extinguish the irreparable damage inflicted on his intellectual and character development. He lost the chance of the education which his superior intelligence warranted ; he will never be able to live down his court record, and this stigma was inflicted upon him without serving any remedial purpose. If a boy of 13 is caught trying to take down a little girl's knickers, it would be "common sense" even for the layman not to be astonished. After all, magistrates will probably remember their own school-days when other boys may have boasted about their exploits in that direction without having been caught and punished for their misdeeds. It is difficult to imagine what was the theoretical idea behind the decision of the court. How could a probation officer prevent a repetition of a sexual offence? Did it not strike the magistrate at the second court appearance that the boy had an excellent home, very understanding parents, and that his conduct in school and at home was irreproachable? That there were no antisocial activities of any kind, nothing, in short, in the behaviour of the boy which could be disciplined in an approved school? Was the idea perhaps that the boy should be denied the sight of a girl? It is difficult to understand the Court's decision from any point of view except that of punishment ; and the boy's feelings of guilt were certainly satisfied by this attitude : but it led to the development of a perversion. It is hard to see any difference between the official management of his case and the case of a doctor who fails to diagnose a malignant tumour.

PSYCHIATRIC INVESTIGATION AND TREATMENT FOR ALL SEXUAL OFFENDERS.

Richard's history at puberty is the typical story of the later "incorrigible rogue". Given a different character development, with more overt aggression and a less stable home background, this treatment by the authorities might have induced the boy to become a rebel and to refuse social adaptation altogether. Probably such a history will convince the public and the authorities more than would any theoretical explanation that all cases of sexual offences belong to the domain of the psychiatrist and not to that of penal methods, and that from the very beginning. East and Hubert (13) maintain that only a percentage of sexual offenders respond to psychological treatment. This may be due to the fact that their material consists of the prison population, of sexual offenders who have already been punished repeatedly and who are seen in a situation where their guilty feelings are completely relieved by punishment. In contrast to this, Mullins (27) quotes mostly cases of sexual offenders as having responded well to psychological treatment. East (13*b*) maintains that a number of sexual offenders, after being in prison once, do not make a second appearance in court. This in itself does not show that detention in prison had any beneficial effect on the sexual abnormality, or that the same effect could not have been achieved with less damage to the offender and less cost to the community. Sexual offenders very often suffer from an excessive sense of guilt and are caught for that reason.[1] A relief of these guilty feelings by psychotherapy leads to better results than imprisonment, and in a safer way. Even if the offender's sense of guilt is relieved by being imprisoned, he has almost always a strong resentment at being punished for something which he feels he cannot help. This does not imply that all sexual offences are committed under compulsion ; they are not. But very often the offending act is the only way in which the person concerned can obtain real sexual satisfaction. It has also to be borne in mind that sexual aberrations are very often originally caused by too much punishment for the expression of instinctive desires.[2] It is unlikely that further punishment will do away with the disturbance.

Mullins (27) draws attention to the fact that it is very difficult for the magistrate to dispose of sexual cases by probation and treatment, as public opinion calls for punishment, and he also sees very clearly that the " victim " is often in as much need of treatment as the offender. It is perfectly true that public opinion is specially unenlightened on the question of sexual offences ; this is due to the fear of our own sexual desires, which in the unconscious are exactly the same as those which the offender expressed overtly. But this fact should not be used as an excuse for inflicting irreparable damage on the lives of a number of people because, through no fault of their own, they have not succeeded in developing socially accepted sexual desires. The rational course would be to modify public opinion and not to gratify it by imposing severe sentences on sexual offenders.

Instances do exist—though statistically very few—when a sexual offender may be a menace to the public. Such people must be segregated if treatment for them is impossible. If cases of sexual offences are considered from this point of view it will appear that the number of dangerous persons is so small that it cannot possibly warrant the punishment of all those offenders who are harmless. The risk that sexual offences would increase if they were not severely punished is non-existent, as Alexander

[1] Part II, Ch. VII (*a*), p. 162. [2] Part I, Ch. VI, p. 42.

and Staub (5) have already pointed out. After all, the normality or abnormality of one's sexual desires is decided very early in life.[1] Nobody who is able to derive sexual satisfaction in a socially accepted way would wish to change this satisfaction for a perverted one. Most perverts who do not manifestly live out their perversion refrain from doing so not for fear of punishment by an outside authority but for fear of their own conscience. And other perverts again live out their perversion without ever coming into conflict with the law.

CHOICE OF TREATMENT.

The decision as to what kind of treatment is most appropriate to each individual case can be made only after a thorough psychiatric examination, and, for the reasons enumerated above, every sexual offender should be examined before trial. In some cases one interview with the patient and certain explanations to him may be all that is needed. This course was adopted in Case 10 [2] and Case 11.[3] A follow-up showed that in both cases no further sexual difficulties were encountered. In some cases, especially those of young offenders still at or shortly after puberty, a short psychotherapeutic treatment may be sufficient to help the normal genital desires to come to the fore. Psychotherapy may also help offenders who cannot be cured of their perversion to avoid coming into conflict with the law, by relieving their feelings of guilt or mitigating their aggression. In the majority of cases, again especially of young offenders, psycho-analysis will be the only treatment which can change the abnormal into a normal sex life.

The decision as to treatment and its application calls for long experience not only in the diagnosis but also in the treatment of neurotic and sexual disturbances ; not psycho-analysis alone, but also psychotherapy should in such cases be undertaken only by psychiatrists who have had many years of experience of analytical treatment with neurotic and perverted cases. Nothing but experience of this kind will enable one to decide on the possibilities of cure, the strength of the feelings of guilt, and the addition of antisocial tendencies ; such experience alone makes it possible to advise psychotherapeutic short cuts. Freud (16*c*) discovered that every neurotic patient is suffering from a sexual disturbance as well. Very often these disturbances are inhibitions, such as impotence in the man or frigidity in the woman. But the analysis of the neurotic symptoms reveals unconscious

[1] Part I, Ch. VI, p. 162.
[2] Part II, Ch. VII (*a*), p. 168. [3] Ibid. (*b*), p. 172.

phantasies of a perverse nature, as for instance homosexual, sadistic or exhibitionistic desires. Freud therefore stated that " the neurosis is the negative of the perversions ". These findings aroused interest in the treatment of patients suffering from perversions, and this in turn led to the theory of perversions.

PROBLEMS OF THERAPY.

Psycho-analytical and psychotherapeutic treatment can be successful only if the patient can co-operate, that is to say, if he really is suffering as a result of his condition. This happens much more often than can be seen from superficial examination. Very often these patients, especially if they have come into conflict with the law, have built up intellectual rationalizations around their disturbance and will not admit that they are dissatisfied. Treatment is impossible only if the patient derives full satisfaction from his perverted sexual activity. Then it is a threat : for the patient it means giving up the only way in which he can find sexual satisfaction. Of equal importance for satisfactory treatment is the age and general personality of the patient. A manifest homosexual between the age of 40 and 50 cannot really change his love object.

PSYCHOTHERAPY WITH MR. C.

Psychotherapy may give valuable help in cases where for practical reasons psycho-analytical treatment cannot be undertaken. Such treatment was given in Case 8. Mr. C. lived and worked outside London and could attend the clinic only once a week. The case history disclosed that this man had a very strong urge to acquire normal sex habits, otherwise his experiences would have prevented him from ever going near a psychological department again. As in Richard's [1] case sexual difficulties had existed from very early on, so that the boy came to the notice of the police at the age of 14. He was put on probation and psychotherapy was advised,

PREVIOUS ATTEMPTS AT TREATMENT.

but not carried out. The probation officer should have influenced the father's attitude and induced the boy to attend the clinic. Mr. C.'s second attempt at psychological treatment was no more successful ; he cannot be blamed for preferring prison to confinement in a mental hospital. This rather ambitious and intelligent young man felt insulted at being put into a ward with mentally defective patients. For various reasons an in-patient department in a mental hospital is not a suitable place for a man suffering from a sexual disturbance. The cessation of normal

[1] Part II, Ch. VII (*a*), p. 165 ff, and this chapter, p. 225 ff.

activities and of heterosexual activities wherever they exist can only aggravate the discontent and increase sexual tension, while the segregation amongst men is apt to strengthen homosexual tendencies. In the case of Mr. C. the asylum environment had a special psychological significance : he felt very guilty for masturbating and had a strong fear lest he had damaged his brain and might therefore become insane. Prison was preferable to having the image of this fear constantly before his eyes.

Nevertheless Mr. C. persisted in his efforts, and some time after his release from prison he went to the outpatient department of a leading London hospital. Again the psychiatrist's proposal was to certify him as insane or mentally defective. If this fact had not been confirmed by the patient's wife and father, the suspicion would be aroused that it was a paranoid idea of Mr. C.'s and not a fact. Mr. C., very glad to have escaped this fate, as neither his wife nor his father would sign a petition for his certification, made no more attempts to be treated until he again got into difficulties. This time his probation officer sent him to the I.S.T.D. Mr. C. was examined and the facts described above[1] came to light.

RESULT OF PSYCHO-THERAPY.

Mr. C. attended the Clinic for months, never once missing an appointment. He obtained immediate relief from his state of tension by being able to discuss his difficulties freely without encountering a moralizing attitude. He felt much more guilty about his masturbation than about his exhibitionistic activities. It became clear that his exhibitionism served to express his aggressive tendencies as well as his libidinal desires, and that this was one of the few outlets for his very strong hostile feelings. It was possible to relieve Mr. C.'s guilty feelings about masturbation and to undermine his inhibition of socially accepted aggressions. He succeeded in sublimating some of his instinctive energy by trying to satisfy his ambitions through his work. He began to take a correspondence course in engineering which he passed with much success, and he is making preparations to go abroad after the war. Before he came for treatment he did not attempt any intellectual work because he was afraid that he would find himself unable to learn. The only real safeguard against committing a further sexual offence would be a satisfactory sexual relationship with his wife. It is doubtful whether he will achieve this without psychoanalytical treatment. A change has occurred in this relationship,

[1] Part II, Ch. VII (*a*), p. 163 ff.

unnoticed by Mr. C. himself and reported only by his wife ; he respects her own desires and does not want intercourse merely in order to assert himself. His wife also reported that he was much quieter and less irritable at home. The fact that Mr. C. is married to a very sensible woman who has never reproached him for his misdemeanours is of course very helpful.

EFFECT OF PUNISHMENT.

It seems very probable that a few more experiences of punishment or misunderstanding would have turned Mr. C.'s attitude into one of open resentment against society, with criminal behaviour added to his sexual offences. Mr. C. knew that he had a sexual disturbance which it was not in his power to overcome, and punishment only increased his conflicts. His sexual disturbance developed on the basis of a passive relationship to a severe father who had ill-treated him. His treatment at the hands of the authorities, indistinguishable from that which he had received from his father, only increased the tension under which he was labouring, and because of it he was more rather than less liable to repeat his sexual offences.

Summary

All cases of sexual offenders should be examined by an analytically experienced psychiatrist at the first possible moment.

With some cases at puberty, a few interviews may be sufficient to help towards normal sex developments.

Psychotherapeutic treatment in an older offender may succeed in relieving a strong sense of guilt and thereby help him to avoid further contact with the law.

A cure of sexual abnormality, especially it if is already firmly established, can in most cases be achieved only by psycho-analytical treatment.

The co-operation of the patient is essential for the success of any method of psychological treatment, but can be gained more often than would be suspected on superficial examination pending trial.

CHAPTER V

ENVIRONMENTAL METHODS OF TREATMENT

(*a*) General Principles of Re-education

EXAMPLE 1. CHANGE IN HOME ENVIRONMENT.

The psychiatric interviews with Peter [1] led to the attempt to modify the parents' attitude. By giving the father some understanding of the nature of the boy's hostility towards him, it was anticipated that the boy would be able to express some of his aggressiveness without immediately being reproved. This slight change in the father's attitude prevented a further repression with its dangerous results. At the same time a slight change in the mother's behaviour (less overt expression of her affection for the boy) enabled him to loosen his fixation to her. By working with the parents in this way a change in the environment, in this case in the atmosphere of the home, was achieved which made it easier for the boy to cope with his adolescent conflicts.

EXAMPLE 2. CHANGE OF WORK.

Psycho-analytical knowledge of the conflicts at work in Richard's case [2] gave rise to the proposal of a change of work which helped Richard considerably in sublimating his desire to look. At the time of the investigation Richard had developed a compulsion to go to the pictures, a compulsion which led to instability in his behaviour towards his uncongenial work. The assumption that Richard, if given the opportunity of using some of this instinctive energy in social activity throughout the day, would cease to be compelled to satisfy it in an antisocial way, proved correct.

These two examples illustrate the method of environmental treatment. The mere removal of an offender from his home, or the mere change of job, though it brings about a change in the delinquent's environment, cannot in itself be called treatment. An environmental change can have a remedial effect only if the alteration is based on the offender's needs in his particular psychological situation.

[1] Part II, Ch. V (*c*), (2), p. 133 ff.
[2] Ibid., Ch. VII (*a*), p. 165 ff.

MEANS OF EDUCATION DURING FIRST FIVE YEARS OF LIFE.

Broadly speaking, environmental treatment aims at the re-education of the offender. Antisocial behaviour, if based on the antisocial character formation, is primarily a failure of education in its widest sense. Naturally, therefore, in order to combat this disturbance, the original process of education has to be repeated in a better setting. But let there be no misunderstanding. The disturbance in education occurred first and foremost during the first five or six years of life, when the task of education—possible only if there is a strong and firm emotional relationship between parents and child—consists in training the child to wait for satisfaction and in modifying the primary antisocial or perverse instinctive urges of the child by careful administration of gratification and frustration. Education during the first period of life is therefore directly connected with the child's instinctive life and takes account of the fact that the child himself does not want to forgo instinctive pleasure. This education therefore can succeed only if there is an emotional bond between the child and the adult, and if this intimate relationship continues without interruption over a long period of time. This primary and most important step in education will proceed satisfactorily only if a large amount of time and patience is allowed for the modification of instinctive urges during each stage of instinctive development. We have seen that success in this first attempt at education leads to social adaptation and its failure to the antisocial character formation.

METHODS OF EDUCATION IN LATENCY PERIOD.

The methods of education during the latency period and at puberty are entirely different, as they are adapted to a different phase of emotional development in the child. After the age of 6, education aims at the strengthening of the Super-Ego.[1] Though it is still important that the child should be on good terms with the educator, this relationship is by no means of the same nature as that of the small child to the mother. At this age the child tends to identify himself with persons in authority and by obeying them to find support for his own wish to " be good ". The child himself is now eager to be helped to combat his instinctive urges, provided he has emotionally, and not only in actual age, reached the latency period. Ordinary methods of discipline in schools can achieve their purpose only with children whose Super-Ego is at least in the process of

[1] Part I, Ch. IX, p. 57.

becoming independent. The delinquent whose emotional life is like that of a very much younger child will not respond to the methods of education appropriate to his age, and this fact can be used to diagnose the state of latent delinquency. I would remind the reader of Billy's reaction [1] to the ordinary methods of education and the detailed discussion on why in his case these methods could not achieve their aim.

The failure to achieve re-education in many cases of delinquent behaviour, even if the offender is removed from his home and lives for years in an institution, is due to the fact that the educational methods used are not in accordance with the emotional development of the offender but with the age group to which he belongs. Many educators, especially in institutions, fall victims to the fallacy that as ordinary discipline has no effect, the discipline for the offender should be more severe. It is not laxity of discipline which makes the offender rebel against his environment: it is that the educational methods applied find no response in the delinquent's own mental make-up.

CONDITION OF RE-EDUCATION.

We are now faced with a very difficult problem. In order to re-educate the child, the educational methods of the first five years have to be applied; but the object of re-education is not a small baby but a child or young person who is no longer entirely dependent on an adult for fulfilment of his desires. There are many wishes which these young people can satisfy for themselves against their parents' will—by means of their greater strength and independence as compared with the small child. Moreover, there is not the same willingness in the older child as in the baby to centre his emotions on a single adult. The young offender has experienced so many disappointments in his early emotional relationships that a person in authority will find it difficult to arouse affection. But if re-education is to be achieved at all, the establishment of a firm object-relationship, similar to that between the baby and its mother, is the precondition for further educational work.

TRANSFERENCE.

Fortunately, the innate urge to transfer old emotional relationships constantly to the persons of the environment, the transference,[2] paves the way for the establishment of a strong emotional relationship between the offender and the educator. It will depend on the skill and the personality of the educator how quickly the transference situation is established and how soon it is sufficiently developed for re-education

[1] Part II, Ch. II, p. 68 ff.

[2] Part III, Ch. III.

to begin. Each worker will have to develop his own particular methods in making contact with the offenders in his charge. Aichhorn (2*b*) describes in detail his method of effecting a quick transference with different types of offenders and with different types of parents. Intuition and a scientific knowledge of the emotional needs of offenders of the varying age groups will help the educator in this first stage of treatment.

No hard-and-fast rules can be applied to the first approach to a delinquent, with the one exception, that a moralizing attitude will at once arouse a negative transference which it will be difficult to combat later on. It can be taken for granted that an offender who has come before the court has met many people in authority who have tried to modify his behaviour with the usual methods of education, that is by appealing to his better self. As this better self does not exist, these methods have been unsuccessful, and have aroused in the offender a thorough hatred of every person who wants to induce him " to be good "

There are certain signs which show when the transference has been established. The offender may enjoy the educator's company and may confide in him of his own free will. Or he may start to provoke the educator in the way he used to provoke his parents. Though in such cases the negative transference is in the foreground, owing to the mental structure of such offenders, they can express their affection only in this distorted way. Or the first signs of the establishment of this relationship may be expressed in jealousy of other children and in the desire to show off in front of the educator, either by achievements or by naughtiness.

Once this relationship is established, the process of re-education can begin. It will vary according to the needs of the offender and the kind of environmental treatment which is applied.

Offenders who show a high degree of antisocial character formation, expressed in manifest delinquent behaviour over a long period of time, will probably have to be in continuous contact with the person who undertakes their re-education, and as in such cases the home is often irreparably bad, they often find their way into institutions.

AICHHORN'S EXPERIMENT IN RE-EDUCATION.

The best controlled experiment in re-education inside an institution has been undertaken by Aichhorn (2*a*), and it is of interest to study his experiment in detail as an example of re-education in general. Aichhorn took over an institution for wayward boys in Vienna after World War I. Trying to form groups of boys not more than 20 years old who showed similarities in their mental make-up and could therefore be dealt with in a similar way, he was left with twelve boys between the ages of 15 and 20 years who would not fit into any of the groups. Wherever they were, they disturbed the growing community spirit by their intense aggressiveness. So he decided, for practical purposes at first, to form a group of these twelve hooligans whose only common characteristic was their intense destructiveness. When faced with these boys the social workers who otherwise shared Aichhorn's psychological approach thought that in their case stern discipline and hard work alone could make any impression. Kindness and friendliness would be interpreted as weakness and would only lead to greater difficulties. Though Aichhorn agreed that this would happen, he felt differently about treatment, since he had already formed some idea of their problems. In discussions with these boys he had found that they had other things in common besides their aggressiveness : there was a certain similarity in their early experiences. In all these cases there had been severe and constant quarrels between the parents or between the child and the parents. The boys either hated father, or mother, or both, or the people who represented parent figures for them. None of them had ever been treated with friendliness and tenderness. In some of these lads the tender feelings were entirely transferred from human beings to animals. They talked about their rabbits with real affection while they attacked their best friends. All these boys had been beaten mercilessly and repeatedly and they themselves behaved in the same way towards those who were weaker.

Aichhorn knew that these boys owing to their early experiences had never had the opportunity of normal emotional development. He knew that they were out to satisfy their impulses all the time, and he also knew that a regression had taken place to the anal-sadistic phase of development. Their destructiveness was due to these two disturbances : the failure of the Ego to adopt the reality-principle with the ensuing failure of Super-Ego development, and the need for satisfaction of impulses on the sado-masochistic level of instinctive development. He laid his educational plans accordingly : he wanted to allow these youths to satisfy their impulses as much as possible and to let them experience the results of such behaviour for themselves. He himself took the group over with two women workers, who in time, being entirely worn out, had to be replaced by others. The boys, living by themselves in a hut, were allowed to do whatever they liked. There was no set timetable, they were not pressed to do any work, but there was ample opportunity for games and other amusing occupations and the social workers encouraged them to talk to them. The attitude of the adults was uniformly friendly and kind ; they avoided arousing jealousies by being strictly impartial. They agreed among themselves not to interfere with the destructiveness of the boys unless there was danger to one of the people living in the hut. No damage to property was considered important enough to justify the interruption of the experiment.

During the first weeks the pessimistic predictions of the workers were amply justified. The furniture, windows, doors, etc., were soon destroyed, the educators were regarded as weaklings, and if there was any fear it was the social workers and not the boys who experienced it. Aichhorn still wanted to carry on because he could already see a slight change in the boys' behaviour. They were still very destructive, even more so than in the beginning, but their aggressiveness seemed at times to be staged for the benefit of the adults. One incident was particularly instructive : in the presence of Aichhorn one of the boys attacked another with a large bread-knife, screaming that he meant to kill him. Aichhorn, noticing the exaggeration, did not look round and did not move. The boy, unable to impress his leader, threw the knife on the floor in despair and started to cry bitterly. For days afterwards he was quiet and amenable to discussion. Some such breakdown occurred with every one of these youths. There followed a period of great emotional instability, violent scenes alternating with good social behaviour. When the periods of good social behaviour grew longer, Aichhorn took the boys into a new house with good furniture and entirely new decorations. This time the pessimists were wrong ; there was no new outburst of destructiveness. Though the boys were still very unstable, and especially sensitive to every change in attitude of the adults, they were now in a condition which made re-education possible. During these first violent weeks they had formed a firm relationship with their leader, and he could now use his influence for educational purposes. Slowly but surely the boys became able to bear a certain amount of frustration ; they grew less sensitive towards changes in the adults' attitude. They were given certain tasks to perform which grew progressively more difficult. It was observed that with this change in attitude the boys suddenly seemed to be more intelligent. They had already begun to sublimate some of their instinctive energy, and the attempt was made to train each boy for the work for which he seemed most suitable. Very slowly the claims on working capacity and endurance were increased. Impossible demands were no longer fulfilled, but the need for frustration was discussed. The boys did not become socially adapted between one day and the next, but Aichhorn succeeded in the course of many months in re-educating these boys, all of whom became useful citizens and remained so after they left the institution.

THEORETICAL CONSIDERATIONS.

The change perceived by Aichhorn in the attitude of these boys after the first few weeks was due to the establishment of the transference. The aggressiveness was not just acted out; the person of the educator became an important factor in it. The boys clearly wanted to provoke him to punish them, and were therefore specially destructive when in his presence. This punishment would have provided them with an instinctive gratification on the sado-masochistic level, which they had been able to obtain in all their former environments. When the punishment did not come the boys grew dissatisfied. Not only did they not derive sufficient gratification when destroying inanimate things, but the unforeseen reaction of their educators put them in a difficult position: there was no longer any justification for their hatred. They still tried to get what they wanted by being more and more aggressive, but in the end they had to give in: they began to feel guilty (the first signs of Super-Ego development) and they broke down. Behind their aggressiveness and their wish to be punished, which had been transferred to the educators, there now appeared a fierce longing to be loved. This was still very untamed, their demands for the affection of the leader being insatiable, but they now had an emotional relationship to the adult which made education possible. At the same time, the frustration of their instinctive wishes on the sado-masochistic level led to a progress of instinctive development to the genital phase. This allowed them in time to establish a firm, friendly relationship with the adults in the institutions and among themselves. It was considered very important that as soon as this change began there should be ample opportunity for sublimation of the pregenital instinctive urges by the offer of all kinds of work, intellectual activities, and hobbies.

This experiment proves the correctness of the statement that the re-education of the offender has to be achieved by the educational means used in training the small child and not by means of severe discipline. These hooligans were made into useful citizens without any application of force or actual punishment. Nevertheless, their antisocial instinctive urges were frustrated all the time, in the first place by the educators' kindness and friendliness. The time factor is of course of great importance: it took weeks for the transference to be properly established and months before the results of re-education were visible in greater stability and greater working capacity. The boys were then able to fall in with the normal routine of the institution without being forced to obey the rules.

RE-EDUCATION OUTSIDE AN INSTITUTION.

This is an example of re-education with boys who showed an extreme degree of antisocial character formation. Very often, probably in the majority of cases, and in all those cases who are not sent to an institution, much less effort is needed to bring about re-education. The measures taken may occasionally seem insignificant, for instance the change of work in Richard's case, but they may effect a profound alteration in the delinquent's attitude. This will occur if the environmental change is chosen not arbitrarily but after careful insight into the psychological needs of the offender. In many cases of more superficial disturbance re-education can be effected by offering possibilities of sublimation, especially if the offender has outstanding abilities. In this connection it is interesting to study Mary's [1] development.

MARY'S DEVELOPMENT.

This child never came under the notice of the authorities, and her delinquent behaviour during the latency period was investigated only when she underwent psycho-analytical treatment as an adult. It will be remembered that she had not been punished for her delinquent acts and that her mother never knew about them. There was no upheaval of any kind within the family. Her last act of stealing was the expression of an unconscious conflict in which her hostility against her mother played the most important rôle. But at that time Mary had already succeeded in sublimating some of her instinctive desires by trying to do as well as her brother in school. This ambition did not remain

[1] Part II, Ch. V (*b*) (1), p. 123 ff.

an empty wish. Mary had the ability and the environment which allowed her to fulfil her intellectual desires. With her entrance into secondary school some of her ambitions were gratified, as she was very soon able to get reports as good as and even better than her brother's. Her attitude towards society changed rapidly after her first term in school, when the same aunt who knew about the stealing gave her a beautiful present with the remark that no fuss need be made about the elder brother since she, Mary, was even more successful than he.

SUBLIMATION AND RE-EDUCATION.

In this case, for constitutional and environmental reasons, the antisocial character formation was rectified by the opportunity of sublimating instinctive urges which found expression in the delinquent symptom. With Mary—as in many other cases of delinquent behaviour which never come to the notice of the authorities or the parents—a cure occurred by chance, but in Richard's case a similar procedure was actively adopted with great success. The opportunity of sublimating those instinctive urges which must disappear on account of their antisocial nature may constitute a treatment in itself, but it will play a part in all cases where other means of re-education are adopted as well. Without sublimation of the antisocial urges there can be no guarantee that the young offender will not fall back into his old attitude. In order to effect this quickly, it is not sufficient to give the offender work : the work must be of a kind which will permit the sublimation of those antisocial urges which are most pronounced and most disturbing in the case. Aichhorn (2*a*) describes the case of a schizophrenic boy whom he trained as a gardener in order to help him to sublimate his anal tendencies, and that of a homosexual boy who could sublimate his perverse tendencies as a tailor.

POSSIBILITY OF SUBLIMATION IN APPROVED SCHOOLS.

Approved schools, especially those for girls, do not usually consider the training from this angle. Most of the girls are trained for some domestic job or other. In my view, domestic work is the most unsuitable kind of training for such girls, unless they marry. They have invariably come to the approved school because conflicts with the members of their family have driven them into antisocial behaviour. The infantile pattern of relationships is very strong and is apt to influence all later human contacts. In the family atmosphere of a domestic job the old conflicts are bound to be revived and transferred to the members of the new household. Invariably there will be a repetition of the most common conflict, namely that the girl who did not get sufficient attention from her parents now feels the same about her employers. In giving an antisocial girl a job of this kind we are almost bound to undo the benefit she may have derived from her stay at school. Some of the girls may have a preference or a special gift for housework, and they can be trained for it. With the majority of antisocial girls, vocational guidance will be faced with the problem of choosing a training which makes use of these girls' excessive tendency to show off, to exhibit themselves and to be admired. Once this tendency is successfully sublimated (by dancing if there is special talent for it, by jobs like hairdressing, millinery, and so on) there is less danger that it will have to be satisfied by leading a " glamorous " life, which in the end leads to prostitution.

RE-EDUCATION AT HOME.

Very often, re-education can be achieved by a modification of the parents' attitude, in particular of those parental traits which have caused the antisocial reaction in the child. It has to be borne in mind that the change of attitude in the parents cannot be achieved at once, as they have to be given some insight into their own and their children's problems. This is especially true at puberty when the adolescent's desire to become independent of his parents may be the most pressing conflict.

To sum up : environmental treatment aims at re-education. If the antisocial character formation is pronounced and the home is bad, re-education can be achieved only by the establishment of an emotional relationship with a person other than the real parent. In other cases, changes of environment, if based on the offender's psychological needs, may in themselves achieve re-education of some instinctive urges ; the offer of opportunities for sublimation is one example of an environmental change which may have a remedial effect.

(*b*) Probation

HOME VERSUS INSTITUTION.

Fundamentally, all methods of environmental treatment of the young offender aim at the same thing, namely his re-education. The means by which this can be achieved differ slightly with different methods and different types of delinquents. The decision as to the type of treatment in any given case calls for the most careful diagnosis, based on intimate knowledge of the offender's environment and psychological make-up. A knowledge of the influences leading to social adaptation is necessary if we are to create conditions which come nearest to a child's normal upbringing. An institution, however well run, offers an environment entirely different from that of the home, a factor which has recently been scientifically investigated by Anna Freud and D. Burlingham (9). At puberty, however, the removal from home may not cause any disturbance, but on the contrary may help the adolescent to become more independent of his infantile love objects. Treatment differs not only according to the type but also to the age group to which the offender belongs. But it would be entirely erroneous to conclude that there is any hard-and-fast rule that children up to the age of 12 should never be removed from home, and that older children can easily be sent away. In each case the various factors emerging in the investigation have to be carefully weighed against each other before the real solution can be found. As has been mentioned already,[1] in some courts the decision whether a child is to be sent away from home or not is not based on a careful consideration of all the facts, but is made dependent on the number and the severity of offences; institutional treatment is considered to be the more severe form of punishment and is therefore applied only to repeated offenders. In theory it has always been maintained that institutional treatment is necessary only if the home environment is such that the child cannot possibly recover in it. This may apply to first offenders in exactly the same way as it does to repeated offenders, and it does not make the task of the approved school easier if children are sent there as a last resort.

With the official introduction of the probation service, a situation was created in which an offender could be influenced without being removed from home or taken away from his school or work. The enlargement of this service on scientific lines will make institutional treatment unnecessary in many cases where it is still applied owing to lack of other possibilities.

TASK OF PROBATION.

How is it possible that the probation officer, by seeing his charges once a week or once a fortnight, can bring about re-education, when the fact has been stressed that a change of educational methods has to continue from morning till night in order to be effective? How can he establish a good relationship to the offender by so erratic a contact? The task of the probation officer differs with

[1] Introduction, Ch. I, p. 2.

the different age groups, and his method of re-education has to be adapted to the various types of offenders.

(1) WITH CHILDREN.

With the child up to the age of 11 or 12, and especially with children between the ages of 6 and 9, direct influence will be most difficult to achieve. Children of that age are still most intimately bound up with their parents, and the influence of an outsider will be very small indeed as compared with the constant influence of the family atmosphere. The first task of the probation officer, a task in which he should be helped by a psychiatric examination of the case, consists in defining the factors in the family atmosphere which have led to the faulty development.

It will be particularly important to discover inconsistencies in behaviour, represented perhaps by differences of approach on the part of the parents—one parent always prohibiting, the other always permitting freedom—or by jealousies among the siblings, or by inconsistency between the real and the apparent relationship between the parents, and so on. This is a difficult task, as the home atmosphere cannot be assessed by simple inspection. Children may be very happy in a dirty home, because they may have a very satisfactory relationship with their mother or among themselves. It is important not to be deceived by appearances and by the economic status of the family. Though bad economic conditions may have decisively influenced the upbringing of the child, good economic conditions do not counteract emotional disturbances in the parents. Billy's home was economically sound, very clean, the mother very much concerned with the boy's physical health, and the father's rôle in the home could not have been recognized in a single visit. Yet from a psychological point of view the home was very bad, and a probation officer would have had no chance to effect a change.

ASSESSMENT OF HOME CONDITIONS.

The task of the probation officer is to grasp the emotional undercurrents in a home, to evaluate their importance for the special problem of his charge, and to find a way of modifying the faulty attitude of the parents. This is difficult, and becomes possible only by means of transference. Not only the child, but first and foremost the parents will establish an emotional relationship with the probation officer which will correspond to their own personalities. The probation officer must help to develop this relationship ; he should not

TRANSFERENCE.

respond to it emotionally, but should use it for his own ends. He must know that the parents' attitude towards the child will change only if they think that the modification in behaviour has originated in their own mind. Aichhorn describes in detail how he succeeded with various types of parents in establishing a transference situation, in using it for the modification of the mother's or father's attitude, and how he managed to let the parents take the lead again.

To give an example : let us say the probation officer knows that the constant nagging by the mother will make any modification in the child's behaviour impossible. To explain this to the mother directly will only annoy her. But if the mother's relationship with the probation officer is such that she gives him her confidence, she may begin to talk about her own upbringing and about the way in which her mother was constantly nagging her. By agreeing with the mother that this method of education is very unpleasant, the probation officer may be able to make her aware of her own methods, and the mother may of herself alter her method of education. Such a roundabout method may not always succeed, but it will do so more often than the direct method. A positive transference situation can be established only if the parents understand that the probation officer is a friend and not an enemy. It is true that this is explained to them in court, but only the probation officer himself can establish a friendship. It is of paramount importance for the treatment of the child that the probation officer should state his position. Then there will be less danger of his being used as a bogy man to frighten the child, and the parents will not try to shield the child for fear that it will have to appear in court again. In his relationship with the child it is often sufficient for the probation officer to succeed in convincing it that it can confide in him without any fear of being punished and that in misunderstandings between child and parent the officer sides with the child.

In the case of children up to the age of 11 or 12 the probation officer's task is therefore concerned at least as much with the handling of the parents as with that of the child. The re-education has, in these cases, to be accomplished by the parents or foster-parents themselves, as they are in constant contact with the child. The probation officer must also be in contact with the school, which forms the other side of the child's life. He has to be able to judge whether the child's bad progress in school is due solely to its inability to concentrate (to sublimate its instinctive energy) or whether changes in school conditions would be sufficient to guarantee a change in the child's interests. Much emphasis is laid on the supervision of the child's spare time, and one very often hears that the provision of more clubs would solve the problem of juvenile delinquency. There are certainly some cases in which the impossibility of satisfying the pleasure in adventure leads to delinquency. But these are the exception. The antisocial child cannot get on with other children of the same age, a fact which has been discussed in detail in Billy's case.[1] Club life, at a time when the child is not yet able to form friendships, will add a further burden and will not relieve its difficulties. As soon as the child is able to react more normally it will probably want to mix with other children, and it should then be helped to find the right companionship. There is no wholesale cure for the antisocial child, and at the present stage of our knowledge it will be necessary to study each individual case carefully and to try to satisfy its needs.

(2) WITH YOUNG BOYS AND GIRLS.

With the young offender at puberty, boys and girls between the ages of about 12 to 16 years, the probation officer's task is slightly different. At this age the process of becoming independent of the parents has already made some progress and should soon be completed. Difficulties at this age are often due to the clash of opinions between the older and the younger generation, between the desire of the parents to treat their young boys and girls as children and the children's wish to be grown up. These clashes are particularly strong if the young boys are still very infantile and their claims on the attention and love of the parents are still those of small children. For young people in this emotional situation the probation officer represents a parent figure, and it will be his task to become a more adequate leader than the parents ever were. At this age it will be the first task of the probation officer to establish contact with the offender and to convince him that he is absolutely on his side. It will still be important to understand the emotional background of the family atmosphere and perhaps to a certain extent to modify it. It is also desirable that the parents should not become hostile to the probation officer. But in gaining the parents' co-operation it has to be remembered that the offender may suspect the probation officer of siding with the parents against him,

[1] Part II, Ch. II, p. 89.

and it is usually of greater importance to gain the confidence of the boy than the co-operation of the parents.

PROBLEMS OF SEX.

The probation officer has to be aware of the problems uppermost in the minds of boys and girls of that age [1]; he has to avoid repeating the parents' mistakes and frightening the young offenders in regard to sex. Probation officers probably mean well if when discussing sexual questions they emphasize the danger of venereal disease. But they should realize that in doing so they increase the fear which is already present in the mind of these adolescents, and which, as we have seen, drives them into abnormal sexual activities. At puberty, the preoccupation of boys and girls is not so much with the opposite sex as with the problem of masturbation. Irrational fears should be dispelled and it should be made clear, at least by implication, that masturbation is the normal sexual activity at that age. I do not imply that normal boys and girls, when feeling guilty about masturbation, become delinquents. But in a boy or girl with an antisocial character formation, additional conflicts are apt to increase delinquent behaviour. It needs tact and experience to approach the question of sexual conflicts in the right way, to be able to judge whether this is really the conflict uppermost in the mind of the boy or girl or whether other problems, for instance their relationship with their parents, are more pressing. The first prerequisite for undertaking the task of discussing sexual questions with the young offender is the absence of inhibitions and conflicts regarding this problem in the probation officer himself. So long as he believes that masturbation causes damage to the brain and hinders a later sexual life, it would be better for him not to attempt any enlightenment or any discussion on questions of sex morals.

TRANSFERENCE.

The emotional relationship of the young offender to the probation officer, which has to be established if progress is to be made, may take unpleasant forms. There may be a time when the distorted relationship with the parents will be transferred to him.[2] There may be times of a highly positive transference, when the young offender demands too much attention, or there may be intense hostility. Knowing the psychological basis of such appearances, and realizing that neither love nor hatred has originated in the relationship with himself, but is already a second, third, or fourth edition of

[1] Part I, Ch. X, p. 63. [2] Part III, Ch. III, p. 203.

similar infantile ties, the probation officer will be able to handle these difficult situations better, and in doing this skilfully, will have taken a great step towards the end he seeks to achieve : a modification of these infantile desires. Scientific knowledge of the psychological forces behind the offender's actions will prevent disappointment and a sense of failure. Often it is believed that once a boy is put on probation his conduct should be normal, or, in other words, a repetition of the offence is considered to be due to a failure of the supervision. The same idea is prevalent when an offender is sent for psychological treatment. But the process of re-education takes a very long time, and it is not to be expected that the result should be apparent before the attempt has been made. The probation officer is legally entitled not to bring a child before the court again so long as he believes that he can achieve results in the future. Very often it is the sense of failure, much more than the conviction that the boy cannot recover under the probation order, which induces the officer to ask for a change in the original order.

SELECTION OF CASES.

The probation officer can achieve satisfactory results only if the children placed under his supervision are of a type which will respond, and if the home conditions are such that improvement is possible. The types of children which will most readily respond to this kind of environmental treatment are those classified under Group I (1), and under certain conditions, those under Group I (2),[1] if the home is not too bad. The antisocial character formation can be influenced if the home can be modified ; then the forces which have actuated this particular development cease to exist. Mentally defective children, neurotic and organically sick and psychotic children cannot be influenced by probationary supervision. The diagnosis should be made before the verdict of the court is pronounced so as to avoid unnecessary work and disappointment. It is quite useless to expect the probation officer by a fortnightly visit to counteract the influences of a vicious home, simply because the boy from this home has only been before the court once. Sometimes it will be very difficult to decide which course to adopt.

CASE 14: REGGIE

Reggie was an attractive boy of 6 years 10 months when he was examined for the first time. He had been brought before the court as being "beyond the control" of his mother. He had played truant

[1] Part II, Ch. IX, p. 186.

since the age of 5, stolen money on various occasions from home and from school, usually in order to treat other boys, and had run away from home on frequent occasions, being picked up by the police after 9 o'clock at night at various places miles away from his home. At his first court appearance his joy at seeing his mother again after having been in a remand home was so genuine and he was so afraid of being separated from her that he was allowed to go home, only to run away again the same day. He was of normal intelligence but backward in school ; it was quite impossible for him to concentrate on any school subject. He was disliked by other children, and he tried to bribe them into friendliness by distributing stolen goods among them.

HOME ENVIRONMENT. Reggie was the second of four children, the others being 8, 6, and 3 years of age. His mother was a particularly nice, friendly, unaggressive woman ; she was very fond of the boy and tried as hard as she could to satisfy his incessant clamour for her love and attention. Reggie's father had been in the army for a year. He was sterner than the mother, and used to thrash the boy occasionally, but on the whole Reggie's relationship with his father was good.

The mother had had two children and several miscarriages since Reggie was born. Until three years before, Reggie slept in a cot in his parents' bedroom. The mother had not noticed any signs of sexual curiosity or precocious sexual interest in the boy, and therefore had not explained to him about the arrival of the new children. But when one night the mother asked her husband to fetch a nurse because she was having a miscarriage, Reggie had already left the house and came back with another nurse. The whole family suffered under the constant questions which Reggie asked, and apparently he was never satisfied with the answer. This obsessional questioning is very often a result of unsatisfied sexual curiosity. During his stay in the remand home Reggie used dirty language and tried to find out what little girls look like. He was able to hide these interests very carefully from the eyes of his mother, who, he knew, would not approve of such interests.

DIAGNOSIS. Reggie had a typical antisocial character formation which, owing to war and the absence of the father, made its appearance in antisocial action very early. He was only 10 months old when his younger brother was born, and his exacting attitude towards his mother showed that he had never overcome this setback in his relationship to her. Though of a loving disposition, this woman had no time to devote herself sufficiently to her young son.

TREATMENT.

The decision to take this child away from home was not easily made. He was very attached to his mother, and the home was, regarded superficially, a good one. The mother's personality was such that one could be certain of her co-operation and help. But she would have been quite unable to spend the time necessary to re-educate this boy without neglecting her other children. Also, the boy's habit of running away was rather dangerous for him and could certainly not be prevented at once by the supervision of a probation officer. For these reasons it was decided to send the boy to a small school in the country where he would have ample opportunity to satisfy his craving for adventure in a socially acceptable and less dangerous manner, and to arrange for his mother to see him at frequent intervals. The boy himself, who was terrified of being separated from his mother, was quite thrilled when he heard he would be sent to the country and would be able to care for animals. Though he was most interested in tigers and crocodiles he was quite prepared to have rabbits instead. He has been away for a year and is developing satisfactorily. He has not attempted to run away.

In this case, all the general rules which one is inclined to lay down, namely not to separate small children from their families, and not to send a child away from home if the parents are co-operative, had to be discarded. This case is no great exception, and at least at our present stage of knowledge, individuality in treatment is essential.

THE TASK OF THE PROBATION OFFICER.

The work of the probation officer is highly skilled. He has to be able to judge the home atmosphere correctly, to assess the factors which have primarily caused the antisocial behaviour, and to find ways and means of counteracting these influences. In addition to this he has to supervise not one, but perhaps fifty or sixty cases. He is constantly dealing with a most difficult group of human personalities and has to be able to remain unaffected by emotional upheavals of which he will be made the centre. Such a task calls for an excellent training in various fields of science, not least in psychology.[1] But even

[1] Part III, Ch. VI.

the best training does not make his job an easy or comfortable one.[1]

There are various ways in which the work of the probation officer can be made easier and more interesting. In the first place, a psychiatric diagnosis before the probation order is made will prevent unnecessary work and disappointment with cases which cannot possibly improve ; an outline of the causes of delinquent behaviour will be available. Moreover, the probation officer should have the opportunity of discussing his cases with a psychiatrist familiar with delinquency work. Delinquency clinics, in this country the I.S.T.D. and some child guidance clinics, make a point of discussing cases sent for examination with the probation officer. But these are only isolated instances, and the cases discussed are usually those which need psychological treatment in addition. The author has begun to work with a group of probation officers in weekly or fortnightly seminars in order to give them an opportunity of discussing their problems in a number of cases. This work has proved very satisfactory. The probation officers gain a fuller understanding and learn about the work and methods of other probation officers ; they also get some insight into personal difficulties which may develop with one or another type of case. It is impossible to assume that each probation officer is equally well able to deal with the various types of cases. Probation officers are human beings and may have their idiosyncrasies. It is much better to give a certain type of case to a colleague than to be constantly unsuccessful and dissatisfied with these offenders. A division of labour of this kind, if more widely employed, will do much towards a closer co-operation of the various agencies concerned with delinquents. It also opens up the possibility of handling many more cases on psychological lines than would otherwise be possible. At present there are no facilities for providing psychological treatment for those offenders who may be able to do without it. By explaining their difficulties to the pro-

[1] Miss Wilcox (33) recently brought forward arguments to show that it is doubtful whether it will ever be possible for the probation officer to do intensive case work of the kind described above. Amongst other problems she lays emphasis on the probation officer's divided loyalties under the present system (to the court and to the probationer) and on the large number of cases with which one officer has to deal and which permits intensive work on only a small number of his probationers.

One solution of this problem would lie in an extension of psychiatric social work, by workers attached to a delinquency clinic to the majority of all cases under probation. This would leave the probation officer free to deal with more external problems, of course in close co-operation with the psychiatric social worker dealing with the case.

bation officer, better means of influencing these young offenders can be devised than were hitherto possible. After all, the probation officer is not a psychiatrist and has very little opportunity in his training of seeing mentally disturbed children. Neither does he apply psychological treatment. But environmental methods of treatment will have better results if they are based on psychological insight. The psychiatrist also gains by close contact with the work of 'the probation officer. He becomes familiar with types of offenders which he usually does not see, and can observe how environmental changes influence their behaviour.

Even if an offender is sent for psychological treatment, the work of the probation officer is not finished.[1] The closest co-operation is necessary if weekly interviews with the offender at the clinic are to have any lasting effect. This co-operation will enable the probation officer to decide much earlier than usual that environmental methods are in certain cases ineffective, and he will send many more offenders to clinics than he has done hitherto. At present there are not sufficient clinics to deal with an increasing number of cases, but if the need is fully recognized, they will probably be provided.

SUMMARY. If extended on scientific lines, probation will be successful with a great number of young offenders and there will be less need for institutional care. In order to achieve this result, the training of the probation officer has to be appropriate to the task he has to fulfil, remuneration for his services must be granted on a professional scale, and ample opportunities provided for the closest co-operation with psychiatrists. This will create the possibility of influencing a greater number of cases than was hitherto possible and of bringing about a genuine re-education.

(c) Removal from Home

1. *Foster-homes*

In the last chapter we told the story of little Reggie and why he could not be left at home with his mother. We also stressed that the decision to send this small boy away was not taken lightly. The family atmosphere is an important factor in the development of social adaptation,[2] and still exerts its influence during the latency period. We have seen that Reggie and his mother were

[1] Part III, Ch. V (*c*), p. 224.

[2] Part I, Ch. XI.

very fond of each other, and to disturb this first and most intimate relationship is always a grave step. In the majority of cases the decision to separate a child under the age of 10 from its parents is taken because their character is such that it exerts a bad influence on the child ; for instance, drunkenness, ill-treatment by a step-parent, or neglect are sound reasons for separation.

So far as children under 10, and in exceptional cases older children, are concerned, it would be more in keeping with normal development if they could live in another family. Boarding out in foster-homes is a legally recognized form of disposal if a child has to be removed from its own home, and if this could be arranged on a larger scale and with the necessary precautions it would in a large number of cases result in complete recovery. To fulfil its function a foster-home must offer more than a family atmosphere. The personality of the foster-parents must be such that the damage already done can be undone ; in other words, that a process of re-education can take place.

REQUIREMENTS OF FOSTER-HOMES.

TRANSFERENCE.

It is only to be expected that after a few weeks in the new home, during which the child may behave quite normally, the old difficulties will reappear ; they will disappear only if the foster-mother's attitude towards the child is entirely different from that of its parents ; if it is sustained by real affection and an understanding of the child's problems. During the wartime evacuation this development might be observed over and over again : it can be understood on the basis of the psychological background. Very many children are " good " if they are in a strange place and have not yet formed any real relationship with the people surrounding them. As an emotional relationship to the foster-parents develops, the old conflicts originating in the relationship with the real parents are transferred to the person who is now the centre of affection. The child cannot help but bring with its affection all the difficulties which have developed in its own home. This is the moment when the foster-mother can start to exert her influence over the child, but she will be able to do so only if she understands why the child has to behave in such a way, what the difficulties in the home really were, and in what way the child can become socially adapted.

Taking Billy as an example, he would certainly after a longer or shorter period have started by constant disobedience to provoke his foster-mother to punish him ; he would have transferred his love relationship with his mother, which, according to his instinctive development, was on the sado-masochistic level, to the foster-mother. If she had reacted in the same way as his mother, namely by punishing and nagging him, she would have lost the game before beginning to educate the boy. Only constant friendliness with a consistent attitude towards Billy's antisocial desires, and an encouragement of every sign of sublimation, could have had any effect on him.

SUPERVISION.

The ordinary foster-mother is not a trained psychologist, and the problems of the child under her care will have to be explained to her. She will have to know what kind of behaviour to expect and whether she will be able to deal with it. That means that the psychiatric social worker would have to remain in contact with the home, and under the guidance of the psychiatrist help the foster-mother step by step to evolve a plan of action. It would not be practicable for the psychiatric social worker or the psychiatrist to dictate the behaviour to be adopted by the foster-mother. No one who has to deal with a difficult child day in, day out, could carry out someone else's methods. The foster-mother will have to develop her own methods on the basis of facts and suggestions made to her by a trained psychiatrist. The question of contact with the real parents will need very careful handling, and will have to be decided in each individual case. Often it will be necessary to find a foster-home a long way from the real home in order to avoid difficulties, especially if it is thought that contact with the parents would spoil the chance of success. The number and age of other children in the house, and their effect on the child, will also have to be considered.

SELECTION OF SUITABLE FOSTER-HOMES.

From these comments on some of the difficulties which arise it will be apparent that the choice of a suitable foster-home is a formidable task involving the co-operation of various agencies. Foster-homes have to be found, and then to be thoroughly investigated, before the right child can be sent to the right home. In other words, boarding out in foster-homes can be undertaken on a bigger scale only with the help of a large organization. Healy and his colleagues (22) have published the results of boarding out in foster-homes delinquent children and those with behaviour difficulties. They had at their disposal a child-placing agency with a large staff of home-finders, visitors and supervisors, all of whom were in constant touch with the psychiatric team. The results with antisocial children were excellent—showing cures between 75 per cent. and 85 per cent. They describe the very complicated technique of child placing in detail, and it is quite clear that the good results were due to the great care taken in the choice of foster-homes and in the diagnosis of the disturbance. Without an organization of this kind, placing in a foster-home can either be undertaken only on a very small scale or will remain a gamble. At the I.S.T.D., only foster-homes well known to the staff are chosen, but the demand is much greater than the supply.

2. *Institutional Treatment*

The success of institutional treatment for the young offender depends entirely on whether the stay in the institution has brought about re-education. This depends not merely on the time he has spent there, but also, and far more, on the choice of cases and the methods of education adopted.

SELECTION OF CASES.

Diagnostically speaking, offenders whose delinquent behaviour is due to their antisocial character formation and not to neurotic or organic illness, and whose home environment does not allow of sufficient modification, need to be sent away from home. Children under 14 years of age, for whom the family atmosphere is still of great importance in their psychological development, should, if possible, be sent to foster-homes. Psychiatrists are very reluctant to send young offenders over the age of 14 to approved schools and later to Borstal institutions. This reluctance is based on two different reasons. As Mannheim (26) has pointed out, a social stigma is attached to a stay in an institution, and though the Borstal Association, with its excellent after-care, tries to minimize the effects of this, it is not able to do so fully. Mannheim discusses the social stigma attached to the various forms of penal treatment and makes some proposals for alleviating it in the case of the young offender.

The second reason for this reluctance to send suitable cases to institutions lies in the doubt whether re-education will really be achieved under the institutional conditions of to-day. This doubt is justified by the many cases which have a very good record during their stay in the approved school, but afterwards continue their antisocial behaviour as if they had not been touched by any process of re-education. Some of these cases, Richard,[1] for instance, should never have been sent to an approved school, but

[1] Part II, Ch. VII (*a*), p. 165.

others, judging by their mental make-up, ought to have benefited from it. What are the reasons for these failures?

CONDITIONS OF RE-EDUCATION.

Perhaps it would be best to consider briefly under what conditions re-education can be achieved in an institution. Unlike the position when re-education is brought about by the efforts of a single adult dealing with one child—the situation which would occur in the home if the parents' attitude were modified, or in a foster-home—in an institution one adult will have to deal with a number of offenders. In order to create a situation in which this adult can enter into an emotional relationship with a number of children, the latter will have to be divided into small groups comprising those of a similar type, so that the same educational methods can be adopted with all of them. Under such conditions, a group feeling is bound to develop and the leader of the group will be able to exert his influence on more than one child at the same time. This grouping will have to be done very carefully, for one misfit may prevent the development of the transference in the whole group. Aichhorn (2*a*) has worked on this principle in a State institution with very good results. Makarenko (25) arrived at the same conclusion in an experimental way; Wills (34) devoted much thought to the development of the group spirit in Q Camp, and the Borstal system is built up on the principle of classification and small units, though in some Borstals up to forty boys are under one house-master (21).

GROUP SPIRIT.

TRANSFERENCE.

The development of a group feeling paves the way for the establishment of transference, which —as we have seen—is only the first step in the process of re-education. Aichhorn (2*a*) lays great stress on the necessity of allowing the boys to live out their hunger for pleasure at first. He had recognized the failure of the offender to develop towards the reality-principle, and knew that only very careful handling over a long period of time would lead him to achieve this important step in development. It is interesting to note that this factor is recognized by heads of private establishments whose interest in delinquent youth has led them to undertake the task of re-education, as for instance Homer Lane (7), Wills (34), and Makarenko (25). It is not officially recognized as the working principle in approved schools and Borstal institutions, though in the latter individual head-masters do occasionally work on it to a certain extent.

Without this period between the first development of the

transference and the time when the first steps in re-education can be taken—a period during which the offender will be as antisocial as he was before he entered the institution—re-education cannot take place at all. The obligation of the offender to behave as if he were socially adapted from the moment he enters the institution and to comply with the rules and the discipline of the school, is based on the mental make-up of the normal and not the abnormal child. The offender, as we have repeatedly shown, cannot comply with discipline. He can be forced to do so by superior strength, but this will not achieve a real change of attitude. Or he may very willingly and obligingly do whatever he is told to do in order to avoid difficulties, but he will not be able to develop an independent conscience—and that is one of the aims of re-education. Every institution knows these types. They are boys who have a good record in the institution yet underneath remain antisocial the whole time. In Borstals this danger has been recognized, and some of the more modern institutions have therefore abolished the system of marking (21).

This obligation to allow the offender to display his antisocial attitude before the attempt at re-education can be made, calls of course for larger and better-trained staffs. It is certainly true that in large institutions with an inadequate staff the only means of running the institution is severe discipline. On the other hand, the offender is sent there not to be disciplined, but to be re-educated. And the effect of re-education cannot be estimated by the offender's obedience in complying with the rules under pressure.

STAFFING.

ATTITUDE OF EDUCATORS TO OFFENDER.

During this first period of instability the offender has to feel that the leader of the group is on his side, understands his problems, and is willing to help him. Aichhorn (2*a*) regards this attitude on the educator's part as the most important ingredient in the process of re-education. The educator can adopt such an attitude towards the offender only if he has a real understanding of the causes of his delinquent behaviour, and realizes that it is through no fault of his own that the child has failed to develop normal standards of behaviour. It is equally important to realize that the child cannot possibly, likewise through no fault of his own, comply with over-exacting demands for discipline and tidiness. A short period of kindly treatment cannot induce the offender to become socially adapted; as we have seen, the process of re-education takes not weeks but years. A knowledge of the structure of the offender's mind and of the scientific principles of re-education will guard the educator against expecting too much in too short a time, and therefore prevent disappointments which in turn create an unfavourable attitude towards the delinquent.

BORSTAL IDEAS. It is interesting to note that the staff of Borstal institutions have, after years of experience, come to very much the same conclusions as those here outlined in theory. The principle of the Borstal authorities is to learn the offender's needs by experiment and observation. Though the idea of the beneficial effect of severe discipline and hard work still exists in the minds of the Borstal authorities, observation of the boys has led to the foundation of open Borstals. The fact that fewer boys run away from these open institutions (21) will influence future policy. Usually when the youth first comes into a Borstal institution he is given time to become acquainted with the routine; probably further observation will show that this period has to be extended over a longer time and that the offender works better when he starts work of his own free will. More and more emphasis is laid on the development of the group spirit and the relationship of the youth to the house-master.

TRAINING. Once the process of re-education has begun and the offender has become more stable it is of the utmost importance that enough facilities should be available for intellectual activities and training of various kinds. The importance of sublimation during the process of re-education should not be underestimated. It is the surest safeguard against falling back into the old antisocial attitude when the offender leaves the institution. If sublimation has really taken place, the offender will enjoy his work, and there will be no need to enforce rules in order to keep him at it. The group spirit and his wish to achieve something are sufficient incentives to him to fulfil his daily duties, especially if there is no wide gap between the duties of the offender and those of the staff.

CLASSIFICATION. Re-education is possible only with certain types of delinquents. The work of institutions is made much more difficult by the lack of diagnosis before children are sent to them. The Borstal authorities are careful to observe the youths for weeks before they allot them to one institution or another. In their observation centre there are facilities for psychological as well as for physical examination and treatment if necessary. It is a great step forward that classificatory schools have been introduced into the approved school system, and it is to be hoped that enough facilities will be available after the war for children to be sent to the school which suits their mental make-up and not to the one where there is a vacancy.

But even if classification were effective, and only those offenders who could really be cured by a process of re-education were sent to institutions, there would still be many problems calling for psychiatric advice. Often the antisocial character formation may be so pronounced and the home so bad that institutional treatment appears to be necessary, although the offender may show signs of a neurotic disturbance as well. Or problems may arise during the process of re-education with which the staff of an institution is not equipped to deal if severe disciplinary measures are to be avoided. In such cases it is very desirable that the staff should have the chance of discussing their problems from time to time with a psychiatrist trained in delinquency work. This contact between the staff and the psychiatrist would be especially necessary if some of the children were being sent for psycho-therapeutic treatment. The knowledge of the offender's conflicts and former history which the psychiatrist gains in such interviews can be most valuably employed in devising re-educational methods in co-operation with the staff. As said above,[1] such co-operation between the staff of institutions and the psychiatrist would permit a much wider application of psychological principles than would otherwise be possible.

CO-OPERATION WITH PSYCHIATRY.

HOSTELS.

Owing to the superiority of small units over big establishments and to the social stigma attached to approved schools and Borstal institutions, the introduction of small hostels for offenders as envisaged by the new Criminal Justice Bill (12) may help considerably towards the achievement of better results. The hostel permits of removal from home without an inevitable interruption of work or removal from the community. The seclusion of some institutions constitutes a grave danger for the offender, who often, before he is entirely cured, has to go back to a world different from that in which he has spent important years of his life. The hostel system will allow the offender to remain in the real world, to carry on with his work, to keep up old friendships and to stand more on his own feet than he could do even in the best institution. If a hostel is properly staffed, re-education can be carried on in much the same way

[1] Part III, Ch. IV (*b*, *c*, *e*).

there as in the institution, and if the plan is carried out on a rational basis, the offender will not be ostracized.

SUMMARY. Summarizing, it can be said that cases whose delinquent behaviour is due to an antisocial character formation and whose home background is beyond repair should be removed from home, and if a foster-home is impossible, or if they are over the age of 14, should have some kind of institutional treatment. The smaller the unit, the closer the relationship with the leader of the group, the more skilful the adjustment between the type of education given and the actual faults of character, and the greater the emphasis on redirecting instinctive energy into socially accepted channels, the better will be the results. Small establishments with an adequate staff will meet these requirements better than big institutions with an insufficient staff which can be run only by the application of severe and uniform discipline. Close co-operation between psychiatrists and the staff of institutions or hostels would considerably increase the chance of successful treatment.

CHAPTER VI

THE TRAINING OF FIELD WORKERS

THE PROBLEM. Scientific research in various fields has led to a radical change in the fundamental ideas about the causation and treatment of juvenile delinquency. So far this change is known only to a small circle of professional workers; it has filtered through to the authorities dealing with the problem of delinquency, but it has not yet reached the public to any great extent. Further research and experiment are necessary in order that ideas now held may be discarded and much of this research will have to be done by the workers in the field. These workers have different tasks to perform and come from different strata of society, have had a different training and have therefore a different background. This might be an advantage, since it would permit ideas of all kinds to be brought forward and experiments of various kinds to be carried out. But the fruitfulness of the varied background can be realized to the full only if these workers are in contact with each other and if there is some common ground on which they can meet. In some spheres of delinquency this standard has been achieved, although the units do not comprise the whole field. In this country the Borstal authorities form a unit with constant interchange of ideas and experiences between all the members of the staff of the various institutions and the personnel of the after-care authorities. There is the unit of the I.S.T.D., in which psychiatrists work together in a team with psychiatric social workers and psychologists, keeping in contact with the probation officer, the home, and whoever else is concerned with the case. There is very little contact between the magistrates of Juvenile Courts and these various units except for the probation officer who is attached to the Court. The policy adopted with regard to the treatment of juvenile delinquency in the various juvenile courts in this country is by no means uniform.

Each of these units acquires experience in one particular field of delinquency, restricted usually to certain age groups and certain types. Outside these units are the professions which deal theoretically with the problem of delinquency, criminology and sociology, and their findings are so far not embodied in the more practical fields of work. The workers in these various units are not enabled to see the problem of delinquency as a whole and from all its various angles except through their private efforts. There is, for practical reasons, no interchange of staff between the various branches. It is not possible to-day for a probation officer to become, for a time, a member of the staff of an approved school, a Borstal institution or a prison, and then to go back to probation work, neither does such a possibility exist for the workers in other units. That is to say, except by great exertion, it is impossible for any workers in the field of delinquency to follow up the careers of criminals from their early youth to manhood except on paper. The prison official has no conception that the hardened criminal was once a boy like Billy, and those who deal with the Billys have often no clear idea what their later development will be like unless they spend much time and attention on them when small. The psychiatrist sees these types who seem strange to others or who do not respond to ordinary methods of treatment. These are usually the neurotic types, and if the psychiatrist is not very careful he may come to the conclusion that there is no difference between neurosis and delinquency. On the other hand the psychiatrist working in prison sees criminals of a certain type and under prison conditions only, and is therefore likely to generalize when his deductions should apply only to these particular conditions.

PROBLEMS OF TRAINING OF PSYCHIATRISTS.

As far as psychiatry is concerned, the I.S.T.D. has made the attempt to collect within its organization all psychiatrists interested in the problem of delinquency from any of its various angles. It has been known for some time that forensic psychiatry is a special field within psychiatry, and one for which special experience is necessary. East (13*b*) stresses this point and underlines the danger of the psychiatrist being an expert witness unless he has acquired this special body of knowledge and experience. But forensic psychiatry is mainly concerned with the problem of criminal responsibility, and it is only in recent years that the so-called " normal delinquent " has been made a special psychiatric study. This development has arisen out of Healy's work in America and Burt's in England. It is not yet fully recognized that special experience is needed in diagnosing the different types of " normal " delinquent, and that the diagnosis and treatment of juvenile delinquency is becoming a speciality within a speciality. The training of psychiatrists in this special field of work meets with great difficulties. The I.S.T.D. is the only organization in this country which devotes itself entirely to the study of the criminal of all ages. Psychiatrists working in it do so on an honorary basis and cannot devote much of their time to this particular kind of work, especially as each case demands not only an investigation lasting for at least an hour, but often several interviews and discussions with the psychiatric social worker and psychologist. A further difficulty arises out of the fact that work of this kind can be done satisfactorily only by psychiatrists who have already had years of experience in the diagnosis and treatment of neurotic and psychotic illness in patients other than delinquents. At the time, then, when they begin delinquency work, they have already many other duties on their hands. Psychiatrists working in Child Guidance Clinics have the advantage of being already familiar with work with neurotic children, and gain experience with the delinquent children sent to the clinic as well. But they have had only rarely experience with adult offenders. Apart from the special psychiatric knowledge necessary for satisfactory work with delinquents, a knowledge of the legal aspect, of the possibilities of environmental treatment, and some knowledge of criminology and the sociological aspect of crime is needed.

PROBLEMS OF TRAINING OF OTHER FIELD WORKERS.

Very similar difficulties are met with by all workers in the field. Owing to the fact that criminal research is a borderline science, a much wider training than in most other fields is needed if the work is to be done efficiently, and is to produce scientific research. To take a few examples: the probation officer has to be conversant with legal methods and court work, with administration, with the sociological and criminological aspects, and last but not least, with the psychological aspect of his work; he ought to have some knowledge of the motivation of normal and abnormal human behaviour. The staff of the approved school, apart from all those aspects of the work, have to have some knowledge of teaching and of institutional methods in general, while the staff of Borstals, in addition, have to know something of vocational guidance and one or another trade, as the case may be. The magistrate, to take one worker from the legal field, in addition to his legal knowledge, ought to be thoroughly conversant with penology and the psychological aspect of delinquency.

We have shown [1] that the antisocial character formation is caused by the inconsistency shown by the mother or by both parents in their first educational efforts. It would therefore be a factor of the greatest magnitude in the treatment of antisocial behaviour if, from the time of the delinquent's first appearance before the authorities, the treatment applied to him were absolutely consistent until the time when he can be said to be cured and can stand on his own feet. This would be possible only if all the personnel who come into contact with the delinquent throughout his criminal career had a uniform training, at least so far as their part in his treatment is concerned.

A SCHEME OF TRAINING.

Psychiatrists, psychiatric social workers and psychologists can gain the special knowledge of delinquency in clinics, such as the I.S.T.D. or Healy's clinic, where they work in a team.

The probation officer, the staff of approved schools and of Borstal institutions, wardens of hostels, club leaders and similar personnel should have a uniform training in certain subjects. The fundamental principles of the motivation of normal and abnormal human behaviour, the psychiatric and psychological aspects of delinquency, modern as opposed to old methods of treatment, the psychological factors of re-education, early symptoms and signs of antisocial behaviour, and the signs of neurotic illness complicating delinquent behaviour should be the main subjects of this uniform training, which should be undertaken after the specific training for one or the other branch of delinquency work has been completed. Such training would not only give the uniform background which is essential if the delinquent is to be treated consistently and on the same principles, whether he is on probation, in an approved school, or in a Borstal institution. It would also have the advantage of bringing the various workers together and establishing fundamentals of co-operation between them which at present are almost entirely lacking.

FUNDAMENTALS OF COMMON KNOWLEDGE.

This consistency in treatment does not mean that every worker must use the same methods, or that the aim of probation is the same as that of a Borstal institution. According to the environment in which the delinquent lives and the personality of the worker who has to deal with him, the means used to bring about re-education will be very different. The probation officer may for instance try to effect this re-education by establishing contact

[1] Part II, Ch. V, p. 117.

with the parents, and so indirectly influence his probationer, while in a Borstal institution the emphasis on group spirit may achieve the same result. But there should be unanimity that antisocial behaviour cannot be cured by punishment and discipline, that re-education can come about only if the offender has a chance of establishing an emotional contact with an adult, and that means have to be devised of directing instinctive energy into socially accepted channels once the process of sublimation begins. With the school child this will only mean a follow-up of his school record and perhaps a change of school, while with the adolescent and older offenders it entails careful vocational guidance and ample opportunity for as many training schemes as possible. This last factor is recognized in Borstal institutions, but is neglected in many approved schools, especially in those for girls.

A common training in the needs of human beings, in the necessity in the normal human being for some direct instinctive satisfaction, and the increased need of this direct satisfaction in the delinquent would avoid the haphazard way in which nowadays the different workers in the field advise their charges or train them for their occupations.

Apart from this universal course of training, which would probably have to extend for over a year, as certain subjects cannot merely be studied theoretically but involve familiarity with case material, a two-years course in social sciences for probation officers and some of the staff of Borstal institutions would probably be required, and a two years' course in teaching for the staff of approved schools and for some of the staff in Borstals. All of these workers must have practical experience in either social work, teaching or allied subjects.

LONG AND VARIED TRAINING.

To put these or similar proposals into practice would involve a four-years course of training for all the workers in the field. This would have the advantage of providing a uniform background, and the further advantage of interchange of workers between the various branches of delinquency work. To-day this interchange is made impossible not only by the very different training but also by the fact that the various branches of delinquency work are administered by different authorities. But surely, once the advantage to the worker of having to deal with different types of delinquents during his or her career is understood, such an interchange could easily be arranged.

SELECTION OF SUITABLE PERSONALITIES.

The handling of offenders for the purpose of re-education is one of the most difficult tasks of social work. The worker engaged in such an enterprise must not only have a sufficient training to equip him for the task, but also the characteristics which make such work possible. All the authorities dealing with the choice of workers for their particular branch of delinquency work place great emphasis on choosing the "right" kind of personality, and maintain that personality is much more important than training. It would be wiser to emphasize that training and personality are equally important, especially as the choice of the right personality is very difficult and at best erratic. It is very difficult to describe a suitable personality for such work in psychological terms, though it is easy to say what he should *not* be like. He should not be rigid, he should not have preconceived ideas and prejudices, he should be able to learn by experience, he should, on account of his special personality, command respect without having to use artificial means of achieving this end. Added to these negative and positive qualities there must be a genuine interest in the motivation of human reactions without the constant urge to divide these reactions into "good" or "bad" ones, and together with this, the possibility of establishing contact with as great a variety of people as possible. None of these attitudes can be acquired by training, and this is the reason why such emphasis is laid on the choice of a suitable personality. But though the training cannot be a substitute for necessary personality traits, whatever they may be, it imparts knowledge which the most suitable person must acquire in order to do his work satisfactorily. And the extension of the training would have another advantage which it is difficult to over-emphasize.

SELECTIVE POWER OF ADEQUATE TRAINING.

As with all work in which contact with human beings and their eventual management is concerned, people are attracted to it for motives which do not further their work and which may even make them into a danger for their charges. To give only one example: We have shown [1] that pity is a reaction formation against cruelty, and that this modification of aggression occurs in every human being. But there are people whose feelings of pity for the "underdog" seem grossly exaggerated and form their main object in life. The psycho-analysis of such personalities has shown that their exaggerated pity

[1] Part I, Ch. V, p. 29.

corresponds with an equally strong cruelty underneath, and that by exercising their pity on their usually helpless charges they are also able to express their aggressiveness, though in a more or less hidden way. Such people are very friendly and compassionate to their charges so long as they allow themselves to be managed, but become rather angry and stubborn if they refuse to be made happy for their patrons' sake. Such attitudes are especially dangerous when dealing with antisocial persons who need so little encouragement to be rebellious. To be able to decide when examining a prospective candidate for probation service, for instance, whether his or her wish to work with offenders is based on pity of this kind would be extremely difficult; for without an interest in and a certain amount of identification with the offender such work cannot be done satisfactorily. It is again not quality but the quantity of certain characteristics which distinguishes the suitable from the unsuitable personality. But this distinction cannot be established merely by interviewing the applicant, or by studying his former achievements. If the training for delinquency work is extended over three to four years, those personalities whose main interest lies in the satisfaction of their own instinctive urges will no longer be attracted, or will drop out during the course of training, as it will take too long for them to achieve what they really want.

It has to be borne in mind, however, that the interest in this or any other kind of work is always based on emotions. This in itself does not prevent success in work. Success and failure are a question of sublimation. The further removed from direct instinctive gratification the interest in the work has become the more chance there is of successful social achievement. Training helps towards this end. Other aspects of the work will become apparent, and the horizon of knowledge be widened. Delinquency is seen in its historical, sociological and economic background, and does not remain merely a problem of unhappy or disturbed individuals.

TRAINING AS BASIS OF RESEARCH.

An extensive training will give the theoretical background without which scientific research is impossible. This interest in scientific research should be fostered among workers with offenders. Not only is work of this kind essential if progress is to be made, especially in the treatment of offenders; but it will give the worker a wider interest than dealing with his or her immediate charges. This is important for the mental equilibrium of the worker. To be in constant contact with emotionally unbalanced human beings and not to be allowed to react emotionally oneself causes a great mental strain. By having a scientific interest which extends over and above each individual case disappointments can more easily be borne, failure will not be taken in so personal a way, and new ideas will be created.

It would probably help the workers greatly if after they have finished their training course they could work for some time under the supervision of experienced officers in their own branch. This would help them to deal better with the practical difficulties they are bound to meet with, and would enable them to avoid mistakes which every novice is bound to make.

REMUNERATION. Naturally, if such long years of training are needed in order to become a probation officer, approved school teacher or Borstal officer, the remuneration for such work will have to be in accordance with the professional standard of the worker. Though this will at first increase the Government's expenditure on its delinquents, it will pay in the long run: the qualified worker has more chance of coping with the difficult task of re-educating the offender than has the unqualified one, save in exceptional cases. It is certainly true that there are some outstanding personalities who have a special gift for dealing with offenders and who, by reason of their special ability, accomplish their work much better than do very many fully qualified people. But only a small minority of offenders will be dealt with by such people, and more often than not such outstanding personalities will eventually land in one of the professions concerned with remedial treatments. Aichhorn is one such example.

It has been argued that such training schemes for workers in the field of delinquency are excessive, as the workers dealing with normal children are not equally well equipped, and the "naughty" child should not be given preference over the "good" child. Apart from the fact that the training of workers dealing with normal children ought to be equally thorough, it has to be borne in mind that the process of re-education is a much more difficult task than that of education. And if it is realized that delinquency work succeeds not only in keeping the offender away from the court but in making him into a useful citizen, the community will have to take the necessary steps to achieve this end.

The training scheme here put forward would therefore

SUMMARY.

briefly be as follows: psychiatrists, psychiatric social workers and psychologists would in addition to their specific training gain experience in delinquency work by being attached to such a clinic as the I.S.T.D.

Probation officers, staff of approved schools and of Borstal institutions, wardens of hostels and similar workers would have a two-years course in social sciences or teaching or a combination of both. They ought to have at least a year's experience in ordinary social work, and then a further year's training in delinquency work, including the subjects mentioned above. All these workers should be given the opportunity of obtaining some clinical experience with neurotic and psychotic patients, and should understand the working of child guidance clinics and similar institutes dealing with delinquents from the psychiatric and psychological point of view.

CHAPTER VII

THE PROBLEM OF PREVENTION

Treatment of already established antisocial behaviour is long, tedious, expensive, and not always successful. Though the establishment of facilities for the treatment of delinquents on more modern lines and their application in each individual case at the first possible moment is imperative, this alone will not materially decrease the incidence of delinquency. It has long been recognized, especially by sociologists, that preventive measures are urgently needed. A scientific scheme for the prevention of crime will not succeed in altogether abolishing it ; but it will prevent it from spreading, in the same way as preventive medicine has succeeded in substantially decreasing the frequency of large epidemics, though it cannot prevent the sporadic incidence of infectious diseases.

The great advance in delinquency research during recent decades is to be seen in the scientific facts brought forward to show the environmental causes of antisocial behaviour in all cases except those where there is an organic disturbance. The material brought to light by the psycho-analytical investigation of individual cases has made clear in what intricate ways environmental factors can bring about disturbances in mental development resulting in antisocial behaviour. This fact has been demonstrated in the preceding case-histories, and it has probably become evident that in all these cases antisocial behaviour might have been avoided by a different upbringing. Alexander and Healy (4) state that even in their " desperate " cases the uncovering of unconscious material indicated that environmental factors were responsible for the development of criminal behaviour, and they maintain that psycho-analytically guided help in early childhood could have prevented these criminal careers.[1]

(1) ABOLITION OF PRIMARY FACTORS.

A rational scheme for the prevention of crime will therefore have to concentrate in the first place on the abolition of the primary factors leading to antisocial behaviour.[2] Though these factors, as we have seen, are purely psychological ones, so far

[1] Part III, Ch. IV (*b*), p. 210.
[2] Part II, Ch. III (*b*), p. 96 ff.

as the influence of the parents on the child's character development is concerned, the parents' attitude may to a large degree be dependent on external circumstances.

It will be the task of sociology and its allied sciences to emphasize the necessity for the creation of external conditions which will allow the mother to bring up her children in a satisfactory way. Good economic and housing conditions, a comprehensive health service and the abolition of unemployment will be among the most urgent necessities. Under conditions such as those described in *Our Towns, a Close-Up* (28), which are said to be prevalent among a large section of the public, external circumstances alone make the development of social adaptation impossible. To give only a few examples : bad housing conditions influence the mother's attitude towards cleanliness training,[1] overcrowding exerts its influence on the instinctive urges of the child in various ways,[2] and the atmosphere of the early family setting will be decisively coloured by the regularity or irregularity of the father's work, the presence or absence of economic stress and the security or insecurity of the future.

The influence of environmental factors of this kind on the incidence of delinquency has been stressed by various authors (H. Mannheim (26), Bagot (6), East (13*a*), Burt (10), Healy (20*a*)), but they have hitherto been thought to influence the older child and the adolescent in a much more direct way. This explains the disparities between the various investigations as to the correlation of each separate environmental factor with the incidence of delinquency.[3]

(2) EDUCATION OF PARENTS.

Hand in hand with this sociological endeavour to create favourable conditions for the upbringing of children, psychiatrists and psychologists must make plans for the education of parents. Mistakes in the upbringing of children are made for two reasons : one is a lack of knowledge, the other is the fact that parents, owing to neurotic disturbances of their own, cannot apply correct methods even when they are aware of them. The first difficulty is easier to overcome than the second.

It is often assumed that mothers, so long as they are healthy, will know by instinct how to bring up children. This assumption seems to be very generally accepted, otherwise the entire lack of training or guidance for this task in our social system could

[1] Part I, Ch. V, p. 37. [2] Part I, Ch. XI, p. 68 ff.
[3] Introduction, Ch. IV, p. 9.

not be explained. On the other hand, every change in social conditions produces a change in education, and especially during the last decades fashions in the early upbringing of children have changed with great rapidity. Such fashions are usually confined to a small section of the community, while the majority of mothers still work with older methods. Though some books have recently been written on the subject, and some periodicals are endeavouring to enlighten the public, no general plan of education for the parents of under-fives is in action.

I do not suggest that mothers should be given a psychological training in order that they may be able to bring up their children so that they can become useful and law-abiding citizens. Provided the mother develops normal feelings for her children, she will instinctively avoid gross mistakes. She will not willingly be separated from her child, she will be patient and will avoid harsh punishments, she will be consistent in her attitude towards the child's instinctive manifestations. But even the best mother cannot help being influenced by her environment and may, for lack of better knowledge, make mistakes which will prove fatal in the later life of the child. We have witnessed one such situation in our own time : at the beginning of the Second World War propaganda made it appear the moral duty of the mother to have her children evacuated. Many mothers who would otherwise never have dreamt of separating from their children did so under this environmental influence, and at the time this attitude was probably a national necessity. We have witnessed the disastrous results of such separations in many cases and the difficult problems which confronted social workers. A little more knowledge on the side of the authorities of the emotional needs of the small child, and a little more knowledge on the mother's side of the correctness of her own emotions, would probably have done much to avoid an increase in antisocial behaviour caused by the child's separation from the mother.

INFLUENCE OF MOTHER'S OWN EXPERIENCES.

Mothers are influenced in their attitude towards their children not only by environmental factors but also by their own experiences. If not taught otherwise, the tendency of each mother will be to bring up her child exactly as she herself was brought up if she had a happy childhood, or in exactly the opposite way if her own was unhappy. Neither the same nor the opposite upbringing may be in conformity with modern requirements.

So we conclude that the education of the mother will be a

useful means of avoiding the development of antisocial behaviour. This education should do two things: first, it should give the mother some idea of the emotional needs of the child, with special emphasis on the necessity for an uninterrupted relationship between mother and child, the normality of the appearance of certain antisocial or perverse instinctive urges at the various age levels, and the slowness with which such impulses tend to disappear. Secondly, on the basis of such information, which can be given in very simple terms, an outline of the best educational methods in their widest sense should be provided, emphasizing the need for absolute consistency in dealing with the child's instinctive urges and the patience which has to be shown if instincts are to be modified in a satisfactory way. Such explanations, if based on the child's needs, will allow the mother to spend sufficient time over the training in cleanliness, and will prevent her from feeling inferior if her neighbour tells her that her child was clean at a much earlier age. In my experience, such explanations have better results when the emphasis is laid on the reasons why feeding or cleanliness training should be carried out in a certain way rather than when the mother is given advice on how to deal with the child in certain situations and this advice is carried out blindly. The explanation of the child's emotional needs will also give the mother an inkling of the conflicts which are going on in the child's mind and the way in which even the very small child already understands incidents in its environment. If the mother realizes this, she will prevent the child from witnessing quarrels and sexual scenes without being expressly told to do so, and she will generally be able to cope with situations which had not been foreseen by her educators.

EXPLANATION OF THE CHILD'S EMOTIONAL DEVELOPMENT.

PRINCIPLES OF EARLY EDUCATION.

SEX ENLIGHTENMENT.

Some elements of the child's sexual development will also have to be described, with special emphasis on the child's sexual curiosity and the need for satisfying it as far as possible by simple explanations. Though the child will still cling to its own phantasies at least until the age of 6,[1] it is important that co-ordinated with these phantasies there should be also the knowledge of reality. The first sexual enlightenment will have to take place at home, because the child's preoccupation with this subject begins at the age of 3 and not when it goes to school.

[1] Part I, Ch. III, p. 20.

MEANS OF PROPAGANDA.

How should this education be transmitted so that it will reach a wide section of the public?

(1) If the school-leaving age is raised to 16, the last year's syllabus should include a course in child psychology and the upbringing of children, for boys as well as girls. If given in simple terms this is a fascinating subject for adolescents, and of more importance than anything else for their later life. In this way essential knowledge could be universally distributed. Even if it does not go further than to make the boy or girl aware that there are problems connected with the upbringing of children, this would be sufficient. It would recur to their minds when they themselves have children and would urge them to seek for further enlightenment.

(2) Ante-natal clinics, maternity wards and infant welfare centres should have personnel to provide this education for all prospective young mothers who make use of such facilities. This is the time when the mother is usually most anxious to learn how to deal with her baby. The work in these clinics could be facilitated by teaching the mothers in groups, being careful to arrive at a good method of selection. Such group teaching with the ensuing discussions will probably be more fruitful and more likely to impress the mother than would explanations given to individuals. In cases where mothers do not visit any of these clinics the district nurse could begin the education and interest the mother in taking part in such group discussions.

(3) Day nurseries could organize similar group teaching. The staff of the nursery meets the mothers when they bring and fetch their children, and could arouse their interest by discussing the individual problems of their own children first.

(4) Child-guidance clinics could extend their propaganda work by including the education of mothers of normal children as well as those of disturbed children.

(5) Every social worker who comes into contact with a family could advise the mother to take part in group discussions at one of the above-mentioned centres.

If this plan were adopted, a large section of the public would benefit from these educational efforts. It is needless to say that the training of the workers who undertake this education would have to be entirely uniform. The advice given to the mothers should be based on the theoretical knowledge of the child's emotional development as outlined above.

(3) MODIFICATION OF ATTITUDE OF NEUROTIC MOTHERS.

Those mothers who are bound to fail in their educational efforts, not so much on account of their lack of knowledge as on account of emotional disturbances, could also be helped to a certain extent. They could be detected in ante-natal clinics, infant welfare centres, maternity hospitals and child-guidance clinics. Some of them would have to be given psychiatric help. But the majority would probably be able to modify their attitude if the worker approached them in a way appropriate to their disturbance. Over-anxious mothers have different conflicts from "possessive" mothers or from mothers who feel hostile towards their children. Psychiatric social workers have the necessary training and experience to modify the attitude of such mothers, and the experiment could be made of having them together in small groups and attempting a kind of group therapy.

Individual mothers with difficulties in their attitude towards their children have been helped by psychiatric social workers in child-guidance clinics with very good results. A pooling of these experiences may make it possible to devise means of attempting such modifications in the attitude of emotionally disturbed mothers on a wider scale, and before this attitude has caused an emotional disturbance in the child. These mothers have to be given the same education as the more healthy mother, but apart from this they have to be helped to apply this knowledge, often against their instinctive tendencies. The methods described may not succeed in every single case, but they will be helpful in some cases. With greater experience of this particular kind of work more and more disturbed mothers will be enabled to create a more healthy family life.

These educational efforts, in conjunction with such economic and sociological changes as will enable the parents to put the advice given them into action, are the best means at our disposal of avoiding antisocial character formation. If successfully applied, they will considerably decrease the incidence of the "state of latent delinquency" (2*a*) or "susceptibility" (11) towards delinquency, and they will be more potent in lowering the incidence of delinquency than any other measure, applied to the older child. This latter can only do away with "secondary" factors,[1] that is, prevent the state of latent delinquency developing into manifest delinquency. In passing it should be borne in

[1] Part II, Ch. III (*e*)., p. 105.

mind that such a scheme, attempting a sound education of the child during the first years of life, will not only decrease the incidence of delinquency, but will lower the incidence of neurotic illness and similar disturbances which also originate in faulty education during the first five years of life.

II. PREVENTION OF "MANIFEST DELINQUENCY". (1) IN LATENCY PERIOD.

The next step in a rational scheme for the prevention of crime must be to take measures safeguarding those children and adolescents who are already in danger of becoming delinquent. The first signs indicating an antisocial character formation make their appearance either in the latency period or, in cases where the antisocial character formation is not very pronounced, under the emotional stress of puberty.

FIRST SIGNS OF ANTISOCIAL BEHAVIOUR.

These first symptoms are not necessarily antisocial actions in the legal sense of the word. Often these children show inability to conform to the ordinary methods of discipline applied in schools, a difficulty in realizing the rights of other people, and in conjunction with this a difficulty in fitting into community life, a lack of interest in school subjects and learning in general, and a futile rebellious attitude towards authority. The first signs of antisocial character formation are usually noisy and are felt to be a nuisance to the environment. This is due to the fact that the antisocial child is still dependent on the actual persons in its environment for learning how to behave, and will frequently provoke punishment by living out its instinctive urges.

There are degrees of severity in the antisocial character formation; and education during the latency period and certain environmental adjustments in puberty may still be sufficient to rectify the faulty development.

PREVENTION IN SCHOOLS.

(1) The significance of the school in the emotional development during the latency period has been discussed, and the importance of the schools offering the antisocial child more pleasures has been touched upon. In schools, ways and means can be found to help the child to modify its instinctive urges, a process which in antisocial children has not proceeded normally at an earlier stage, and thus a chance will be offered of curing the antisocial character formation or of completing the development towards the independence of the Super-Ego. The majority of antisocial children like to show off. They are usually, on account of their lack of interest, unable to shine in ordinary school subjects. Ways and

TEACHING METHODS.

means should be found for such children to excel in some way, perhaps in games or drawing. Such an experience will make school more attractive to them and will in time bring about some interest in other subjects as well ; the process of sublimation has been set in motion, perhaps because of a special talent, and is likely to spread to other subjects. These children would need special tuition in those subjects in which they were bad, in order to avoid the setting up of a vicious circle. But in general, if the teaching tried to arouse the instinctive interests of children, the normal child would benefit together with the antisocial child, and both could be treated equally (23).

New methods of teaching on the lines described will help towards sublimation of antisocial instincts. The personality of the teacher is of great importance in conscience formation, especially if this is not yet complete.

INVESTIGATION OF HOME ENVIRONMENT.

But it is of the greatest importance that in those cases which show signs of antisocial behaviour in school, contact should be established with the home, the conditions which have led to the faulty character development should be examined and if possible modified. Such a task cannot be undertaken by the teacher, though the teacher will be the first person to notice the symptom. The contact with the home and the modification of the home atmosphere should be undertaken by a person with the training of a psychiatric social worker. The school medical officer will have to decide whether better teaching methods and home contact by the psychiatric social worker will be sufficient in any given case to modify the disturbance or whether the child should be sent to a child guidance clinic.

Apart from measures taken generally in schools to help children to rectify an antisocial character formation, facilities for group activities outside school will do much to guide the development into the right channels. The Boy Scout movement,

CLUB FACILITIES.

extending downward to the age of 8, with the Cub and Brownie organizations, do not merely offer children the chance of sublimating their aggressive tendencies but also help them to conform to community life much more easily than can be done at school. Extension of such facilities by making clubs and sports available for children from the age of 7 onwards will not only help towards a consolidation of character development, but will also enable the workers to spot a more severely disturbed child much earlier than would be possible if it were playing alone in the street. The same holds good for clubs and similar organizations as for the school: activities inside the club have to be more attractive than the life in the street if antisocial children are to be induced to take part in these activities.

(2) AT PUBERTY.

The problem of prevention at puberty is similar in theory, though different in practice, according to the different stage of emotional development.

At present puberty is the time when the boy or girl leaves school and starts work. It would be of the utmost importance in the prevention of antisocial behaviour if more attention were to be paid to the abilities of young people when choosing their work. If facilities were open for the sublimation of instinctive energy there would be much less danger of antisocial impulses finding an outlet in action. Here again the sociological and psychological aspects are intermingled. If there are no facilities for work the most careful vocational guidance will not achieve any result. Even if facilities for varied occupations are open to every young boy and girl, the problems to be solved will be extremely difficult. It will very often be found on psychological examination that the interest of the young boy or girl does not lie in the direction of their greatest abilities, and the decision will have to be made whether to be guided by interest or by ability. Often one will succeed in persuading young people to begin a job for which they have a special aptitude and hope that in time their interest will fasten on to it. Such will be the decision if the work in which they are interested demands abilities which the boy or girl does not possess at all. If their gift lies in the direction in which they are interested the choice should follow the interest. Interest in an occupation always has an instinctive basis, and shows that sublimation in this direction has already been achieved.

VOCATIONAL GUIDANCE.

The chances of a rectification of the faulty character development at puberty are very small if the occupation which fills the whole day is boring for the young person, especially if there are no other facilities for sublimation such as hobbies or clubs.

SEX EDUCATION.

The choice of occupation is one important problem of prevention at puberty. The other problem is the help which can be given to the adolescent in dealing with his emotional problems. Sex education, appropriate to the emotional development of that age, may ease severe conflicts. The problem of masturbation, as being of immediate concern at this age, and that of sex morals, should be made the centre of such educational efforts. It is certainly a bad mistake to start sex education at puberty by giving warnings of the dangers of venereal disease. Boys and girls at this age are normally not concerned with adult sex life, and such instruction will only increase their fears connected with masturbation and thereby lead to conflicts and perhaps to antisocial behaviour.[1]

SEPARATION FROM PARENTS.

Finally, the young boys' and girls' attitude towards the parents may be causing conflicts, and help could be given by creating facilities, in the form of hostels, for boys and girls who cannot conform to the atmosphere of their home, to live away from home. This may be so even if the home is not really bad. Occasionally the normal conflicts of puberty are very violent, and removal, even from a good home, and with the consent of the parents, may help the adolescent more quickly to regain his balance.

If boys and girls leave school at the age of 14, it will be much more difficult to spot any difficulty in their behaviour before it comes to the notice of the authorities. Teachers should be able to notice instability during the last year in school, and welfare officers in the places of work should be aware of the first symptoms and not wait until the boy or girl stays away from work altogether.

CHILD GUIDANCE CLINICS.

If the behaviour of the child, either during the latency period or at puberty, seems to tend towards antisocial behaviour, and if the preventive measures so far described do not achieve any modification, the children should be sent to child-guidance clinics before they become delinquent. During the last decade psychiatrists have laid emphasis on the similarity between delinquent and neurotic behaviour, mainly in order to stress the fact that such children should be treated psychiatrically and not be punished. At our present stage of knowledge it is important once more to stress the differences between the two disturbances. Antisocial behaviour, if not complicated by neurotic illness, should be treated by environmental methods, under psychiatric guidance, while neurotic disturbances, especially in the older child and in the adolescent, will have to be treated by psychotherapeutic methods. The emphasis on the similarities of the disturbance

[1] Part I, Ch. X, p. 63.

often leads to overlooking the inadequacy of psychotherapy as the sole method employed in a case of antisocial character formation. This fact is very well known at the I.S.T.D., but it is less well known in child-guidance clinics which deal mainly with neurotic children. The special problems involved in the treatment of offenders are not yet fully recognized.

PREVENTION AT FIRST COURT APPEARANCE.

Proposals for dealing with the young offender in a more rational way at his first court appearance still belong to the field of prevention. The way in which the delinquent is handled in his first clash with the law of the community will often decide whether a criminal career shall result or not. This is a problem which demands the co-operation of criminologists and psychiatrists. Watson (33) shows how much an enlightened court can do to prevent further delinquency by studying the problems of the individual child. Mannheim (26), as already mentioned, makes a series of most interesting proposals of a preventive nature. Among other measures he proposes to raise the age for criminal responsibility to 12 years, thereby avoiding the question of punishment and stigma altogether up to that age, and he thinks that treatment after the conviction of older offenders should be decided upon by a committee consisting of the magistrate, a psychiatric social worker and a psychiatrist.

DIAGNOSIS IN EACH CASE.

This comes very close to the proposal already made above: that each case ought to be examined at the time of the first court appearance, and treatment should be decided upon only after all facts concerning the case have been taken into account. It is to be hoped that the facilities for environmental treatment for the young offender, which are envisaged in the new Criminal Justice Bill, as for instance the provision of hostels of various kinds, will be conducted on scientific lines, and that they will not be stigmatized as penal institutions, in principle even if not in name.

TRAINING OF FIELD WORKERS.

In a way, the training of workers in the field of delinquency also concerns the field of prevention; it will depend on the attitude of these workers whether the first offender is rehabilitated or whether he will be driven towards a life of crime.

Summary

I. A rational scheme for the prevention of crime has to concentrate in the first place on the abolition of "primary factors" leading to antisocial character formation or to the "state of latent delinquency". This can be done by—

(1) economic changes,
(2) education of parents,
(3) treatment of maladjusted parents.

II. In order to prevent the occurrence of manifest delinquency in cases where the antisocial character formation exists, measures should be taken—

(1) in schools by—
- (*a*) new methods of teaching (furthering sublimation),
- (*b*) immediate investigation and if necessary treatment at the first signs of antisocial behaviour,
- (*c*) furthering pleasurable spare-time activities in groups.

(2) after school-leaving age by—
- (*a*) provision of work for all,
- (*b*) vocational guidance,
- (*c*) sex education,
- (*d*) separation from home wherever necessary.

III. If a child or young person comes before the court, prevention of recidivism can be furthered by—

(1) correct diagnosis at first court appearance,
(2) institution of treatment on scientific lines,
(3) effective training of field workers so that the proposed treatment can be carried out consistently over a long period of time.

CHAPTER VIII

EPILOGUE

If a rational scheme for the prevention of crime such as that set out in the preceding chapter should come into operation, sociologists, economists, criminologists, and education authorities will have to co-operate with psychologists and psychiatrists in working out the details.

In this book I have set myself the task of showing which problems can be solved by psycho-analytical theory and practice. The contribution of psycho-analysis to the various fields of criminal research can be summarized very briefly: psycho-analysis furnishes a scientific theory of the working of the human mind, in health and illness, and should therefore play an essential part in every branch of delinquency research.

Sociological research, especially the further compilation of statistical data, will bear fruit only if from the outset of any given investigation psychological factors are taken into account. The most important example of this necessity has been shown to lie in the separation of the primary from the secondary factors causing delinquency.

Economic changes will not bring about a significant decrease in delinquency unless at the same time a scheme for the education of parents comes into operation.

Teachers have to understand the normal emotional development of children if they are to spot disturbances at the earliest possible moment. A much more intensive training in the working of the human mind and the manifestations of mental ill-health is necessary for the workers in the field, as interest in human beings and a desire to help them are not sufficient qualifications for the treatment of delinquent boys and girls.

We have shown that the case for or against the punishment of the delinquent can be decided on rational grounds only if the emotional attitude of the public is fully understood and allowance is made for unconscious motives influencing "common-sense" decisions.

Delinquency figures are rising. This is usual during a war, for sociological and psychological reasons. Let us meet this threat to our community life by helping these young boys and girls to become useful citizens in the post-war world : they have suffered, through no fault of their own, in their emotional development by the insecurity of family life in a world at war. They are victims as much as the wounded soldier or the bombed-out citizen.

By realizing the emotional needs of these boys and girls and by working out plans for their re-education on scientific lines, we shall not only prevent an increase in criminal careers but also increase the number of happy, socially adapted and therefore, useful citizens.

BIBLIOGRAPHY. PART III

1. Abraham, K.: "Die Geschichte eines Hochstaplers im Lichte psychoanalytischer Erkenntnis." *Imago*, Bd. XI, Heft 4. 1925.
2. Aichhorn, A.:
   (a) *Wayward Youth.* London, 1936.
   (b) "Zur Technik der Eriehungsberatung: Die Ubertragung." *Zeitschr. f. psycho-analyt. Päd.*, Vol. X. 1936.
3. Alexander, F.:
   (a) *The Psychoanalysis of the Total Personality.* Nervous and Mental Disease Publ. Co. New York, 1930.
   (b) "The Neurotic Character." *Intern. Journal of Psycho-analysis.* July, 1930.
4. Alexander, F., and Healy, W.: *Roots of Crime.* New York, 1935.
5. Alexander, F., and Staub, H.: *The Criminal, the Judge, and the Public.* London, 1931.
6. Bagot, H.: *Juvenile Delinquency.* London, 1941.
7. Bazeley, E. T.: *Homer Lane and the Little Commonwealth.* London, 1928.
8. Breuer, J., and Freud, S.: "Über den psychischen Mechanismus hysterischer Phenomene." *Neurolog. Zentralblatt*, 1893, Nos. 1 and 2.
9. Burlingham, D., and Freud, A.: *Infants without Families.* London, 1943.
10. Burt, C.: *The Young Delinquent.* London (4th edition), 1944.
11. Carr-Saunders, Mannheim, Rhodes: *Young Offenders. An Enquiry into Juvenile Delinquency.* Cambridge, 1942.
12. Criminal Justice Bill, 1938.
    Revised Criminal Justice Bill, 1939.
13. East, Norwood:
    (a) *The Adolescent Criminal.* London, 1942.
    (b) *Introduction to Forensic Psychiatry in the Criminal Courts.* London, 1927.
14. East, Norwood, and Hubert, W. H. de B.: *Home Office Report on the Psychological Treatment of Crime.* H.M.S.O., 1939.
15. Freud, A.: *Introduction to the Technique of Child Analysis.* Nervous and Mental Disease Monograph Series. New York, 1928.
16. Freud, S.:
    (a) "Freud's Psycho-analytical Method." *C.P.* I, 1924 (1904).
    (b) "The Dynamics of Transference." *C.P.* II, 1924 (1912).
    (c) *Three Contributions to the Theory of Sexuality* (1905). New York, 1910.
17. Friedlander, K.: "Early Signs of Antisocial Behaviour." *Mother and Child.* April, 1945.
18. Glover, E.: *The Diagnosis and Treatment of Delinquency*, being a Clinical Report of the work of the Institute during the five years 1937 to 1941. I.S.T.D. Pamphlet. London, 1944.
19. Glueck, S., and Glueck, E. T.: *500 Criminal Careers.* New York, 1930.
20. Healy, W.:
    (a) *The Individual Offender.* London, 1915.
    (b) *Mental Conflict and Misconduct.* London, 1919.
21. Healy, W., and Alper, B. S.: *Criminal Youth and the Borstal System.* New York, 1941.
22. Healy, Bronner, Baily, Murphy: *Reconstructing Behaviour in Youth.* New York, 1929.

23. Hill, J. C.: *The Teacher in Training.* London, 1935.
24. Hoffer, W.: *Discussion on Psycho-analytical Approach to the Problem of Delinquency.* Psychoanalytical Society. 20th May, 1942. (Unpublished.)
25. Makarenko, A.: *Road to Life.* Lindsay Drummond, London.
26. Mannheim, H.: *The Dilemma of Penal Reform.* London, 1940.
27. Mullins, C.: *Crime and Psychology.* London, 1943.
28. *Our Towns, a Close-Up.* A study made during 1939–42. Oxford University Press, London, 1943.
29. Paneth, M.: *Branch Street.* London, 1944.
30. Reik, Th.: *Geständniszwang und Strafbedürfnis.* Vienna, 1925.
31. Schmiedeberg, M.: "The Psychoanalysis of Asocial Children." *Intern. Journal of Psycho-analysis.* Vol. XVI, 1935.
32. Watson, J. A. F.: *The Child and the Magistrate.* London, 1942.
33. Wilcox, G. M.: "What is the Function of a Probation Officer?" Paper read at Staff Meeting of I.S.T.D., February, 1945. (Unpublished.)
34. Wills, D. W.: *The Hawkspur Experiment.* London, 1941.
35. Zulliger, H.:
    (*a*) *Heilung eines Prahlhanses.* Z.f.P.P. II. 1927/28.
    (*b*) *Eine kleine Lügnerin.* Z.f.P.P. V. 1931.

INDEX